EAVESDROPPING

on

TEXAS
HISTORY

EAVESDROPPING

on

TEXAS HISTORY

edited by

Mary L. Scheer

University of North Texas Press

Denton, Texas

10 9 8 7 6 5 4 3 2 1

Permissions:
University of North Texas Press
1155 Union Circle #311336
Denton, TX 76203-5017

The paper used in this book meets the minimum requirements of the
American National Standard for Permanence of Paper for Printed Library
Materials, z39.48.1984. Binding materials have been chosen for durability.

Library of Congress Cataloging-in-Publication Data

Names: Scheer, Mary L., 1949- editor.
Title: Eavesdropping on Texas history / edited by Mary L. Scheer.
Description: Denton, Texas : University of North Texas Press, [2017] |
Includes bibliographical references and index.
Identifiers: LCCN 2016042095| ISBN
9781574416756 (hardcover : alk. paper) |
ISBN 9781574416879 (ebook)
Subjects: LCSH: Texas--History.
Classification: LCC F386 .E28 2017 | DDC 976.4--dc23
LC record available at https://lccn.loc.gov/2016042095

The electronic edition of this book was made possible
by the support of the Vick Family Foundation.

DEDICATION

For Jane and Diane, who left us too soon,

and once again, for Richard

CONTENTS

ACKNOWLEDGMENTS

THIS VOLUME WAS A TEAM effort. As an editor of four anthologies, I can attest to the importance of assembling a top notch group of contributors who are consummate professionals, engaging writers, and can also tell a good story. All those who wrote chapters for this volume fit that bill, and I am profoundly grateful for their willingness to become members of the "fly on the wall" gang and eavesdrop on Texas history. From the inception of this project, Ron Chrisman, sponsoring editor with the University of North Texas Press, supported me and the book's premise that history can be both academic and fun. For its support of faculty research, allowing funds and travel for such pursuits, I am indebted to Lamar University. I am also obliged to my husband Richard, who not only served as a sounding board for my ideas and potential eavesdropping topics, but volunteered to write an index for this book. He also provides steady guidance, editorial assistance, and good natured support, allowing me to continue having fun in the sandbox of history. Finally, as editor, it has been a distinct privilege working with the "fly on the wall" gang, who entertained, enlightened, and even surprised me at times with their stories of Texas history. Herewith, my heartfelt thanks.

INTRODUCTION

THIS ANTHOLOGY GREW OUT OF the premise that history is inherently interesting, intriguing, instructive, and fun. Like many other historians and writers, I have often thought about a particular event or moment and amusingly wished I'd been there to eavesdrop on history. For example, who would not like to have been a "fly on the wall" at some great historical event, such as the debates in Philadelphia in 1787 to draft a new constitution, or the surrender of Confederate General Robert E. Lee to Union General Ulysses S. Grant in 1865 at Appomattox Court House, or the decision by President Truman to use the atomic bomb to end World War II? Even lesser known or less significant events merit such fly musings, such as riding the Chisholm Trail at the height of the cattle drives, or traveling a historic byway to experience a distant time, or witnessing baseball great Babe Ruth hit a home run in Yankee Stadium. Invariably, such "fly on the wall" moments lead to a research trip to locate an exact spot, a specific house, a certain government building, a particular church pew, or a precise location of a singular event that I would have liked to have witnessed. Such journeys into the past have the potential to augment ongoing research or spur new efforts, thus providing the social and cultural context for telling a good story. As writer and publisher

Bryon Hollinshead has observed: "The best historians have to be there." And so do the contributors to this volume.[1]

History is littered with many such engaging moments. Some take place in minutes, many occur over days and weeks, while others last months, even years. All, however, alter the way we understand the past, recognizing that events and their results could easily have gone another way. For example, the momentous decision by Christopher Columbus to sail westward, instead of the usual sea lanes, led to the discovery of a New World. The decisive moment when George Washington resigned as commander of the Continental Army, rather than retain power, led to civilian control of the armed forces. And the critical moment when General Dwight D. Eisenhower sent a massive Allied naval force across the English Channel began the ultimate defeat of Nazi Germany. Each of these dramatic events and thousands of others held grave consequences for those living at the time and for future generations.

Texas history also provides many captivating Lone Star moments. Its rich and storied past has proven popular with readers, particularly if measured by the tremendous number of titles published each year in a wide variety of genres. Much of this scholarship is rooted in the widespread assumption that Texas is a colorful, unique, and exceptional place with larger-than-life heroes and narratives. At the same time newer historical writings about Texas have incorporated newer themes within the developing currents of regional and national trends, such as the growing ethnicity, diversity, and globalization of the state. As a result, the list of possible compelling moments is endless and the opportunities to eavesdrop on Texas history are unlimited.

Thus, to test my hypothesis that eavesdropping on some historical event is intrinsically valuable and compelling, I invited fourteen prominent historians to choose events from Texas history that they would like to have witnessed. The criteria for these "fly on the wall" moments were relatively simple. First, the moment should be a compelling narrative, one that provokes interest both for the author and the reader alike. Second, the essay should be grounded in primary sources, scholarly documentation, and the most recent available evidence. And third, it should be fun. Each contributor who took up the challenge good naturedly endorsed the concept and embraced the prospect of being a "fly on the wall" at a particular Texas moment.

On both personal and professional levels, in one way or another, I know and have ties to each of the participants in this project. Some contributors, such as Light T. Cummins and Watson Arnold, were fellow students during my graduate school years, others collaborated on previous anthologies, such as Bill O'Neal and Patrick Cox, and several have served with me at conferences on scholarly panels, such as Dan K. Utley and Heather Green Wooten. All are my friends and distinguished scholars. By my count there are two State Historians of Texas, two Texas State Historical Association (TSHA) past presidents, three East Texas Historical Association (ETHA) past presidents, two West Texas Historical Association (WTHA) past presidents, five TSHA fellows, three ETHA fellows, two WTHA fellows, two Fulbright scholars, three Piper recipients, and at least seven award-winning authors. Collectively, they are experts in their respective fields and provide in some fashion answers to the following questions: What pivotal moment in Texas history would you liked to have eavesdropped on as the proverbial "fly on the wall" and why?

The choice of each moment reflected the contributor's own interests and individual inquisitiveness. For many contributors a personal connection or sense of place with his or her chosen topic determined their particular moment. Other contributors selected subjects based on a long-standing interest and an opportunity to finally write about it. The only requirements in choosing each topic were that it should be something that intrigued the author and, at the end of each essay, they tell the reader why. For example, Watson Arnold wanted to be a fly on the Alamo wall, March 6, 1836. Chuck Parsons wished to be an eyewitness to a Texas Ranger gunfight in 1877. And Michael Collins would have liked to have been aboard Air Force One on November 22, 1963, to witness the first few hours of the presidency of Lyndon Johnson. All provide a brief narrative that connects their Texas moment to a personal story.

The diversity of topics chosen in this volume covers a broad spectrum of Texas history. They range from the familiar to lesser known topics. For example, Paul H. Carlson and Tom Crum examine the well-known abduction of Cynthia Ann Parker on December 19, 1860, while the editor of this volume revisits the secession crisis and the famous refusal of Governor Sam Houston to take a loyalty oath to the Confederacy on March 16, 1861. Lesser known subjects include the 1909 environmental meeting in the deep woods of East Texas, as engagingly related by Dan K. Utley; the firing of Homer Price Rainey, U.T. President, on November 1, 1944, as expertly written by Light T. Cummins; and the unique circumstances surrounding the establishment in 1947 of Texas Southern University in Houston, as skillfully told by Merline Pitre.

Varied chapter subjects also span both the nineteenth and twentieth centuries. The book begins with Victoria H. Cummins's analysis of a significant but little known event, the New Madrid earthquakes in 1811-1812 that resulted in the formation of Caddo Lake, and ends with Nancy E. Baker's chronicle of the passage of the Marital Property Act in 1967. Political, social, and sports history are included as well: Patrick Cox eavesdrops on the conversations between Speaker Sam Rayburn and President Harry Truman as they learn of the death of President Franklin D. Roosevelt, April 12, 1945; Heather Green Wooten describes the environmental disaster and impact of Black Sunday, April 14, 1935; and Bill O'Neal reports the play-by-play action of "the greatest football game ever played" between TCU and SMU on November 30, 1935. For the general reader each chapter can be read as a stand-alone essay. For the classroom student the chapters can be read separately or as part of a comprehensive course of study.

On behalf of all the contributors—Vicki, Carolina, Watson, Paul, Tom, Chuck, Dan, Heather, Bill, Light, Patrick, Merline, Michael, and Nancy—it has been informative and fun researching, reading, writing and eavesdropping on these Texas topics. It was an opportunity to "loosen the reins a bit" and reflect on events that in most cases we knew intimately and about which we wanted to know more. In each case we simply wished to have been there as the proverbial "fly on the wall" at a particular Texas moment. Every author, to a person, collectively referred to as the "fly on the wall" gang, stated that she or he had fun doing it. We hope that shows in the final product.[2]

NOTES

1 Byron Hollinshead, *I Wish I'd Been There: Twenty Historians Bring to Life Dramatic Events that Changed America* (New York: Random House, Inc., 2006), ix-xi.
2 Ibid.

CHAPTER ONE

"The Earth Had Chills and Fever": The New Madrid Earthquakes and Caddo Lake, 1811–1812

Victoria H. Cummins

CADDO LAKE IS A MYSTERIOUS and haunting place unlike any other in Texas. Here, once out on the lake, the sounds of modern life drop away and the visitor finds herself enveloped in an eerie silence, broken by the occasional sound of an alligator or turtle breaking the surface or water birds taking wing at the boat's approach. Fantastic scenery greets the eye. Oak snags and clumps of cypress stumps obstruct navigation. Giant cypress knees rise from the muddy water, looming so large and high as to suggest the gothic cathedrals of old. The landscape suggests that the man-made environment has ceased to exist and the swamp has returned animals and humans to the primitive pre-historic past. From the 1930s to the 1950s Texas artist Don Brown fished these waters and loved this lake. He experienced how the spooky stillness and exotic flora could suspend time and warp the imagination. He once

Caddo Lake

COURTESY OF DAVIDCUTTS/DREAMSTIME.COM

wrote that in this strange and wondrous place "you can easily imagine a dinosaur floundering in the murky depths . . . or a pterodactyl banking for a clumsy landing."[1] The lake's history is as mysterious as its ambiance.

Caddo is Texas's largest natural freshwater lake (or rather complex of lakes and bayous), extending from Harrison and Marion counties in northeast Texas eastward across the border to Caddo Parish in northwest Louisiana. Bayous flowing from the west feed it and today the lake ends at the Mooringsport, Louisiana, dam. Historically, it issued into the Red River at Shreveport through Twelve Mile Bayou and has been important to the European settlement of the area. For a thirty-year period in the nineteenth century the lake was navigable by riverboat from Shreveport, Louisiana, to Jefferson, Texas, and was the major transportation route to northeast Texas. This ended in the 1870s when water levels fell after the Corps of Engineers eliminated the "Great Raft," a colossal logjam blocking and backing up the Red River north of Shreveport. Since that time the lake on the Texas side has been a sparsely populated maze of swamps and shallow ponds with deeper channels used as boat lanes. The "Big Lake" has served mostly for recreational purposes while the Caddo's wetlands are known for their exotic plant and animal life, drawing hunters, fishermen, artists, and conservationists for over a century.[2]

Very little is known about Caddo Lake's origins. Was the formation of the lake sudden and catastrophic or gradual and peaceful? Or was it something in between? Native-American legend seems to ascribe its birth to the catastrophic series of earthquakes that devastated the Missouri boot heel and nearby territories in 1811-1812. There is some archaeological and biological evidence to support this. However, most scientists now discount the legends and support the idea that the lake formed gradually, either from spring flooding or with water backed up from the Red River, covering swamplands and alluvial plains along its course. It is also possible that both explanations are partially correct and neither is wrong.

Scarcity of historical and scientific data explains the lack of surety about Caddo's birth. No direct eyewitness accounts exist of the lake's formation. The Native Americans who lived on the shores of Big Cypress Bayou must have known, but they left only orally transmitted legends and no written records. The science of seismology hadn't been invented when the New Madrid earthquakes happened, so measurements of intensity and magnitude have been extrapolated from the unscientific accounts of distant eyewitnesses. Only since the late nineteenth century has seismological data been systematically collected from the area.

Thus, while there are some definite opinions among scholars and local historians, there is no consensus about whether the earthquakes that hit the Mississippi Valley in 1811-1812 or the Great Raft of the Red River caused the lake to form over the alluvial flood plain of Big Cypress Bayou in the first decades of the nineteenth century. The only way to know for sure would be to have been there and observed what happened. When did the flooding bayou become a lake? Did it exist before December 16, 1811, the date of the initial quake? Would the Caddo Indians have felt terrifying shaking, heard loud inexplicable noises, and witnessed unbelievable changes in the land and water on that cold clear December night? Does their legend accurately describe the topographical and hydrographical changes they saw that evening? In short, what impact did the New Madrid earthquakes have on northeastern Texas?

The New Madrid earthquakes of December 1811 to February 1812, which destroyed towns near the epicenter, were powerful enough to have impacted northeast Texas and northwest Louisiana some 370 miles to the southwest. The small town of New Madrid in the Missouri Territory was located on a ridge above a horseshoe bend in the Mississippi River. George Morgan founded the port town in the late 1780s. Its 400 or so inhabitants prospered on the trade with flatboats heading downriver to Natchez and New Orleans. As night fell on December 15, 1811, a number of these boats tied up below the river bank.[3] Without warning, at about 2 a.m. on December 16, the night erupted with a loud noise and strong movement, causing the astonished inhabitants to scurry from their cracking and crumbling abodes. After suffering a series of milder aftershocks, which kept them terrified and outside on the cold December night, two more heavy earthquakes hit the area later that morning. Aftershocks continued for nearly a year in the region of the epicenter with two additional temblors as intense as that of December 16 on January 23 and February 7, 1812. By the time this cycle of earthquakes ended, the banks at New Madrid had collapsed into the river and the town had been swallowed up by the new channel of the Mississippi River created by the quakes. These strong quakes of December 1811 to February 1812 created topographical and hydrographical phenomena so singular as to seem fantastic even to those who witnessed them. Yet, modern scientific and historical research has confirmed most of what firsthand accounts described.[4]

Eyewitnesses saw the earth undulating in a wave-like motion, pitching trees horizontally, causing blowholes and opening deep fissures. Bluffs crumbled; some land was lifted up while other areas sank and were filled with water, either pushed up by pressure from below the earth or from water rushing in from the river.[5] The naturalist John James Audubon, who was out riding his horse in Tennessee to the east of the epicenter, described how "the ground rose and fell in successive furrows like the ruffled waters of a lake . . . the earth waved like a field of corn before the breeze."[6] Another witness similarly described "undulation of the earth resembling waves, increasing in elevation as they advanced, and when they had attained a certain fearful height the earth would burst."[7]

Along the river high banks caved in, causing waves that swamped boats and drowned rivermen. The riverbed lifted up. Islands vanished and new ones appeared. The shifting land caused the mighty Mississippi River to flow backward for a short period and created falls above New Madrid, which remained until spring floods washed the underlying sand ridge away.[8]

In May of 1812 Texas's founding father Stephen F. Austin passed through New Madrid by boat. He reported in his diary that at Cape Girardeau, some forty-five miles north of

New Madrid, "the Earthquakes were felt severely here having thrown down, or cracked every chimney in the place and
ruined two handsome brick buildings which were not quite
finished."[9] Moving south past the juncture of the Mississippi
and Ohio rivers, Austin's boat arrived at New Madrid.

> On landing at New Madrid the effects of the earth-
> quake were so prominently visible as well in the sunken
> and shattered situation of the houses, as in the counte-
> nance of the few who remained to mourn over the ruin
> of their prosperity and past happiness. . . . The effects
> of the earthquake began to be visible about 20 miles
> above this place by the shattered state of the bank of
> the river .6 miles above this the bed of the river rose on
> the night of 7 February the most severe shock which
> has been felt, and formed a kind of falls very similar
> to the falls of Ohio, and rendered the navigation very
> dangerous until the spring floods had washed it away
> being only sand—There were a number of boats lost at
> this place, And many lives. The banks are very much
> shattered and sunken from this place to N.M. where
> the bank has sunk about nine feet which reduces the
> former site of the town, below high water mark . . . the
> earth is very much cracked . . . and perforated with
> holes of different sizes out of which immense quanti-
> ties of white sand has been discharged.[10]

One reason that the event was so destructive was that
there was not one New Madrid quake, but a whole series of
them. Hundreds, even thousands, of aftershocks followed in
the year after the initial quakes on December 16, 1811. The
largest earthquakes—those of December 16, 1811, January 23
and February 7, 1812—were felt over more than 5,000,000 sq.
km., as far away as Detroit to the north, New Orleans to the
south, Washington, D. C. to the east, and the Texas-Louisiana
border to the southwest.[11] These three great quakes, with mag-
nitudes of M_w 8.0 (February 7, 1812), M_w 8.1 (December 16,
1811) and M_w 7.8 (January 23, 1812) respectively, constitute

three of the ten strongest earthquakes ever experienced in the lower forty-eight states.[12] Using the Modified Mercalli Intensity Scale, seismologists estimate that they would have been felt on the Texas-Louisiana border (where Caddo Lake is located) at the level of MM VII, "difficult to stand . . . hanging objects quiver . . . furniture broken. Weak chimneys broken at roofline. Fall of plaster, loose bricks, stones, tiles, cornices, unbraced parapets, and architectural ornaments. . . . Waves on ponds; water turbid with mud. Small slides and caving along sand or gravel banks."[13] Even in areas remote from the epicenter the tremors would have a notable impact for those living in the alluvial river valleys: "the shocks were much more distinctly felt by those living in the alluvial flats of the valleys than by those on the rock uplands."[14]

No eyewitness accounts exist of the impact of the New Madrid quakes on the area where Caddo Lake connects northeast Texas to northwest Louisiana. In 1811-1812 Native Americans populated the area, leaving no written records. The Caddo Indians who inhabited the area that became Caddo Lake had migrated there only at the end of the 1700s. They settled on the shores of a bayou to the west of the Red River to escape epidemic diseases, alluvial flooding, and slave raiding by the Osage Indians. The Caddos comprised a federation of loosely related villages tied together by common language and culture. They were a sophisticated tribe of agriculturalists, cultivating corn as their main crop along with beans and squash, and hunters, tracking deer, bison, rabbits, fowl, and other animals to provide meat for food and skins for clothing and other uses. Fishing and collecting wild berries and nuts further supplemented their diet. By the end of the eighteenth century the Caddos had acquired horses from the Europeans and were able to maintain long distance trade contacts. Trade goods connected the Caddos to areas as far away as Illinois, the Gulf Coast, and New Mexico. They used stone, wood, and shells to manufacture tools and weapons and produced fine pottery and baskets. The Caddos were also a peaceable people. They accepted the Alabama, Coushatta, and Quapaw, other indigenous groups being pushed west by white settlement. By 1835, however, under strong pressure from European westward expansion, the Caddos sold their land in Texas to the United States and eventually migrated to Oklahoma.[15]

While the Caddos left no written records about the lake's formation, we can deduce evidence of the earthquakes' impact in their oral tradition. According to Caddo legend the lake was formed by a sudden catastrophic inundation. The Caddo Indians who lived along its shores in the early nineteenth century called the biggest lake (or the whole series of connected lakes) Tso'to, which the white settlers corrupted to Sodo (now Caddo). One translation of Tso'to is "water thrown up into the draft along the shore by a wind."[16] In her book *Caddo Indians: Where We Come From,* Cecile Elkins Carter, a tribal historian, recalls the legend of the lake's sudden formation.

> The legend, remembered in the present time, is at least as old as Tso'to itself. The traditional sequence of Turkey Dance songs that relate past events includes one about two brothers who saw the creation of Sodo Lake. Several tribes were gathered for a dance when the high water came. The brothers were worried about the rising waters and went to higher ground. They looked to the east and saw a ridge of land moving like a great snake. The ridge was holding back the water in the valley, blocking the stream running through, and making a lake where the people were dancing. The older brother called out to warn the dancers of the danger, and a few were saved by climbing up the hill to join him. The others paid no attention and were lost to the high water.[17]

In the 1930s the WPA Writers' Project collected a variant version of the legend of the lake's origin:

> There is a legend of the Caddoes who once had a populous village in this [Caddo Lake] vicinity, of a chief who was warned by the Great Spirit to take his tribe to high ground, or see his people destroyed by earthquake and flood. The chief paid no heed to the warning, and one day a party of warriors returning from a hunting expedition found the village gone and a lake covering the place. They referred to the region as the "trembling ground," and maintained that it was the predicted earthquake that had formed the lake.[18]

Caddo resident and conservationist Fred Dahmer gave a similar version in his 1989 history *Caddo Was . . . A Short History of Caddo Lake*, but in his retelling the Caddo chief took the warning seriously and saved his people. Dahmer's version adds that when the flood came it was accompanied by loud sounds and flashing lightning.[19]

These Caddoan accounts parallel a Chickasaw Indian legend regarding the origins of Reelfoot Lake in Tennessee, which all agree was a product of the New Madrid quakes, and which shares some similarities with Caddo Lake. According to the oral tradition, Reelfoot Lake was named for a club-footed chief who caused trouble by kidnapping a Choctaw princess for his wife, "despite warning in a dream that if he did so the earth would tremble in rage. During the wedding ceremony the ground shook, the town sank, and the Mississippi gathered its waters and flowed backwards over it, drowning everyone."[20]

Don Brown was an artist and freelance journalist who published articles about the history and folklore of the area. Brown had grown up in Marshall and hunted and fished Caddo Lake in his youth. As an adult, he spent many hours on the lake sketching and painting its moss-covered cypresses, its exotic wildlife, and its local inhabitants. He taught art at Centenary College from the mid-1930s to his death in 1958. In articles written in the 1950s he gave several versions of a story he had heard since boyhood: "An old Indian had returned for a last visit there [Caddo] many years before and told how 'the earth had chills and fever and shook in the night and the waters rolled over our village and we fled to the hills.' He also pointed out the wide expanse of lake lying in front of Long Point where the water now averages five or six feet deep, and said that he had seen herds of buffalo grazing on the prairie there."[21]

A few months later, Brown published this version of the lake's creation, a story told in 1903 to Carnegie Institution researchers by a Caddo informant named Wing:

> One day, Wing related, a man went down to the bayou to get a drink of water and saw this great creature moving through the water. He started running along the bank in the direction it was swimming and ran nearly two miles before he caught up with its head. The man then went back to camp and told his grandfather what he had seen. "You have seen something wonderful, my son," the old man said. "This has been sent as a sign to our people." The old man called all of the men of the tribe together and told them the story. Some did not believe him but others went to the bayou and saw the creature. There was one man in the camp who was old and blind but very wise. The chief asked him the meaning of what had happened. The old man sat silent for a long time then said, "The sign is a very bad one for it signifies that the waters shall rise in a short time." The waters rose soon and formed a large lake. The lake was very dangerous. When one crossed he had to cross without saying a word to anyone.[22]

Despite the consistency of the core story in the variations of the Caddo legend, the earthquake theory has many detractors. These authors discount the "catastrophic" origin and favor a more gradual creation due to the buildup of the "Great Raft" of the Red River. The Great Raft was a log jam, or rather a series of log jams, made up of trees, driftwood, and other detritus being carried down river that got stuck in sand bars and piled up more flotsam behind them. The reason the Red River picked up all this debris was that its banks were made up of soil, not rocks. In times of rain and high water they easily crumbled into the river, taking trees along with the silting earth. The river's slow current and sand bars added to the problem. The buildup of blockage caused the Red River to spill over its banks and flood surrounding valleys while raising the level of the creeks and bayous that drained into the river. Overflow also created new flows from the river to inundate the valleys, making prairie and swamp into lakes. This is how Caddo Lake gradually formed. A raft was reported as early as 1722 at Natchitoches and in 1805 Dr. John Sibley reported it had reached Campti, twenty-five miles to the north. The Great Raft was notable in that, having formed near Natchitoches, it back built upstream, expanding further by catching more debris. It expanded upstream with flotsam, renewing it at the top as older decayed materials at the bottom broke loose and washed harmlessly downstream. At about 1800 the raft extended from about eight miles below to seventeen miles above present-day Shreveport. It continued to build until it reached its zenith of about eighty miles in length.[23]

Indian legends support the earthquake origin theory. Some dismiss these legends as baseless superstitions or fanciful and entertaining fictions to be told around a campfire, but this shows a fundamental misunderstanding of the function of oral tradition in pre-literate societies. In these cultures stories passed down orally conveyed beliefs, customs, sayings, wisdom, and history to the group. Although orally transmitted folk legends have variant versions, are not verifiable, and often

The Red River Raft, ca. 1871

combine supernatural elements with ordinary ones, the people who tell these stories believe that they have an historical basis, as well as natural evidence for the legend.[24]

Writing in the 1940s, J. G. Burr, who had been Director of Research at Texas's Game Fish and Oyster Commission, cited as evidence supporting the earthquake theory the reported fact that the Caddo Indians called Caddo Lake "the Trembling Ground" and that even after the Great Raft of the Red River was permanently removed in the 1870s, the lake complex remained, although with low water levels until the first dam was built in the early twentieth century. He also cited Indian artifacts found under ten feet of water, far from the shore. How could they have gotten there if the lake formed gradually? Wouldn't the Native Americans have taken their possessions in an orderly fashion? Finally, he points out the large submerged trees and stumps in the lake, which could not have grown under water.[25]

Don Brown gave credence to the impact of the New Madrid quakes: "There is definite evidence that the great New Madrid earthquake of 1811, when the earth broke open and swallowed whole houses and the Mississippi ran backwards, affected Cypress Bayou and its chain of small lakes . . . and that the ground here subsided to form the main body of Caddo."[26] Brown backed up his belief in earthquake formation from personal experience. In addition to painting the lake and collecting stories about local history, he also hunted for Indian artifacts in his meanderings around Caddo. In 1938 he found near the Texas-Louisiana border "the remains of the original Caddo Indian Village" in two to three feet of lake water. These artifacts included arrowheads, flint chips, stone hammers, and some of the stones the Caddos used to heat in the coals and throw into pots to warm water. He claimed that when University of Texas scientists looked at his find they said it confirmed the Caddo legend.[27] In another article, Brown characterized the professors' reaction as that they had opined that they (the Indians) "did not leave in orderly fashion but fled for their lives, leaving their most treasured possessions,"[28] thus supporting the occurrence of an unexpected and disastrous inundation. He also cited oak snags standing in deep water where their growth could never have begun as further evidence for a sudden catastrophic formation. The lake also experienced continuing shocks. Brown recounted that in 1921 his father experienced one of these. Fishing in the absolute stillness of a hot summer day, the elder Brown looked up and saw a two-foot high wall of water heading across what had been a dead calm lake. Frightened by the fact that he had no idea why it had appeared, he nonetheless rode it out and saw the water return to its former stillness.[29]

N. Ray Maxie, a native east Texan and former Texas Ranger, added to the discussion that the lake "is said to have been caused by a large sinkhole appearing there in the ground overnight many years ago."[30] Of course, the question is what would cause a sinkhole so large as to create Caddo Lake. Could it have been caused by anything less than a major earthquake? Mildred Gleason, a local historian based in Jefferson, added support in her 1981 work *A Survey of Caddo Indians in Northeast Texas and Marion County 1541-1840.* She noted that in the late 1880s a few Caddos came back to visit Swanson's landing on Big Cypress Bayou. They told a Mr. Josey who was living there that they used to plant corn on the land that was now covered by Sodo Lake, part of the Caddo Lake complex. Yet, she supported the Red River raft theory, believing that the story she recounted described the effect of flooding due to the raft rather than proof that there had been a seismological event.[31]

Jacques Bagur, a professional researcher who has been a consultant to the Corps of Engineers, rejected the impact of seismic activity in the formation of the lake complex. He cited as proof reports from white explorers in 1806 and 1808, years before the New Madrid earthquakes of 1811-1812, mentioning Caddo Indians living on a lake. Instead, Bagur credits the back up of waters by the Red River Raft. His proof is that other lakes of this kind were formed by the raft with some of the upper lakes' formation being witnessed and recorded. They formed as the raft backed upstream, and no lakes formed above the upstream extent of the raft. Finally, as the raft declined and disappeared, so did all these lakes, except Caddo, which was greatly diminished. However, he does not dismiss the Caddo legend. He accepts the great flood recounted as fact, just not connected to the New Madrid earthquakes. He explains that early white settlers, hearing the story of a catastrophic flood, assumed that it must be related to the earthquakes and added this to the story.[32] Instead, he points out, the legend is "rooted in the real experience of the Caddos in their floodplain village on the occasion of the break in the bend of the Red River in 1800 that brought the Sodo Lake complex into existence. The Caddos were too high to be in the direct path of the flood, but they were near enough that the rushing waters precipitated a retreat to higher bluffs on the newly formed Caddo Lake."[33]

Plant Biologist Robert Mohlenbrock, writing in *Natural History*, concluded that the lake did emerge close in time to the New Madrid earthquakes, but earlier, in about 1800 "and was simply the result of dead trees piling up in what was a relatively slow-flowing, shallow section of the river."[34] Cecile Elkins Carter agreed, but placed the time of formation between 1806 and 1811.[35]

A number of writers hesitate to choose between one explanation or the other. They find ways to reconcile what at first appear to be mutually exclusive explanations. Fred Dahmer mostly agrees with Jacques Bagur. He discounted the earthquake theory, but tried to reconcile the Indian legend with the Great Raft by pointing out that the inundation described by the Caddo legends "accurately describes what would have occurred in a tremendous flood causing a sudden breakthrough in the already overloaded bank of the Red River, with its soft, fertile soil."[36] Moreover, while he found the idea that the lake formed overnight due to a catastrophic inundation "about 80 to 90 percent wrong," he admitted that it is "quite possible" that the Caddos felt the New Madrid quakes and that "trees may have overturned, and minor changes in the course of the Red River may have occurred."[37] Seismologists Cliff Frohlich and

Scott Davis acknowledged that the presence of Indian artifacts far below the lake's surface might be proof of a catastrophic, sudden inundation caused by an earthquake, but might also only represent things left behind by Indians moving on as water levels gradually rose. They also pointed out that "Caddo Lake apparently existed as a large swampy area long before 1811 and was caused by a great logjam known as the Great Raft that was noted as early as 1722." They allowed, however, that whether the lake area pre-existed the earthquakes or not, the quakes might have deepened the lakes.[38] In her book *Caddo Lake: Mysterious Swampland* (1974) Mildred McClung found some truth in all the theories, seeing gradual geological change, the backup of water due to the Great Raft and even the 1811-12 earthquakes as contributing to the lakes' formation.[39]

As the above discussion bears out, there are definite opinions, but no consensus, about the formation of Caddo Lake. Were the New Madrid earthquakes felt, or not, in northeast Texas? Does the Caddo Indian legend refer to the earthquakes, or not? Did the quakes or the Great Raft of the Red River play the only or greatest role in creating Caddo Lake? No one really knows, but to have eavesdropped among the Caddos on Big Cypress Bayou at about 2 a.m. on December 16, 1811, would have provided answers to these questions that constitute my fly on a Texas wall moment.

———◆◆✕◆◆———

I became interested in the debate over the origins of Caddo Lake through my research on Don Brown, a Texan who lived most of his life close to Caddo Lake. As a boy living in Marshall he camped, hunted, and fished the "Big Lake," absorbing the stories told by and about its inhabitants. As an adult, Brown became a well-known regionalist artist. Trained in New York and Paris, he returned to Caddo Lake to paint the landscape he knew and loved. In 1934 he founded the Art Department at Shreveport's Centenary College and remained its head until his death in 1958. Brown was a journalist as well as an artist. He wrote and illustrated stories for newspapers in Marshall, Shreveport, New York City, and Paris, France, as well as for American magazines like the *Southwest Review* and *The Ford Times*. His knowledge of Caddo Lake would find its way not only into his drawings, paintings, and prints, but also into his writing. From the 1930s to the 1950s he always had a camp on one side of the lake or the other where he had a rustic cabin and kept a shallow draft boat. He spent a lot of his time cruising Caddo Lake, sketching and painting the haunting beauty of its flora and fauna. A gifted raconteur himself, he collected and retold legends about Caddo's past and tall tales about colorful characters who lived there. He published a number of articles about the lake's history, although he never finished the book he intended to write about it. Several of these articles recounted versions of Caddo Indian legends that attributed the formation of Caddo Lake to the massive New Madrid earthquakes of 1811-1812.[40] What existed of the book manuscript has been lost, so we will never know whether he would have had something definitive to say about the origins of Caddo Lake.[41]

SELECTED BIBLIOGRAPHY

Bagur, Jacques. *A History of Navigation on Cypress Bayou and the Lakes*. Denton: University of North Texas Press, 2001.

Carruth, Viola. *Caddo 1,000: A History of the Shreveport Area from the Time of the Caddo Indians to the 1970s*. 2nd ed. Shreveport, LA: Shreveport Magazine, 1971.

Carter, Cecile Elkins. *Caddo Indians: Where We Come From*. Norman: University of Oklahoma Press, 1995.

Dahmer, Fred. *Caddo Was . . . A Short History of Caddo Lake*. Austin: The University of Texas Press, 1989.

Frohlich, Cliff, and Scott D. Davis. *Texas Earthquakes*. Austin: The University of Texas Press, 2002.

Fuller, Myron. *The New Madrid Earthquake*. 4th ed. 1912. Reprint Gutenberg-Richter Publications, 1995.

Gleason, Mildred S. *A Survey of Caddo Indians in Northeast Texas and Marion County, 1541-1840*. Jefferson, TX: Marion County Historical Commission, 1981.

McClung, Mildred May. *Caddo Lake: Mysterious Swampland*. Texarkana, AR: Southwest Printers and Publishers, Inc. 1974.

Penick, Jr., James Lal. *The New Madrid Earthquakes*. Rev. Ed., Columbia: University of Missouri Press, 1981.

NOTES

1 Don Brown, "Of Caddo Lake: A Chapter of a Book Now Being Written," Shreveport *Times*, March 23, 1955, North Louisiana Historical Association Papers, fol. 136, Archives and Special Collections, Noel Memorial Library, Louisiana State University-Shreveport (hereafter cited as NLHA).

2 Seth D. Breeding and Sallie Starr Lentz, "CADDO LAKE," *Handbook of Texas Online* (http://www.tshaonline.org/handbook/online/articles/roc01), accessed July 15, 2015; Fred Dahmer, *Caddo Was . . . A Short History of Caddo Lake* (Austin: The University of Texas Press, 1989), xi-xii, 3-4.

3 Norma Hayes Bagnall, *On Shaky Ground: The New Madrid Earthquakes of 1811-1812* (Columbia: University of Missouri Press, 1996), 12-19; James Lal Penick, Jr., *The New Madrid Earthquake* (rev. ed. Columbia: University of Missouri Press, 1981), 15-29.

4 Arch Johnston and Eugene S. Schweig, "The Enigma of the New Madrid Earthquakes of 1811-1812," *Annual Review of Earth Science* 24 (1996): 339.

5 Myron Fuller, *The New Madrid Earthquake* (4th ed. 1912, repr. Marble Hill, MO: Gutenberg-Richter Publications, 1995), 9.

6 Quoted in Fuller, 31.

7 Ibid.

8 Fuller, 10.

9 Stephen F. Austin's Diary [May 17-19, 1812?], Eugene C. Barker, ed., *The Austin Papers, Annual Report of the American Historical Association for the Year 1919* (2 vols. Washington, D. C.: GPO, 1924), II, 206.

10 Ibid., II, 207.

11 Cliff Frohlich and Scott D. Davis, *Texas Earthquakes* (Austin: The University of Texas Press, 2002), 113; Fuller, 21-31.

12 Frohlich and Davis, 43.

13 Ibid., 2 (quote), 5.

14 Fuller, 32.

15 The name Caddo comes from the Europeans' abbreviation of the term "Kadohadacho" which means "real chief." According to legend, the Caddos gave us the name "Tejas." The word meant "friend," but the early

European settlers misunderstood it to be the name for the geographical place. Dahmer, 4-5, 10-11, 38; Jacques Bagur, *A History of Navigation on Cypress Bayou and the Lakes* (Denton: University of North Texas Press, 2001), 30-32, 37-38, 43-44, 54; Timothy Perttula, "Caddo Indians," *Handbook of Texas Online* http://wwwtshaonline.org/handbook/online/articles/bmcaj accessed July 15, 2015; John R. Swanton, *Source Material on the History and Ethnology of the Caddo Indians,* Smithsonian Institution Bureau of American Ethnology, Bulletin 132 (Washington, D. C.: GPO, 1942), 234-237; Viola Carruth, *Caddo 1,000: A History of the Shreveport Area from the Time of the Caddo Indians to the 1970s* (2nd ed. Shreveport, LA: Shreveport Magazine, 1971), 1-10.

16 Swanton, 16.

17 Cecile Elkins Carter, *Caddo Indians: Where We Come From* (Norman: University of Oklahoma Press, 1995), 215; Mildred May McClung, *Caddo Lake: Mysterious Swampland* (Texarkana, AR: Southwest Printers and Publishers, 1974), 15.

18 Harry Hansen, ed., *Texas: A Guide to the Lone Star State* (1940; new rev. ed., New York: Hastings House Publishers, 1969), 535. This legend is repeated, with minor embellishment, in Carruth, 41.

19 Dahmer, xii, 6.

20 Penick, Jr., 121-122.

21 Brown, "Of Caddo Lake."

22 Don Brown, "The Strong and Crafty Triumph in Caddo Indian Myths," *The Shreveport Times,* June 26, 1955, NLHA.

23 Carruth, 11-13; Mildred S. Gleason, *A Survey of Caddo Indians in Northeast Texas and Marion County, 1541-1840* (Jefferson, TX: Marion County Historical Commission, 1981), 68; Jacques Bagur, "The Awesome Birth of Caddo Lake," *The Uncertain News* 1, no. 2 (Summer/Fall 1996); Paul's Website www.angelfire.com/journal2/discerner/caddo.html accessed July 13, 2015; Bagur, *History of Navigation,* 61-65.

24 "What is a legend?" American Folklore Teachers Resource www.americanfolklore.net/folklore/2010/07/folklore__definitions.html accessed August 4, 2015; William Haviland, et al., *Cultural Anthropology: The Human Challenge* (14th ed., Belmont, CA: Wadsworth Cengage Learning, 2011), 350.

25 J. G. Burr, "Did Quake Spawn Caddo Lake?" *Texas Game and Fish* 1, no. 6 (May 1943): 10; and J. G. Burr, "The Probable Earthquake Origins of Caddo Lake," *Proceedings and Transactions of the Texas Academy of Science* 26 (1943): 132, Caddo Lake Institute. Caddo Data Server www.caddolake-data.us accessed October 30, 2014.

26 Brown, "Of Caddo Lake"; Don Brown, "Caddo Lake," *Ford Times,* n. d., pp. 46, 48, NLHA 135.

27 Brown, "Caddo Lake"; Brown, "Of Caddo Lake."

28 Brown, "Of Caddo Lake," 48.

29 Brown, "Caddo Lake," 46.

30 N. Ray Maxie, "Uncertain, Texas, Caddo Lake and Cypress Trees," *Ramblin' Ray* TexasEscapes.Com http://www.texasescapes.com/N-Ray-Maxie/Uncertain-Texas-Caddo-Lake.htm accessed July 13, 2015.

31 Gleason, 67.

32 Jacques Bagur, "The Awesome Birth of Caddo Lake." *The Uncertain News* 1, no. 2 (Summer/Fall 1996). Paul's Website www.angelfire.com/journal2/discerner/caddo.html accessed July 13, 2015; Jacques Bagur, *A History of Navigation on Cypress Bayou and the Lakes* (Denton: University of North Texas Press, 2001), 7, 73-75.

33 Bagur, *History of Navigation,* 37.

34 Robert H. Mohlenbrock, "The Two Centuries of Caddo Lake," *Natural History* (May 2001) Caddo Lake Institute. Caddo Data Server www.caddolakedata.us accessed October 30, 2014.

35 Carter, 214.

36 Dahmer, xii.

37 Ibid., 4-5.

38 Frohlich and Davis, 113-115.

39 McClung, 16.

40 Brown, "Of Caddo Lake" and other articles about Caddo Lake, NLHA 135, 136.

41 Victoria Cummins, "Donnell Adair Brown (1899-1958) and the Waterways of Louisiana," *Louisiana History* 56, no. 2 (Spring 2015): 151-155.

CHAPTER TWO

A Fly on Stephen F. Austin's Shoulder in Mexico, 1822–1823

Carolina Castillo Crimm

*I*N THE EARLY MAY SUNSHINE of 1821, a persistent fly perched on the shoulder of Stephen F. Austin's broad-cloth coat. The twenty-nine-year-old did not bother to brush it away. After all, there were always flies in New Orleans. Tired, disillusioned, and depressed, he stared down at a letter from his father, Moses Austin. He studied the words that his domineering father had meant to be uplifting and encouraging. "I hope you will make the trip to Arkansas. By the time I arrive raise your Spirits, times are changing A new chance presents itself Nothing is now wanting but concert and firmness."[1] Stephen felt neither. He did not want to go to Texas.[2]

Almost five months earlier, in January of 1821, Stephen Fuller Austin had left his father in Arkansas and had moved to New Orleans. Moses Austin planned to go to Texas to present his land settlement scheme to the governor in "St. Antone." His son Stephen, although uninterested in the Texas venture, lent his father his slave, Richmond, and a gray horse to take

with him to Texas. Stephen, in "gloomy despair [that] probably would have disappointed, and might have disgusted, his
father,"[3] lamented, "I am entirely indifferent what becomes of
me, or whether I live or die."[4]

Stephen had good reason to flee to New Orleans. He left
behind his father's mortifying losses at the lead mines at Mine
à Burton, Missouri, and the even more devastating losses in
land speculation in Arkansas. The nation-wide Depression of
1819 had dried up all the cash available and ruined Austin's
prosperous mining operation. Those holding promissory notes
or outstanding loans, in particular the Austins, found themselves with useless paper and unpayable notes.

Stephen's move to New Orleans had been occasioned by
the loss of his position as County Court judge in Little Rock.
The Arkansas legislature had abolished the bench on which
he sat.[5] His hopes of finding some kind of employment in the
seething town of New Orleans proved frustrating. The revolu-
tions in Latin America over the previous decade had driven
many of the rebels into New Orleans and everyone was looking for work. He offered to hire himself out "as a clerk, as an
overseer, or anything else."[6] But there had been nothing. He
learned that there were "hundreds of young men who are glad
to work for their board."[7] Meanwhile, Stephen was drifting
further into debt and he was worried about his future.

When Stephen wrote to his family on January 20, 1821, he
reported that his father had just returned from "St. Antone
and was to be back at Natchatoches by 15 of February." He
added, "He is well."[8] In actuality, his father was suffering from
a lingering pneumonia that would eventually take his life five
months later. "I know nothing as to my father's objects or prospects," he concluded and it is likely he did not want to know.[9]

In New Orleans the younger Austin at last had a bit of good fortune. He made the acquaintance of Joseph H. Hawkins, a wealthy New Orleans lawyer from Lexington, Kentucky. To Austin's relief, the lawyer not only offered him a job in his offices, but advanced him enough money to "purchase a few groceries and [send some] for you and sister."[10] Hawkins even agreed to help Austin "read for law until I am well fitted to commence the practice of law in this country."[11]

The problems, from Stephen's point of view, were two-fold. It would take eighteen months to learn the law and the French language, during which time he could send his mother no money at all. The other danger was that "those I owe in Missouri may persecute [me] here."[12] Coming after him would do them no good, he assured his mother, as he had no funds and was not likely to have any for the foreseeable future.

Stephen held out little hope that his father would succeed at his plans to colonize Texas. An unusual combination of factors in Spain, Mexico, and the United States had created political and social instability that would eventually result in Spain's loss of its colonies, the loss of Texas to Mexico, and the eventual loss of nearly half of Mexico's territory to the United States.

By the time Moses and then Stephen Austin embarked on their colonization efforts, there were several "push and pull" forces at work. First, the Depression of 1819 in the United Sates had left many, including the Austins, desperate and deeply in debt. The possibility of land in Spanish Texas and the prospect of speculation in land for profit appealed to many American entrepreneurs. Moses and Stephen had attempted land settlements in Arkansas that had failed miserably because of the Depression.

Second, during 1819 and 1820, King Ferdinand VII of Spain had been forced to accept a return to the liberal Constitution

Stephen F. Austin portrait by William Howard

of 1812. In domino fashion, Spain's New World conservatives and clergy, horrified at the liberalization of the distant Spanish government, determined they were better off without Spain. Forging an uneasy alliance, the conservatives in Mexico joined the rebellious liberals to declare independence from their mother country and establish the new Republic of Mexico.

Third, the Spanish Constitution of 1812 had also had an impact on the United States. Americans had learned of the constitution's liberal attitude toward outsiders. The constitution opened the once tightly closed Spanish Empire to both foreign settlement and international trade. Men such as Moses Austin saw the possibilities for land-hungry Americans to move into Spanish territories, especially since he himself held a Spanish passport from the years during which Spain had controlled Louisiana.

A fourth factor related to the U.S. boundary. In 1819, Don Luis de Onís and Secretary of State John Quincy Adams had (relatively) successfully settled the boundary problem between the United States and Spanish Texas. The United States received Florida, but gave up Texas. Enraged westerners insisted that the Louisiana Purchase had included Texas and were willing to fight to regain it. In July of 1819, General James Long marched for Texas, planning to take possession of "St. Antone." He failed and was eventually shot in Mexico City.[13]

A fifth factor was the desperate need of Tejano settlers to find a way to overcome their poverty. Texas had been reduced from some 4,000 settlers to a population of around 2,100 by the 1813 Battle of Medina and General Arredondo's devastating executions of liberals in Texas. The residents of Texas were of two minds. Some believed that keeping the Americans out would protect their lands from invaders as aggressive as the Goths and Visigoths. Among them were Governor Antonio Martínez in San Antonio and Rafael Manchola, presidial commander at La Bahía. Others, such as Erasmo Seguín and the Baron de Bastrop, hoped to encourage incoming American settlers. They felt the new arrivals would improve trade and create profitable markets for Tejano goods.[14]

Another important consideration was the location of Austin's requested grant. Spain, for nearly three hundred years, had always been wary of letting anyone see maps of their territories. Just because there was a change in the constitution did not mean they were planning to hand out tourist maps at the border. When Moses made a claim for land at the mouth of the Colorado River, he had never seen it and had no real idea where it was. Nor did he take the time to visit his site in the brief week he spent in San Antonio. The Spanish authorities were rightly fearful of intruders learning the route or coming too close to their silver mines in the interior of the country. Over the years, a few maps may have fallen into the wrong hands and been copied, but it is more likely that Moses Austin had never seen an accurate map of Texas. He may have known of the existence of the Colorado, probably from rumor and gossip, but he had never mentioned the Brazos de Dios River.

By the time Moses Austin left Texas in January of 1821, he had given his proposal to Governor Antonio Martínez. The plan was then sent to Commandant General of the Interior Provinces, Don Joaquín Arredondo in Monterrey. One wonders why or how General Arredondo, once the executioner of liberals in Texas, should have done such a complete about face as to accept and approve Austin's plan immediately. Within days, he had sent the papers back to San Antonio with his signature. The requirements included that the settlers swear loyalty to Mexico, prove their Catholicism, and promise to defend the area against Indians and other invaders. When the paperwork came back to the newly established Provincial Deputation of San Antonio, they also agreed. Perhaps they saw the potential profit for this plan to settle Texas. They also appointed Erasmo Seguín, their postmaster, to go after Austin to let him know.[15]

Erasmo Seguín, like many of his compatriots, was ambivalent about the Americans. He opposed open immigration, fearing that the voracious Americans would flood Texas. He was willing to accept Austin's settlement because it would be carefully controlled and he, too, may have hoped for a more profitable Texas. Seguín, however, failed to catch up to Austin who had already headed home to Herculaneum on the Mississippi River. So the paperwork was sent up-river after him. Learning that Austin planned to return by May, Seguín took up residence in Nacogdoches to await the return of the American empresario.[16]

Moses returned to Missouri to find that his financial situation was worse than disastrous. He was about to lose everything. For the next few months he fought hard to extricate himself from the morass of debt. Weak from his efforts to settle his financial problems in Missouri with the Bank of St. Louis, Moses was still euphoric over his plan to colonize Texas. The pneumonia that he had contracted on his trip to Texas, however, returned with a vengeance. At the end of May he was still writing to Stephen, encouraging him and asking him to get "Bacon and flower [*sic*] as they will command money in St. Antone and that immediately."[17]

Throughout the last weeks of May and the first week of June, Dr. Physick blistered and bled Moses copiously. His wife Maria wrote to Stephen at the end of May, alternating between hope and despair. All her prayers were in vain. Moses Austin died just a few days later on June 10, 1821. His deathbed wish, whispered to his wife Maria through phlegm-choked lungs, begged his son, Stephen, to take over the Texas project. She wrote to Stephen and his brother to tell them the terrible news, assuring them, through her tears, that they "would be successful and independent in a few years."[18] Everything was in readiness, save the funding.[19]

One can only imagine what Stephen, and the fly on his shoulder, were thinking when he received the news. His whole life was about to be uprooted. For better or worse, he was going to Texas. Turning to his mentor and friend, Attorney Hawkins, Stephen explained his predicament. He did not have the money to carry out his father's wishes. To his amazement, Hawkins agreed to help fund the project. The lawyer offered to provide Stephen with the money to start for Texas as well as to support the entire colonization plan.[20]

Taking over his father's Texas colonization project gave Stephen "the means of escaping from his father's shadow, recovering the family's lost fortune, paying his own massive debts, and restoring the house of Austin to its former status."[21] He would also be able to leave the depression-ravaged Mississippi Valley and the chaos of his own private life. Texas would be a chance to redeem his personal career and provide him with a calling in life. Stephen's attitude toward the Texas project was changing.[22]

On July 1, 1821, Stephen F. Austin arrived at Natchitoches, Louisiana. He sold Richmond, the slave who had ridden to Texas with his father, for $650. Some of the money went to pay off a tiny portion of his debts in New Orleans and the remainder he used for the trip. Stephen had said he would return to Louisiana by September 25 and then continue on to Herculaneum on the Mississippi to collect his family and bring them to Texas. At Natchitoches, Stephen found Erasmo Seguín. The dedicated postmaster had been waiting patiently for his father since March.[23]

When Stephen Austin and nine companions arrived instead with the news of the death of Moses Austin, Erasmo Seguín gave Stephen the copy of the papers relating to the grant. He "counseled the young Anglo American that 'this most unhappy event will not retard the progress of settlement.'"[24] The older man took Stephen under his wing and spent the next dozen years helping Stephen "open a new page in Texas history."[25]

With Seguín, Stephen and his companions rode for San Antonio to meet Governor Antonio Martínez. Together they would sort out the new situation.[26] They set out along the *Camino Real* or the King's Highway. The "highway" was not much more than a narrow, well-trodden trail through the Piney Woods. Making about fifteen miles a day on horseback, they wound through the dark, dense evergreen forest. It would take them nearly six weeks to cover the distance to San Antonio.

Around them grew hundreds of varieties of trees. Thick stands of loblolly, slash, and yellow pines competed for space with spreading hardwoods. Oaks of a dozen different kinds mixed with sweet and black gum, elms, hickory, ash, beech, and cottonwoods. Southern magnolias drooped with Spanish moss while the forest floor glowed with greenery: ferns, delicate orchids, pitcher plants, sundews, and pipeworts.

The men did not lack for food. They hunted the bears that roamed the woods along with deer, panthers, squirrels, and a host of other animals. In the many rivers they crossed, already named by Spanish explorers as the Sabinas, the Neches, the Angelina, the Trinidad, the Brazos de Dios, and the Colorado, they caught bass, catfish, and crappie in abundance. Otters, beavers, muskrats, and minks splashed in the water while birds flitted from tree to tree. Sparrows, warblers, nuthatches, and red-cockaded woodpecker whistled and twittered, while bald eagles swooped overhead.

At the highest point on the trail, appropriately called Alto, they turned southwest. Nearby they saw the strange mounds left by the Caddo Indians, and the remnants of the old Mission to the Tejas Indians. At last, after splashing across the Neches and the broad reaches of the Trinity, they emerged from the forests onto the rolling grasslands of central Texas.

By the time they reached the *Brazos de Dios* (The Arms of God), Stephen had become enamored with the land. For ten days, 134 miles, they continued southwest, riding across the grasslands between the Brazos and the Colorado Rivers. Covered in grama grass and bluestem, milkweeds and columbines, winecups and mallows, the hills rolled down to the river valleys that crisscrossed the land. There pecans and oaks grew thick, marking the verges of the rivers with dark green stripes. Although he would later explore the Guadalupe and San Antonio river valleys, Austin realized that this was the land he wanted for his empresario grant. This was land that southerners would value for growing cotton or corn. Only later would he learn about cattle and mustangs from his Spanish neighbors.

On July 17, 1821, just as Seguín and Austin headed into Texas, the San Antonio Ayuntamiento had been called together. They were to meet with Governor Antonio Martínez. Word had reached San Antonio that General Agustín de Iturbide had successfully led the conservative rebel forces against the Crown's Army in Mexico City. After three hundred years, Mexico was independent of Spain.

The overthrow of the Spanish crown had been quick and nearly bloodless. One after the other, as news reached them, the provincial governments had fallen into line and sworn allegiance to the new imperial government. In San Antonio, the Council debated their choices. There were none. On July 19 they swore allegiance to the Mexican Empire in the Plaza amid as much pomp and ceremony as San Antonio could muster. The government was to be a constitutional monarchy with a member of the Spanish royal family at its head.[27]

When Stephen and Seguín arrived in the small town, they learned of the changes in the government in distant Mexico City. No one, however, knew what the changes might mean to those out on the Texas frontier. For the governor, who himself felt unsure of his position under the new government, the changes meant that Austin's contract, agreed to under the Spanish government, in all probability had no standing under the new Mexican government.

Stephen might have felt relieved when Governor Martinez accepted his plan to take his father's place, but the acceptance was laced with concerns. The governor wrote to his superiors warning that settlers in the United States considered Austin's grant as opening the door to all. Martínez reported that 500 families, "the worst that the U.S. could produce," were headed to Texas.[28] Years later, even Austin himself would complain that he was "driven to distraction by difficulties with 'backwoodsmen' and 'rough fellows'" since "the Americans were the most obstinate and difficult people to manage that live on earth."[29]

Stephen, with the Baron de Bastrop acting as translator (from Stephen's French to Bastrop's Spanish and back again), was able to work his way through the bureaucracy of the Spanish, now Mexican, red tape. He determined at once to learn Spanish in "a single-minded, almost fanatical fashion."[30]

When his brother, sixteen-year-old Brown Austin, joined him in San Antonio, Stephen left him with the Seguín family with orders to learn Spanish as soon as possible, as he himself was determined to do. Total immersion, as well as Stephen's training in Latin from his youth at Transylvania College, and his latest skill with French from his time in Louisiana, made learning Spanish considerably easier. He also acquired a Spanish grammar book to help with proper construction. He would mention, with considerable regret, the loss of his grammar book to the Comanche several months later. After only a few weeks, "he was writing letters in simple but grammatical Spanish." His fellow Americans soon came to depend on him to intercede between them and the Mexican government.[31]

The colonization plan, as proposed by Moses Austin, still remained to establish a colony on the Colorado and grant each settler 640 acres, a normal American section of land, at a price of 12½ cents an acre. Austin pointed out his need for some income: "Those who have means must pay me a little money on receipt of their titles. From those who have not money I will receive any kind of property that will not be a dead loss to me, such as horses, mules, cattle, hogs, peltry, furs, beeswax, home-made cloth, dressed deerskins, etc. For the balance I will wait 1, 2 or 3 years."[32] He assured his settlers that they would surely be able to sell their land for a quick profit at "50 cents or one dollar per acre"[33] within two or three years. It was evident that Austin did not yet understand the Spanish attitude toward land, but he soon would.[34]

Moses Austin may have chosen the Colorado River as the location for his settlement, but those who lived in Texas knew that there were other, better places to establish a colony. Either Seguín or others in San Antonio informed Stephen of the availability of rich mission lands which were due to be secularized and made available for settlers along the Guadalupe River, the San Antonio River and along the still unpopulated Brazos de Dios River. Austin wanted to see the lands for himself, but he needed a guide.

On August 26, 1821, Tomás Buentello, the Alcade of La Bahía, reported to the San Antonio Ayuntamiento that he had chosen Manuel Becerra to accompany Stephen F. Austin to the Colorado River. Becerra would allow Austin to inspect the Presidio Viejo del Lagarto and the Port of Matagorda since

"Becerra was knowledgeable of the area."[35] The presidial commander, Captain Juan de Castañeda, along with many others from La Bahía, evidently did not trust the Anglos or want them in Texas. Castañeda reported that he could not supply any soldiers for the expedition or provide sustenance for the group. The thirty or forty days they planned to be gone was more than he could provide from his meager supplies. One can almost imagine him shrugging as he pointed out that since Austin had ten Americans with him, Castañeda did not need to protect them. They were on their own, but Becerra would be watching.[36]

According to Manuel Becerra's diary of the trip, Alcalde Buentello and the San Antonio Ayuntamiento ordered Becerra to "observe carefully and report the movement of the Americans while in the Wilderness."[37] On September 3, 1821, after a three-day wait for Becerra to prepare for the expedition, the group of eleven Americans (Austin plus ten companions) left La Bahía. Rather than head straight for the Colorado as his contract required, Austin spent time reconnoitering and "mapping the Guadalupe River, the old Mission of Refugio, the vicinity of the old Presidio, and the port of Matagorda." Becerra complained about the detour, but he believed that he had no choice since he could not force the Americans to follow orders. In the end, Austin and his group were unable to explore the length of the Guadalupe because of "difficulties" and were forced to return to the *Camino Real* and continue their course toward the Colorado.[38]

Councilman Becerra had serious doubts about the legitimacy of this group of Americans. He reported to his Alcalde that "none of those who came with the said Austin appeared to be the legitimate families who were supposed to come [settle]."[39] They were Americans, he felt certain, because he noted that they spoke no other language than English and they were not Roman Catholics as they did not practice any of the rituals of the Catholic Church. La Bahía Alcalde Buentello, based on the reports he was receiving from Becerra, reported to the Texas governor at San Antonio that "being Americans it seems to me that they will be more harmful than beneficial." He ended his report with the comment, "Your Excellency will decide as you think best."[40] Governor Martínez, his hands tied by the lack of a decision-making body in Mexico City, decided not to complain of Austin's out-of-bounds meanderings. Clearly, he did not realize that a tsunami of Americans were about to descend on his territory.

During December of 1821, Austin hurried back to New Orleans. He undoubtedly met with Hawkins, his money man, collected supplies for his settlers and recruited more colonists. By the time he returned to Texas in January of 1822, Austin found settlers already in place on both the Colorado and the Brazos rivers, busily clearing land and planting corn and cotton. The fifty Brazos River colonists were not supposed to have settled there, but their ship, *The Lively*, had been blown off course, missed the Colorado and landed them at the nearby Brazos de Dios. It all looked the same to them. Austin, who had expected the men on the Colorado, had been frantically searching for them and feared that they had been lost. After all their efforts at settling on the Brazos, moving them back to the Colorado was not an option. He now had two settlements to oversee as an empresario.[41]

With the changes in Mexico City, it was now obvious that Austin had no authority to distribute land, determine boundaries or decide how much land was to be handed out. Without these vital functions, Austin could not settle anyone or do anything.[42] Governor Antonio Martínez, who was now certain his days in office were numbered, urged Austin to go to

Mexico City to lay his plea before the Constitutional Congress or Iturbide himself.

In March of 1822, Austin spent two weeks organizing the colonies. He left Josiah H. Bell in control of the settlers. His brother Brown Austin would be his unofficial representative in San Antonio. After gathering supplies, Austin and two companions started on the 1,300-mile trip down the *Camino Real* to Mexico City.[43]

At the Nueces River, fifty Comanche surrounded Austin while his companions were away tending the horses. Alone, but determined not to give up, Austin "expostulated" with the Indians, reminding them that the Comanche had always been friendly to Americans and that it was the Mexicans they hated. His explanations evidently worked because the Comanche returned the saddle bags and saddles they had taken. They kept four blankets, a bridle, and Austin's Spanish language grammar book.[44]

It took Austin another six weeks to make the trek from Texas to Monterrey. There, unable to find a larger group to travel with, he and his companion dressed in rags to avoid bandits. Without further incident they finally reached Mexico City on April 29, 1822.

Austin considered himself a polished and articulate gentleman, but it is still likely that the city appeared breathtaking to him. In 1822, Mexico City had a population of 150,000 citizens, larger than New York City or New Orleans or any city Austin had ever seen. As he toured the three-hundred-year-old city he found magnificent churches, monasteries, and convents; hundreds of dazzling colonial palaces; a dozen hospitals; beautiful botanical gardens; flower-decked plazas; wide, well-lighted boulevards; an art academy, a superb university, and the world's best mining college. For all the luxury, however, Austin also saw poverty with beggars on street corners and in the plazas.[45]

When Austin arrived, Mexico City was at a standstill. No one was interested in his grant. They had larger things to worry about. Iturbide and his governmental junta, as well as the Constitutional Congress, were still waiting for word from Spain about which of the Bourbon royals would be willing to come to Mexico. They had done nothing toward writing a constitution or establishing a stable government.

Back in Spain, Ferdinand VII had overthrown the liberal rebels and reestablished himself on the throne. He absolutely forbade any of his royal relatives from becoming emperor in Mexico. Without a European royal to take over the throne, Iturbide, over his own protests, was named Emperor Agustín I on July 21, 1822.

Two months earlier, Austin had found a room at a Mexico City hotel that welcomed foreigners. There he met two other would-be empresarios, Robert Leftwich and Andrew Erwin. The two Tennesseans were part of the Texas Association from Nashville and like Austin, they, too, sought colonization grants. Unlike Austin, however, they spoke no Spanish. As Austin's Spanish improved with daily practice, Leftwich and Erwin came to depend on him for help. With the government in chaos, and nothing happening, all three men wrote out their lengthy petitions and had them translated into proper Spanish. But there were no government officials who might receive the petitions. Austin and his cohorts would have to wait until Mexico wrote a constitution and reestablished a government.[46]

According to some authors, while he waited, romance entered the life of twenty-nine-year-old Stephen. He met Angelina, the daughter of Don José Manuel Herrera, the Minister of Foreign and Internal Affairs. The minister was a liberal with a positive attitude toward the Americans and their colonization efforts and welcomed Austin into his home. Angelina had just returned from school in England and the young couple were said to have spent considerable time together. Since Austin was "educated, cultured and of a fine appearance,"[47] and she was a raven-haired beauty, the romance blossomed under the watchful eye of the minister and his family. Whether he might have remained in Mexico, or she might have gone to Texas with him, would never be known. The lovely Angelina "fell victim to a plague and died."[48] Austin never married.

As the days and weeks passed, Austin made it a point to make friends with the leaders of the various factions. Among the liberals, those in favor of American settlement, he counted Juan Bautista Arizpe from Monterrey and brother of Coahuila Congressman Ramos Arizpe; Lorenzo de Zavala of Yucatan, who would later go on to become an empresario himself and Vice President of the Republic of Texas; Valentín Gómez Farías, a member of the Congress; and Father Servando Teresa de Mier, who would have a long but varied career in Mexican politics. Wisely, Austin also courted the conservative politicians, who hoped to control colonization tightly from the center of the country. Among his conservative friends he could count on José Manuel Herrera, the father of Angelina and Minister of Foreign Affairs, General Anastacio Bustamante who was then defending the emperor, and Congressman Manuel de Mier y Terán. The conservatives may have opposed colonization by the Americans, but it appears they liked Austin personally.[49]

Finally, with Agustín de Iturbide as emperor, Austin requested an audience to explain his plan. On May 25, 1822, he placed his proposal in the hands of the emperor and assured him that "My property, my prospects and my future hopes of happiness are centered here. This is our adopted Nation."[50]

Unlike his father's plan, his request included all of the land between the Brazos and the Colorado rivers, not just a small port at the mouth of the Colorado.

Colonization formed one of the critical points of discussion for the newly established Constituent Congress. Many of the members of the Congressional Committee on Colonization preferred to leave the whole Gordian knot of how to settle its empty northern lands in the hands of the respective state legislatures. After three months of deliberations, they completed the first draft of a General Colonization Bill in August of 1822.

Among the provisions of this first draft were requirements that colonists could be Mexican or foreigners; they must be Roman Catholic; they must improve their lands within six years; the settlers would not have to pay taxes for those six years; and they were permitted to bring in tools and implements duty free.

The amount of land, however, left Austin stunned. The law called for an eye-popping league of land, or 4,428 acres for livestock, plus one labor, or 177 acres, for farming for each male head of a family. Austin, as the empresario, was to receive 15 square leagues plus 2 labors, or approximately 66,774 acres for each 200 immigrants.[51]

There was, however, a major problem. Austin could not charge for the land, not even 12½ cents an acre. The Spanish view of land had always been based on the belief that land belonged to the king. He could grant it freely to his settlers and citizens. An empresario, as the representative for the king, was to do the same. Land was not for sale. Although Austin himself would be land rich, he would not be able to sell his own lands or make any profit until the colony was completed. Nor could his own colonists sell their lands since he would still be handing out free land to the incoming settlers.

Hundreds of years of Spanish knowledge and experience determined the assessment of leagues and labors of land grants. Arid lands, whether in the American southwest or on the plains in southern Spain or North Africa, required much more land in order to support a cow and calf. The usual American grant of 640 acres would not, in Spanish eyes, have been sufficient to maintain a proper herd of cattle.

As a consequence, Austin's colonists could look forward to receiving three times the land they had expected. If there had been the possibility of a tsunami of settlers before, Austin now knew there would be a flood of Biblical proportions when word reached the Southern states of the amount of land he would be handing out—for free. It is likely that the little fly on his shoulder felt his shiver of dread.

While he waited for some decision on his grant, Austin enjoyed his new friends among the upper classes of Mexican society. It cost him nothing to eat at their homes and he gratefully received invitations to the city's many elegant restaurants and cafés. Wined and dined, he enjoyed all the pleasures of life Mexico City could offer.

Meanwhile, the Congressional Committee on Colonization plodded on through September and October. Austin surely became well acquainted with the members of the committee and quietly attempted to influence their decisions. His efforts to convince them to allow at least a small charge for the land, however, went nowhere. It was simply not the Spanish view of land ownership.

Austin worried, along with the rest of Mexico, when the political spectrum in Mexico began to splinter by the end of October 1822. Members of the Congress, incensed over the emperor's dictatorial views, began to threaten the emperor himself. Nineteen members were arrested for treason.

As the violence increased, Agustín de Iturbide at last shut down the Congress. He established a *Junta Nacional Instituyente* until a new congress could be elected. To Austin's great relief, the emperor's *junta* created its own colonization committee. On November 26, 1822, the committee reported out a bill on colonization for the emperor's signature.[52]

For a few days, Austin experienced his father's euphoria. He almost had his contract in hand. But it was not to be. On December 2, 1822, Iturbide's own generals rose in revolt against him. Calling for the Plan de Casa Mata, Antonio López de Santa Anna, Guadalupe Victoria, Vicente Guerrero, and Nicolás Bravo united against Emperor Iturbide. They proposed a decentralized government with power in the hands of the individual states. Once again, the country would be plunged into war and uncertainty. While revolts took place in the countryside, Iturbide, with the help of General Anastacio Bustamente, remained in power and continued to rule in Mexico City.

Austin could only sit and worry. His little fly may have been suffering from whiplash as he and Austin watched the country's politics shift violently back and forth from liberal to conservative and back again. Fortunately, Austin had made friends in both camps and he could still hope that his grant would be successful.

Austin, now on practically a first-name basis with the emperor, was thrilled to learn that Iturbide had signed the new Colonization Bill on January 4, 1823. All that was left was the confirmation of Austin's own grant. Austin continued to haunt the imperial offices, in particular the offices of his friend, Minister Herrera, lobbying for support.

By the middle of January, the emperor's council, perhaps with encouragement from Austin himself, approved Austin's grant. Now it was just the emperor's signature that was needed.

The rumblings of revolt continued in the distance as Austin paced the halls of the palace.

On February 19, 1823, to Austin's relief, Emperor Agustín de Iturbide signed Austin's colonization grant. But there were problems. The document needed more details. The question of contraband concerned the government. As a result, the boundaries of all land grants would have to be set back twenty leagues from the coast and ten leagues from the border with the United States. The government hoped this would avoid contact with illegal American traders.

Austin accepted the changes, rewrote the grant and took the paperwork back to the council. At this juncture, just as Austin thought he had completed everything, Emperor Iturbide's entire cabinet resigned. Undaunted, the emperor appointed an entirely new set of officials. Austin knew none of them. His carefully constructed connections were gone.

Stephen Austin had never met José de Valle, the new Minister of Relations. He did, however, know General Anastacio Bustamante who was holding off the rebels outside of Mexico City. With Leftwich, Austin rode the twenty-four miles to the general's camp to get a letter of introduction to Valle. To his immense relief, Bustamante received them and gave him the necessary letter.[53]

Racing back to the governmental offices, Austin introduced himself to Valle. Doing his best to remain diplomatic and calm, Austin provided the remaining details that the emperor had requested. With rebel forces outside of the city, and attack imminent, to Austin's amazement, the wheels of government ground on. Day after day passed. At last, March 11, 1823, Minister Valle signed and approved the documents authorizing Austin to establish a settlement in Texas between the Colorado River and the Brazos de Dios. He placed them in Austin's hands. Relieved, Austin could at long last return to Texas, having received approval of his father's Spanish land grant—the only Anglo empresario to do so.[54]

Again, it was not to be. Eight days later, before Austin could even get out of town, Emperor Iturbide abdicated the imperial throne. Austin hesitated. He had the signed contract in his hands. But would his grant hold up? Without the emperor in power, would the imperial signature on the grant have any force? Cautious, Austin decided to stay in Mexico City to await developments. It proved to be a wise choice.

Within ten days, a new revolutionary quorum made up of three men, Guadalupe Victoria, Nicolás Bravo, and Pedro Celestino Negrete, calling themselves the Supreme Executive Power, took over the government. Their first act, just as Austin had feared, was to annul all acts passed since May of the previous year when Iturbide had first declared independence. Among the annulled acts was Stephen F. Austin's colonization contract.[55]

The new three-man junta called a new Constitutional Congress. Austin knew many of the members and his friendly contacts paid off. Determined to gain their stamp of approval on his colonization grant, Austin resubmitted all the paperwork. This time, the grant sailed through. On April 14, 1823, Stephen F. Austin was at last an authorized and legal empresario for Texas. Neither Leftwich nor any of the other empresario contracts were approved. They would have to wait.[56]

After approving Austin's grant, the liberal national Congress put power back in the hands of the state authorities. Specifically, they repealed the National Colonization Law. All colonization grant requests were to be submitted to each of the individual states and it would be up to them to resolve all the problems with the land grants.[57]

According to Austin biographer Gregg Cantrell, "Austin's sincere professions of loyalty to his adopted country, his punctilious deportment, and his seemingly inexhaustible patience, had won him the confidence of Mexicans in places of power."[58] On June 17, 1823, Stephen F. Austin left Mexico City for Texas, ready to begin settling the lands between the Colorado and the Brazos rivers. There would not be a port city on the coast.

On August 24, 1823, Maria Austin wrote to Stephen F. Austin, now back in Texas, congratulating him. His perseverance and fortitude, she said, had won him the contract from the Mexican government. Austin, and the "fly on his shoulder," could not have agreed more.[59]

◆◆◆※◆◆

Stephen F. Austin's first meeting with his Mexican hosts in 1821 is usually covered in the briefest of terms. He came, he saw, he settled. As a student of Mexican history, I realized there was much more to it than that. He arrived in Texas at a time when Mexico was suffering through immense changes. Determined to succeed, even though he had not been in favor of the idea to begin with, Stephen Austin worked hard to carry out his father's mission. That he was able to survive in those turbulent times is a testament to his political and diplomatic skills.

By examining Austin's life and the years from 1821 to 1823 in more detail, it is clear that Austin faced tremendous challenges. Upon reading the Austin papers, I discovered that despite his later claims to the contrary, Austin was reticent about his father's project. I also learned, from a conversation with Estella Zermeño of Goliad, that her ancestor, Manuel Becerra, had served as Austin's guide in Texas. His diary exposes the real story of that trip. And finally, by comparing the dates of Austin's stay in Mexico City with the changes in government, it is evident that Austin's friendship with Mexican men on both sides of the political spectrum enabled him to succeed in carrying out his father's dying wish. His effort to establish the first Anglo-American colony in Texas is a remarkable tribute, as his mother said, to Austin's perseverance and fortitude.

SELECTED BIBLIOGRAPHY

Barker, Eugene C. *The Life of Stephen F. Austin: Founder of Texas, 1793-1836; A Chapter in the Westward Movement of the Anglo-American People.* Nashville, Dallas: Cokesbury Press,1926.

Cantrell, Gregg. *Stephen F. Austin: Empresario of Texas.* New Haven and London: Yale University Press, 1999.

Crimm, Ana Carolina Castillo. *De León: A Tejano Family History.* Austin: University of Texas Press, 2003.

De la Teja, Jesús F., ed. *A Revolution Remembered: The Memoirs and Selected Correspondence of Juan N. Seguin.* Austin: State House Press, 1991.

Gracy, II, David B. *Moses Austin: His Life.* San Antonio: Trinity University Press, 1987.

McDonald, David R. *José Antonio Navarro: In Search of the American Dream.* Austin: Texas State Historical Association, 2010.

O'Connor, Kathryn Stoner. *The Presidio La Bahía del Espíritu Santo de Zuñiga, 1721-1846.* Austin: Von Boeckmann-Jones Co. 1966.

Poyo, Gerald E., ed. *Tejano Journey, 1770-1850.* Austin: University of Texas Press, 1996.

Tracy, Milton Cook, and Richard Havelock-Bailie. *The Colonizer: A Saga of Stephen F. Austin.* El Paso: Guynes Printing Company, 1941.

NOTES

1 Moses Austin to Stephen F. Austin, May 22, 1821; The Austin Papers, Dolph Briscoe Center for American History, University of Texas at Austin, Box 2Q 412. (hereinafter The Austin Papers).

2 Author Gregg Cantrell agrees that Austin lied when he later claimed that he and his father had both been planning for the Texas project since the beginning. Gregg Cantrell, *Stephen F. Austin: Empresario of Texas* (New Haven and London: Yale University Press, 1999).

3 David B. Gracy, II, *Moses Austin: His Life* (San Antonio, TX: Trinity University Press, 1987), 200.

4 Ibid., 197.

5 Ibid., 200.

6 Stephen F. Austin to [his mother, Maria Austin and his sister Emily], January 20, 1821, The Austin Papers.

7 Ibid.

8 Ibid.

9 Ibid.

10 Ibid.

11 Ibid.

12 Ibid.

13 Ibid., 196.

14 Ana Carolina Castillo Crimm, *De León: A Tejano Family History* (Austin: University of Texas Press, 2003), 73; Cantrell, *Austin*, 108; Jesús Francisco de la Teja, editor, *A Revolution Remembered: The Memoirs and Selected Correspondence of Juan N. Seguín* (Austin: State House Press, 1991), 15.

15 De la Teja, *Revolution*, 6.

16 Ibid., 9.

17 Ibid.

18 Gracy, *Moses Austin*, 214.

19 Gracy, *Moses Austin*, 214; Milton Cook Tracy and Richard Havelock-Bailie. *The Colonizer: A Saga of Stephen F. Austin* (El Paso: Guynes Printing Company, 1941). The authors of this latter book indicate that Stephen F. Austin "came through Gonzales over the Old San Antonio Road." Gonzales, the capital of Green De Witt's later colony, had not yet been established. They meant Goliad.

20 Gracy, *Moses Austin*, 217; Cantrell, *Stephen F. Austin*, 3-4.

21 Cantrell, *Stephen F. Austin*, 78.

22 Ibid., 4, 7.

23 SFA to [Mother], July 5, 1821, The Austin Papers.

24 De la Teja, *Revolution*, 6.

25 Ibid., 6-7.

26 Cantrell, *Stephen F. Austin*, 115; Stephen F. Austin to Bastrop, at Natchitoches, July 1, 1821, The Austin Papers; Stephen F. Austin to J. E. Brown Austin, July 4, 1821, The Austin Papers.

27 David R. McDonald, *José Antonio Navarro: In Search of the American Dream* (Austin: Texas State Historical Association, 2010), 90-94.

28 Eugene C. Barker, *The Life of Stephen F. Austin; Founder of Texas, 1793-1836; A Chapter in the Westward Movement of the Anglo-American People* (Nashville, Dallas: Cokesbury Press, 1926), 94.

29 Cantrell, *Stephen F. Austin*, 12.

30 Ibid., 115.

31 Cantrell, *Stephen F. Austin*, 115; Victoria Arbizu-Sabater, *La Habilidad de Estévan F. Austin con la lengua Española* (Doctoral Thesis, University of Seville, Spain, forthcoming, 2016), copy at Rice University, Houston, Texas; Tracy and Havelock-Bailie, *The Colonizer*, 17.

32 Barker, *Life of Austin*, 100-101.

33 Ibid., 101.

34 McDonald, *José Antonio Navarro*, 90-94.

35 Manuel Becerra Orders, August 26, 1821, copy in the possession of Estella Zermeño, Goliad, Texas.

36 Ibid.

37 Manuel Becerra Diary, September 1821, copy in the possession of Estella Zermeño, Goliad, Texas; Manuel Becerra Diary, Bexar Archives, Dolph Briscoe Center for American History, University of Texas at Austin.

38 Letter, Alcalde Tomás Buentello to Governor Colonel Don Antonio Martínez, September 15, 1821, copy of letter in possession of Estella Zermeño; Letter, Buentello to Martínez, September 15, 1821, Bexar Archives, Dolph Briscoe Center for American History, University of Texas at Austin.

39 Letter, Buentello to Martínez, September 15, 1821; Bexar Archives.

40 Ibid.

41 Cantrell, *Stephen F. Austin*, 109,110.

42 McDonald, *José Antonio Navarro*, 105-106.

43 Cantrell, *Stephen F. Austin*, 110; Tracy and Havelock-Bailie, *The Colonizer*, 16.

44 Cantrell, *Stephen F. Austin*, 111-112.

45 Ibid., 112.

46 Ibid., 112-113.

47 Tracy and Havelock-Bailie, *The Colonizer*, 18-19.

48 Ibid. The source for this fanciful romance, according to these authors, came from a letter from Moses Austin Bryan to his son Judge Beauregard Bryan in which he refers to "an infatuation entertained for a Castilian beauty." The other source was the Scrap Book of Emma Tracy Duke which contains a newspaper excerpt that claimed "to love a beautiful Castilian girl could not be accepted as pro-Mexican and in opposition to Americanism." Notes, 376.

49 Cantrell, *Stephen F. Austin*, 120-123.

50 Ibid., 114.

51 Ibid., 123-124.

52 McDonald, *José Antonio Navarro*, 107-110; Cantrell, *Stephen F. Austin*, 124.

53 Cantrell, *Stephen F. Austin*, 126.

54 Ibid.

55 Tracy and Havelock-Bailie, *The Colonizer*, 24.

56 McDonald, *José Antonio Navarro*, 110; Cantrell, *Stephen F. Austin*, 126.

57 McDonald, *José Antonio Navarro*, 110-112.

58 Cantrell, *Stephen F. Austin*, 131.

59 Maria Austin to Stephen F. Austin, 24 August, 1823, The Austin Papers.

CHAPTER THREE

The Fall of the Alamo, March 6, 1836

Watson Arnold

ON MARCH 6, 1836, NEAR a remote Spanish mission, San Antonio de Valero, Mexican soldiers stood quietly in ranks for several hours in the predawn darkness, awaiting the word to advance. Four groups of men, each attacking from a different direction, began marching in silence, slowly at first, and then gathering speed until the excitement of imminent action led them to spontaneously burst into shouts and "vivas." The defenders heard the noise and ran to the ramparts to defend their fort. Gunshots filled the air, cannons began to bellow, the "Yankee yells" and cries of the defenders joined those of the attackers and a cacophony of noise filled the morning as light crept over the horizon.

Three times the Mexican soldiers advanced and twice they were repulsed. The third time they climbed on each others' shoulders, upon the logs of half finished repairs to the walls, and up the few short ladders they had been given. Slowly a trickle, then a stream and finally a flood of troops scaled the walls and entered the courtyard. The noise rose and became deafening as the screams and moans of the dead and dying joined the sounds of gunfire and the roar of the cannons. The attackers gained ground, driving the defenders before them into the secondary defenses constructed in the long barracks, rooms, and chapel. The cannons were overrun and turned on the defenders. Blood-maddened attackers began to search for the remnants of the defenders in every room and closet, killing every one they found. Officers ran about trying to gain control of their army. Even a cat was shot as it scampered from under a board when someone screamed that it was the ghost of a defender.[1]

Finally, there was silence. The fight was over in less than an hour. Every one of the 183 defenders was dead either through battle or execution. The Mexican soldiers wandered among the bodies searching to kill anyone with a remnant of life, while their comrades moaned from their wounds. There were no defenders left alive to tell their story of siege, attack, and death, of heroism and fear, of agony and dying.

In the battle for the Alamo, history has recorded only one side of the story, presented through the distorted descriptions of politically motivated Mexican officers. None of the 183 Texan defenders survived to relate what happened. The noncombatant survivors could only give limited descriptions of the battle seen from their hiding places. Some described one part of an episode while another survivor told a bit more or, hearing the first story, modified his or her story to match. No one could give a coherent report of the events inside the Alamo garrison before and during the battle.

Since that fateful day, many myths have developed, some outright lies told, and numerous exaggerations made, all designed to swell the hearts of the listeners and to celebrate the heroism of the Alamo defenders. Commonly referred to as the Texas myth, it embodied what many Texans hold dear in defining their identity—freedom, independence, patriotism, and sacrifice. This myth has become so imbedded in the Alamo story that it has become difficult to separate truth from fiction. A careful look at the facts, however, can dispense with many of these distortions of the actual events.

The battle played out like this. Mexican General Antonio López de Santa Anna and his troops arrived at San Antonio on February 23, 1836. The Texans retired to the Alamo in haste and the siege began in earnest the next day. The Mexican artillery launched a constant bombardment of the Alamo garrison. On February 25 William B. Travis sent Juan Seguín to General Sam Houston, the leader of the Texan forces, with a letter for help. Meanwhile, Jim Bonham had traveled to Goliad to meet with Colonel James Fannin for reinforcements and returned on February 25. He went again two days later, returning on March 3. Earlier, on March 1, twenty-three volunteers from Gonzales arrived to reinforce those at the Alamo. The Mexican army then tightened the siege to prevent further reinforcements. The last messenger, fifteen-year-old John W. Smith, left on March 3 with a letter from Colonel Travis to Sam Houston. Just before dawn on the morning of March 6 the Mexican army stormed the Alamo. They were repelled initially, but broke through on their third attempt and swarmed over the walls. The final battle lasted less than an hour and all 183 defenders perished.[2]

There were at least five groups of survivors: Joe, Colonel Travis's black slave; Susanna Dickinson and her small daughter, Angelina; the two Veramendi sisters, Bowie's sisters-in-law Mrs. Horace Alsbury and her sister Gertrudis Navarro; several native San Antonio Hispanics, including Mrs. Gregorio Esparza and her four children, Trinidad Saucedo, and Petra Gonzales; and finally Brigido Guerrero, a Hispanic combatant who convinced the soldiers that he had been a prisoner and was released. Guerrero had little to say and quietly disappeared.[3]

These few survivors provided limited narratives and only from restricted points of view. Joe, Colonel William B. Travis's slave, for example, ran to hide in a small room in the long barracks when his master was shot. He saw little after he hid. He related what he saw then disappeared after about a year.[4] Susanna Dickinson, an illiterate twenty-two-year-old with a baby daughter, had been sequestered in the side rooms of the Alamo chapel. She told her story, changing it over time, and then tried to forget the episode. Bowie's two sisters-in-law and their children had hidden in a small room along the south wall. They spoke only Spanish and said little about the battle. The other Hispanic families had withdrawn into the side rooms in the chapel and spoke only Spanish, but some later related what they saw of the battle.[5]

Many of the fallacies and assumptions that comprise the Texas myth concern the major participants on the Texian side. One such question is: How did William Travis, the Alamo commander, die? Did he fall fighting or from a self-inflicted wound to avoid capture? Joe, Travis's slave, was next to him on the wall, manning a cannon. As the only surviving Texan eyewitness, he related the circumstances of Travis's death several times. Shortly after the battle began, Joe explained, Travis was leaning over the wall shooting the Mexican soldiers sheltered there when he was struck in the forehead by a bullet. He was knocked backwards off the cannon parapet to the ground where he sat dazed while a Mexican officer tried to stab him. Travis was able to saber the officer before he died.

The death of Colonel James Bowie has also been mythologized. On the day the Texans pulled out from San Antonio and moved into the Alamo, Bowie had ridden frantically about, ransacking houses for provisions. He was able to move his two sisters-in-law, the Veramendi sisters, safely into the Alamo. The sisters had been frantic. They remembered when the Spanish army took San Antonio (Santa Anna was part of this occupation), killed most of the males, and locked up, humiliated, and assaulted the females. Bowie then became ill that evening and several days later he collapsed and was bed ridden for the rest of the siege. After he relinquished his command to Travis, Bowie continued to decline. A few days later he did not recognize Seguín who came to get permission to borrow Bowie's horse.[6]

Some say that at the time of the siege Bowie lay in his bed with two pistols loaded and his bowie knife in his lap when the Mexican soldiers entered his room. He allegedly dispatched several soldiers with his pistols then gutted several more with his knife before they ran him through with their bayonets, lifting his body and bouncing it in the air. There are no facts to support this story. Actually, Jim Bowie was comatose when he was shot and maybe was already dead. Anyway, Bowie was a large man—six feet tall and weighing over 180 pounds. Not even several Mexican soldiers (average 5'4" in height, weighing less than 140 pounds) could have tossed him over their heads.[7]

Jim Bowie most likely died from acute alcoholic withdrawal and liver failure. Some have espoused that typhoid, viral pneumonia, consumption, or pneumonia from a bacterial infection were possible causes of death, but there is little basis for those diagnoses. Typhoid fever is a waterborne disease caused by salmonella and is usually associated with contaminated well water. It usually attacks the entire household at the same time. At the time Bowie was living with his sisters-in-law in their family home and they would have drunk the same water. But the sisters did not develop typhoid fever. No observers noted a fever, rash, diarrhea, or bleeding that would be characteristic of typhoid.[8]

To support a diagnosis of alcoholic decompensation, Bowie had been on a prolonged drunk just prior to the battle. He vigorously exerted himself the day the Mexican army arrived in San Antonio. And then he suddenly stopped drinking. Shortly thereafter he fell acutely ill, suffered chills and shakes, became increasingly delirious, and slipped into death. Seguín recorded that he visited Bowie several days before the final battle. Seguín stated that Bowie was semi-comatose, unable to talk, and lay in a bed near the chapel annex. Acute alcohol withdrawal fits these descriptions best.

Bowie's place of death has also been an area of contention. Bowie most likely died in a small room in the low barracks next to the chapel near the south entrance. The defenders moved Bowie out of the way of the battle and nearer to his two sisters-in-law, who were in a room in the low barracks along the south wall where they could easily care for him.[9]

After the battle, Dr. John Sutherland showed several people, including Captain Reuben Potter, the room where he said Bowie's brains and blood had spattered on the wall from being shot in his bed—not bayoneted.[10] Travis had earlier sent Dr. Sutherland to Colonel James Fannin at Goliad as a messenger. Captured, Sutherland had had been spared from the Goliad massacre and sent to San Antonio afterwards to care for the wounded Mexican soldiers. Thus, he had viewed the room shortly after the battle, confirming Bowie's final demise.[11]

One debate that has been impossible to expunge from public memory and has contributed to the all-encompassing role the Alamo has played in the construction of a Texas identity is what happened to Davy Crockett? Did he die swinging Ole Betsy? Did he really surrender? Was he captured and then

David Crockett

executed? According to the memoirs of Lieutenant Colonel José Enrique de la Peña, a Mexican officer during the battle, Colonel David Crockett survived the battle and was taken before General Santa Anna. On orders from His Excellency, Santa Anna's aides drew their swords and executed Crockett, along with five other defenders. After reviewing all the evidence, most historians agree with historian James Crisp, who convincingly argues that Crockett surrendered, was captured, and then summarily executed on orders from Santa Anna.[12]

Along with the de la Peña diary, one of the most persuasive pieces of evidence comes from Juan Almonte, a Mexican official and diplomat. He was the illegitimate son of Josè María Moralos, the leader of the 1812 rebellion in southern Mexico. Before his father was captured, defrocked and executed by the Spanish, Almonte was rescued and taken to New Orleans where he was educated. He spoke excellent English and, other than being a staunch Mexican nationalist, he became one of the most honest and respected men in Mexico. During the Texas campaign, Almonte served as Santa Anna's aide and was with him at both the Alamo and San Jacinto battles. He supposedly stated in several interviews while in captivity that Crockett was captured and executed. Although that report has been disputed by some historians, it supported other Mexican accounts of the capture and execution of David Crockett and several other Alamo combatants.[13]

One of the most cherished myths, the line in the sand episode, is also based on shaky historical ground. Did Travis draw the famous line in the sand? This story comes from an article written half a century later by William Zuber, a notorious exaggerator. He related that his story had been told to his parents decades earlier by Louis "Moses" Rose who was present at the Alamo. Not until 1872, thirty-six year later, however, did Zuber publish his account that contains the line in the sand episode.

The story, however, does not stand up to close examination. According to Zuber, Rose supposedly refused to cross Travis's line and escaped before the final assault. In the process of leaving the Alamo, Rose stated that he fell over the wall into a pool of blood. Curiously, why was there a pool of blood before the battle? While not specific whether he was speaking about the line in the sand, Zuber later admitted in a letter dated September 14, 1877, that he had expanded Rose's story to make it sound better. Further, he added that he had made up Travis's speech.[14] Interestingly, the land archives of Texas accepted the testimony of a Rose, recorded as a French immigrant and former Napoleonic soldier and "a survivor of the Alamo," as valid to certify that a person (Rose) was in the Alamo at the time of its fall.[15] Susanna Dickinson does mention a "Ross" who deserted after the line in the sand speech, but only long after Zuber published his article. No survivor mentioned Travis drawing a line in the sand and surely some of the survivors or messengers who left during the last days of the siege would have witnessed such an important event. Evidence does support that Travis talked with his men, telling them that no help would arrive and allowing them to stay or go. Travis also confirmed that Rose was present in the Alamo and slipped over the wall while escaping during the final days of the siege. But most scholars agree that the line in the sand is fiction.

Were there other survivors of the Alamo? Certainly, in the final moments, numerous soldiers slipped over the walls and ran for the woods. Several Mexican participants verify in their memoirs that several Texans escaped.[16] Most were cut down by waiting Mexican cavalry. A Hispanic woman betrayed one escapee who had hidden under a bridge. He was captured and killed. One man, Henry Warnell, probably escaped, but died of his wounds several months later at Port Lavaca.[17] There may have been other survivors, but the scattered reports have not been documented. The fates of the few survivors are well known, except that of Travis's slave Joe who seems to have disappeared several years later. A recent book by Ron Jackson and Lee Spencer White, *Joe, The Slave Who Became an Alamo Legend,* however, documented that Joe walked back to Georgia to return to the Travis family and probably died there.[18]

Andrea Castañon de Villanueva, known as Madam Candelaria, was a Hispanic healer who contended that she cared for James Bowie during the final phase of the battle for the Alamo. She gave numerous interviews that claimed she was inside the Alamo and "was brought in specifically to nurse James Bowie." In other interviews, however, she contradicted earlier statements, thereby calling her recollections into question. Further, no other survivors or contemporary authors described a woman who would fit Madam Candelaria's description. Nevertheless, she did receive a government pension of $120 a year from the Texas legislature for her service to the sick and wounded during the battle of the Alamo. Because her story was inconsistent with some of the evidence and changed several times over the years, Madam Candelaria's presence at the Alamo still leaves behind many unanswered questions.[19]

Which flag or flags flew over the Alamo has also been a subject of contention. There are records of several flags related to the battle. If a flag flew over the Alamo then, traditionally, it would have been a modification of the Mexican flag with 1824 in the middle rather than the eagle. But that flag had gone out of popularity by the fall of the Alamo as the Texians rejected rejoining Mexico and declared independence. Evidence supports that Travis had purchased a flag on his way to San Antonio and he mentioned that a flag flew over the fortification in one of his letters.[20] De la Peña and other Mexican officers reported that one of the officers, Lieutenant José Maria Torres of the Zapadores battalion, was killed at the Alamo while trying to take down a flag.[21] And Santa Anna, in his report to the Mexican government, noted that he was sending a flag to Mexico City as a sign of his victory. After announcing Santa Anna's triumph over the Alamo defenders, Secretary of War Tornel and other members of the Mexican Congress then trampled on the flag in celebration of the Mexican victory.

Dawn at the Alamo *by Henry Arthur McArdle, hanging in the Texas Senate*

In 1934 a flag was discovered in Mexico City that had belonged to the New Orleans Grays, a regiment whose soldiers were part of the Alamo garrison.[22] Dr. Luis Castrillo Lendon, Director of the Mexican Museum of Archaeology, found the flag, which is now kept at Chapultepec, crumbling to pieces in a brown paper wrapper. The blue-gray silk banner belonged to the first Company of the New Orleans Grays. Santa Anna may have chosen the flag of the New Orleans Grays because it was less controversial than other flags.[23] While there may have been other flags flown, this one is the only documented survivor of the battle that can be linked to Santa Anna.

After the battle was over Santa Anna was reported to have said: "It was a small affair." He was wrong! This "small affair" stiffened the resolve of the Texan army to fight at San Jacinto and to defeat the Mexican army. The brutality of the battle crystallized American resolve and welded national sentiment against Mexico. The battle and its aftermath led to the depiction of Santa Anna as a "tyrant," a "butcher," and a "perfidious dictator." Newspapers across the nation called for vengeance. Memories of the massacres at the Alamo and at Goliad led, in part, to the Mexican-American War and the Mexican loss of not only Texas, but also California, New Mexico, and Arizona. A small affair indeed!

The battle of the Alamo lies at the center of the Texas myth. It embodies many of the values and qualities that Texans hold dear in defining their identity. But historians must separate myth from history, ensuring that our narratives are based on accurate historical evidence. This dividing line between truth and fallacy, which often results in the formation of myths, is difficult to discern as events are frequently rearranged, forgotten, or exaggerated by the participants or subsequent historians. Thus, stories may have to be reviewed and revised many times. Historians, therefore, must interpret history in a way that explains the past in a meaningful, useful fashion for the present. The battle of the Alamo, so encrusted with myths, legends, and fallacies, is the perfect, Lone Star moment when a small group of Texians commanded by Colonel William B. Travis faced an overwhelmingly larger Mexican force commanded by Santa Anna and perished, leaving a legacy of heroism and courage.

When I was asked to choose a moment in Texas history at which I could be a "fly on the wall" and eavesdrop on what really happened, I jumped at the chance. I had always been fascinated by the Alamo and wondered how the battle was fought and how it ended. The Alamo is distinctive because so many myths swirl surround its final days. So I chose to be present the last day of the battle of the Alamo, March 6, 1836, during the campaign for Texas Independence, not necessarily as a "fly on the wall," but more as a gargoyle on the roof—on the right front corner of the church chapel. From there I would have had a panoramic view of most of the battle, with only a couple of quick flights for details. How did William Travis and Jim Bowie die and where? Did Davy Crockett survive as de la Peña said or did he die swinging Ole Betsy like Fess Parker showed us in the movie? What was the flag that flew over the walls during the battle? We will probably never know for certain the answers to these questions. But the gargoyle on the roof would know, and for now, he is not talking.

SELECTED BIBLIOGRAPHY

Caro, Ramon Martinez. "A True Account of the First Texas Campaign and the Events Subsequent to the Battle of San Jacinto," in Carlos Castaneda, *The Mexican Side of the Texas Revolution*. Washington, D.C., Documentary Publications, 1971.

Crisp, James E. *Sleuthing the Alamo*. Oxford Press: New York, 2005.

de la Peña, José Enrique. *With Santa Anna in Texas*, edited and translated by Carmen Perry. College Station: Texas A&M University Press, 1975.

Donovan, James. *Blood of Heroes: The 13-Day Struggle for the Alamo—and the Sacrifice That Forged a Nation*. New York: Little, Brown and Company, 2012.

Flores, Richard R. *Remembering the Alamo: Memory, Modernity, and Master Symbol*. Austin: University of Texas Press, 2002.

Jackson, Ron J., and Lee Spencer White. *Joe, The Slave Who Became an Alamo Legend*. Norman: University of Oklahoma Press, 2015.

Long, Jeff. *Duel of Eagles. The Mexican and U.S. Fight for the Alamo*. New York: William Morrow and Company, Inc., 1990.

Lord, Walter. *A Time to Stand: A Chronicle of the Valiant Battle at the Alamo.* New York: Bonanza books, 1987.

Nofi, Albert A. *The Alamo and the Texas War for Independence.* Conshohocken, PA: Combined Books, 1992.

Potter, Captain Reuben. In John Henry Brown, *History of Texas 1685-1892,* Vol. I. 575-585ff.

Rios, John F. *Readings on the Alamo.* New York: Vantage Press, 1987.

Roberts, Randy, and James S. Olson. *A Line in the Sand: The Alamo in Blood and History.* New York: The Free Press, 2001.

NOTES

1 See Ron J. Jackson, and Lee Spencer White, *Joe, The Slave Who Became an Alamo Legend* (Norman: University of Oklahoma Press, 2015); Randy Roberts and James S. Olson. *A Line in the Sand: The Alamo in Blood and History* (New York: The Free Press, 2001), 155-165.

2 The best book for a complete, balanced, and accurate version of the story is still Walter Lord's book, *A Time to Stand.* His narrative is exciting, well written, and accurate. Albert Nofi's *The Alamo and the Texas War for Independence,* and John Rios's, *Readings on the Alamo,* have examined in depth many of the discrepancies in the battle story and offer a plethora of statistics not available in most other sources and serve as the best informational texts. Nofi is especially good on the military aspects of the siege and battle. Captain Potter was the first to write on the Alamo and his essay, though full of what has proven to be inaccurate information, serves as the first and only English source written shortly after the battle. De la Peña's diary and Caro's essay are probably the most accurate of the accounts from the Mexican side of the battle. De la Peña's narrative exploded the story of David Crockett's death. The aftermath of the publication of de la Peña's diary and a well written story of the subsequent controversy and debate is provided by James Crisp's *Sleuthing the Alamo.* Roberts and Olson's *A Line in the Sand* is particularly important for the formation of myth. Albert A. Nofi, *The Alamo and the Texas War for Independence* (Conshohocken, PA: Combined Books, 1992); Procter, *The Battle of the Alamo* (Texas State Historical Association: Austin, 1986), 194.

3 Crystal Sasse Ragsdale, *Women and Children of the Alamo* (Austin: State House Press, 1994). See also Dora Guerra, "Two Silver Pesos and a Blanket: The Texas Revolution and the Non-Combatant Women Who Survived the Battle of the Alamo" in Mary L. Scheer, ed., *Women and the Texas Revolution* (Denton: University of North Texas Press, 2012), 123-152.

4 See Jackson, and White, *Joe, The Slave Who Became an Alamo Legend.*

5 Crystal Sasse Ragsdale, *Women and Children of the Alamo*; Susanna Dickinson's age is usually given as fifteen. But her birthday is given as 1814, making her actually about twenty-two at the time of the battle. Most of the

children remembered little. The Hispanic parents spoke little about their memories.

6   Nofi, *The Alamo*, 124-125.

7   Nofi, *The Alamo*, 69; Procter, *The Battle of the Alamo*, 25.

8   Nofi, *The Alamo*; Rios, *Readings on the Alamo*.

9   Nofi, *The Alamo*, 109; Potter, in *History of Texas 1685-1892*, Vol. I, 575-585ff.

10   Reuben Potter, "The Fall of the Alamo," in John F. Rios, *Readings on the Alamo* (New York: Vantage Press, 1987), 98-112; Potter, in John Henry Brown, *History of Texas 1685-1892*, Vol. I, 575-585ff; Potter must be taken with a grain of salt for he is the source of most of the historical inconsistencies about the battle and the aftermath. Nofi, *The Alamo*, 24-125.

11   Potter, in John Henry Brown, *History of Texas 1685-1892*, Vol. I, 575-585ff; Nofi, *The Alamo*, 69.

12   See José Enrique de la Peña, *With Santa Anna in Texas,* edited and translated by Carmen Perry (College Station: Texas A&M University Press, 1975).

13   Juan N. Almonte, *Almonte's Texas,* edited by Jack Jackson and translated by John Wheat (Austin: Texas State Historical Association, 200), 415-418ff.

14   Nofi, *The Alamo*, 118-119.

15   John F. Rios, *Readings on the Alamo* (New York: Vantage Press, 1987), 354-356.

16   Nofi, *The Alamo*, 130-132.

17   Rios, *Readings on the Alamo*, 359.

18   Jackson and White, *Joe, The Slave*.

19   Nofi, *The Alamo*, 118-119; Guerra, "Two Silver Pesos and a Blanket," 134-136.

20   Procter, *The Battle of the Alamo*, 25.

21   de la Peña, *With Santa Anna*, 49; Ramon Martinez Caro, "A True Account of the First Texas Campaign and the Events Subsequent to the Battle of San Jacinto," in Carlos Castaneda, *The Mexican Side of the Texas Revolution* (Washington DC: Documentary Publications, 1971), 105-106; Miguel A. Sanchez La Mego, *The Siege and Taking of the Alamo,* translated by Consuelo Velasco (Sante Fe: The Blue Feather Press, 1968).

22   Rios, *Readings on the Alamo*, 360-361.

23   Nofi, *The Alamo*, 118-119.

CHAPTER FOUR

"I Was There": The Abduction of Cynthia Ann Parker, December 19, 1860

Paul H. Carlson and Tom Crum

*"I was there, and was an eye-witness to the facts I am re-
lating, and while I have no desire to contradict anyone,
I would like for the people of Texas to know the facts of
history, and not accept the hearsay of any man."—Peter
Robertson, Militiaman*[1]

DECEMBER 19, 1860, BROKE COLD and windy along
Mule Creek in modern Foard County. Winter had set in.
Approximately fifteen Comanches, mostly women and children, were beginning to leave the often-used hunting and
camping ground along the little fresh-water tributary of the
Pease River. On their several strings of pack animals, they had
secured tons of meat plus a large number of bison hides, bones,
horns, and hoofs. They needed the meat, hides, and other supplies to help their band survive the winter.[2]

About two days earlier, Peta Nocona, a Comanche warrior,
and a substantial number of other band members from the
small Noconi (Nocona) division of the Comanches rode away

67

from the popular camping site. As was their custom, they had left the dirty and laborious work of processing, gathering, and packing meat, hides, and other goods to a dozen or so women with their children and a few men who would follow. Nocona and the others pointed their ponies northwest. They headed toward the Canadian River Valley in the upper reaches of the Texas Panhandle where they planned to hunker down for the next few months while women preserved the meat and processed the hides and men fashioned tools and weapons from the bones, horns, and hoofs.[3]

Among the fifteen who remained at Mule Creek were someone the Comanches referred to as a brother (he may have been a cousin) of Peta Nocona, two of Nocona's wives, and his baby daughter. Nocona had taken with him a third wife, a Comanche woman and perhaps his favorite wife. Quanah, or Quanah Parker as Anglos came to know him, and his brother Pecos also accompanied their father to the Texas Panhandle.[4]

Of Nocona's wives remaining at Mule Creek, one by birth and upbringing was a Comanche; the other by birth was an Anglo, a girl whom Comanche raiders had captured in 1836. Nocona's family and friends called the white woman Naudah or Naduah. Her English name was Cynthia Ann Parker. She was the mother of Quanah, Pecos, and an infant daughter named Prairie Flower. Although her two sons had ridden with their father toward the Texas Panhandle, Naudah kept Prairie Flower with her at Mule Creek. They saw the sun set that cold December day. The other wife and at least three additional women—probably four—and two or three of the men, victims of a lightning-like Anglo assault, did not survive the chilly morning.

In the long, often bitter struggle between Anglos moving onto western lands and Native Americans occupying those very same lands, people on both sides became victims. In fact, the

Map showing the battle of Pease River and the route Texas Rangers, Federal troops, and local militiamen took to the Comanche hunting camp.

COURTESY OF CURTIS PEOPLES

fate of the small Indian party along Mule Creek was directly related to events that recently had transpired in Jack, Parker, and Palo Pinto counties in the Cross Timbers region of Texas.

For three days, from November 26 to November 28, Comanches rode through Anglo settlements in those counties. They were looking for horses, but during the foray they killed at least six people, wounded several others, and scalped two women. The Indians left with an estimated three hundred horses and mules and three prisoners. Shortly afterward they released two of the captives and later murdered the third. The raid scared settlers. Farm and ranch activity slowed or stopped. In villages, little business occurred. A few people left the country.[5]

But, the raid also angered people. Men from Palo Pinto, Parker, and adjoining counties created a citizen militia force, elected J. J. "Jack" Cureton, a seasoned frontiersman, captain, and assembled in Loving's Valley along the Palo Pinto-Jack County Line. A Texas Rangers unit under twenty-two-year-old Lawrence Sullivan "Sul" Ross, later a Texas governor, gathered along Elm Creek several miles west of Fort Belknap. There, on about December 11, twenty federal troopers of Company H, Second United States Cavalry, from Camp Cooper, under experienced veteran Sergeant John W. Spangler, joined them. Two days later the Ross and Spangler companies met Cureton and his militiamen along Salt Creek north of Fort Belknap in Young County. They planned to find and strike back at the Comanche raiders.

On December 14 the combined forced moved out, heading northwest along Salt Creek toward the popular Comanche hunting and camping ground in the vicinity of Pease River. Challenged by the poor condition of their horses and by inadequate forage along their route of travel, the command made slow progress. The militiamen and some of the rangers, on account of their debilitated mounts, fell behind the cavalry and other rangers who were better mounted.[6]

Nonetheless, late on December 18 approximately 155 Anglo men—perhaps more—camped along the Pease River. They were several miles downstream from the Comanche camping ground. The majority of the 155 participants were citizen militiamen under Captain Cureton's leadership. Sul Ross led forty Texas Rangers, and Sergeant Spangler directed his twenty federal troops. The militiamen's bivouac lay separate from that of the rangers and cavalry. Some of the men in the determined force were simply doing their duty, some seeking revenge, and some possibly seeking glory or adventure. Most probably shared a combination of such desires.

Early on the morning of December 19, 1860, as had become the normal morning routine, cavalrymen and some rangers started early and ahead of the militiamen. Most of the rangers, however, on account of the poor condition of their horses, remained behind with the militiamen. The twenty cavalrymen and approximately ten to fifteen rangers who started early proceeded west up the Pease River until they discovered the Comanche camp located along the wide, shallow stream's Mule Creek tributary. From where they viewed the camp, they saw that Indian workers had completed the packing and loading of horses and mules, and a few of them had already crossed Mule Creek and were riding toward the northwest. Some in the camping party were just starting, and some were about to mount their horses and lead the heavily laden pack animals. All the horses and mules, even those on which the Comanches rode, were carrying winter supplies. The single exception, possibly, was the horse on which Naudah rode with little Prairie Flower.

Because of the cold north wind, all the Comanches, including Naudah, covered themselves in heavy bison robes. Then, suddenly, to the Indians' great surprise, from over a low hill east of their encampment, they saw horse-mounted men, about thirty in number, racing toward them. Panic ensued. Indians who were not yet aboard their ponies hurried to mount and those who were already on their horses attempted to escape the hard-riding attackers who by this time had split into two groups. The larger group, U. S. troopers of the Second Cavalry, rushed to the right to cut off any further Comanche escape across Mule Creek.[7]

The smaller group, Texas Rangers, rode straight at Comanches still in or near the camp ground. The charging rangers killed four women in camp, their bodies later described as almost being in a pile, and two other people either in or near the camp or some distance away. The attackers may not have been able to tell the sex of the Comanches upon whom they were firing, for all the Indians were wrapped in bison robes. It must have been difficult to distinguish men from women, especially when charging on a galloping horse. Also, Sul Ross had promised a new Colt revolver to the first ranger who killed an Indian, and such a prize may have diminished any concern rangers had as to the sex of that first person killed.

While the rangers attacked Comanches still in or near the abandoned camp, cavalrymen, as indicated, galloped to the right and across the little creek to cut off those people who were attempting to flee. In doing so they killed a man, but were not able to keep six other Indians from escaping. It is unknown whether the six Comanches succeeded in their flight because cavalrymen were not able to stop them or because the troopers, seeing that they were women, decided not to shoot. Or, perhaps, no matter their sex, the troopers simply had no desire to shoot in the back people who were running away.[8]

During the whole affair, which took less than thirty minutes, the Texas Rangers and federal troopers killed seven Comanches and captured three others. Six Indians escaped. No troopers or rangers died or suffered wounds. Two of the three captives were Cynthia Ann Parker and her daughter. The third was an eight- or ten-year-old boy. For the Comanches, the attack proved a disaster: seven people dead, three abducted, and desperately needed winter supplies lost.[9] For Naudah and her infant daughter, the fight forever changed their lives—although neither survived in their new Anglo world for more than a decade.

The encounter, a massacre in some respects, became known to Texans as the battle of Pease River. Hiram B. Rogers, one of the rangers, remembered the affair as a massacre. "I was in the . . . fight," he said about 1928, "but I am not very proud of it. That was not a battle at all, but just a killing of squaws."[10]

Owing to the relatively small number of participants involved and the short duration of the so-called battle, one would expect there to be little controversy as to the facts surrounding the event. Someone laboring under such an expectation would be greatly disappointed, for considerable controversy remains. Not everyone, for example, agreed with Rogers's assessment.[11]

From the Comanche side there is little recorded information. Prairie Flower, of course, did not talk about the event. It seems certain that Pease Ross, the captured Comanche boy whom Sul Ross took home from the Pease River fight and raised among his slaves in McLennan County, said something about what he heard and saw. But there are no extant records of his information, in part because he spoke the Comanche language during his first few years in an alien Anglo world. Comanche oral tradition is based largely on what Quanah Parker said, or may have said, but he was not at the Pease River fight.[12] Thus, except for some statements by Cynthia Ann Parker, given, for the most part, before she regained use of her native English language and made through an interpreter, historians have no extant descriptions of the encounter from any Comanche person at Mule Creek.

As a result, nearly all we know of the battle of Pease River and the abduction of Cynthia Ann Parker comes from only a few Anglos. All the controversy, therefore, originates from reports on their side of the encounter.

Accounts of the December 19, 1860, events do not agree on much. They do not even agree as to the number of people in the Indian camp along Mule Creek. On several occasions, Ross claimed there were fifteen Comanches there, and he wrote that nine "grass tents" stood at the site. Sergeant Spangler reported that about twenty-five Native Americans were at the place.[13]

Benjamin Franklin Gholson's accounts were much different. Gholson, although having served as a Texas Ranger on other occasions, was not a member of Ross's command at the battle of Pease River and therefore did not participate in the fight. Yet, on one occasion he indicated that 500 to 600 Comanches, with 150 to 200 of them warriors, were in the camp along Mule Creek when rangers attacked. On another occasion, although not indicating the total number of Indians present, he stated he and eleven other rangers chased seventy Comanches who were carrying thirty-two of their dead or wounded companions, and on their return from the chase they found the bodies of seven other Indians. In this same statement, moreover, he said twenty-six Comanches were scalped, but another was not mutilated. Thus, assuming the twenty-six figure includes the seven he and the eleven other rangers discovered on their return from the chase, Gholson argues for a total of at least 129 Comanches spread along Mule Creek.[14]

As one might expect, since there is no agreement as to the number of Comanches in the camp, there is also no agreement as to the number of Indians who died in the attack. Sul Ross reported twelve killed. Sergeant John Spangler claimed fourteen dead. Ben Gholson said the total number of people killed was twenty-seven. Jonathan Hamilton Baker, a school teacher, who served as a militiaman and therefore not a participant in the attack, was among those who arrived at the campground several hours after the fight. He stayed at the site until December 25, Christmas day, and he kept a diary. According to the hand-written document, during the six days spent on and around the battlefield, the militiamen found the bodies of only seven Comanches, four women and three men.[15]

The number of rangers involved in the attack is another issue on which the participants cannot agree. Depending on the occasion, Ross gave conflicting accounts as to the number of rangers who rode with him during the early morning charge. In his January 4, 1861, official report to Governor Sam Houston, Ross reported, "Not more than twenty [Texas Rangers] were able to get in the fight, owing to the starved and jaded condition of their horses."[16] The number is approximately the same one Ross claimed in an early 1870s letter he wrote to the *Galveston News*, a letter which he claimed contained a "correct history" of the battle. In the letter Ross wrote, "Twenty of the Rangers were on foot, their horses having broken down . . . . With the twenty Rangers and twenty United States troops, I determined to attack at once." Then, in 1886, when running for governor of Texas, Ross claimed all forty of the rangers were engaged in the fight. He stated: "My command, with the detachment of the Second Cavalry, had out marched and become separated from the citizen command, which left me about sixty men."[17] One can only guess as to the reason Ross changed his accounts, but, like several of Ross's accounts, changes were made.

Sergeant John Spangler offered different numbers. In a December 24, 1860, report he stated, "during the fight we had the assistance of Captain Ross, Lieutenants Callihan [Thomas Killiher] and [David] Sublett, with about ten of his men (state troops) the remaining portion of his command could not give us any assistance on account of poor condition of their animals, they not being able to keep up with us."[18] In a later report, one given on January 16, 1861, he stated prior to the attack, the "State troops were scattered in parties of 6 or 8, and some mile or two in rear of the cavalry." As to the attack itself, Spangler stated, "When the command was given to charge, my men were all in advance of the State troops, in fact I did not see more than 5 or 6 of them at the time the charge was made."[19]

"Numbers" is not the only controversy. In his early 1870s "correct history" letter to the *Galveston News*, Sul Ross wrote that the Comanche he fought during the battle of Pease River was named Mohee. In Texans' collective memory, however, Ross fought Peta Nocona. The principal source for the memory is James DeShields's 1886 book *Cynthia Ann Parker*. In it, the author suggests he quotes Ross as saying after a chase of one-and-one-half miles, he overtook a horse carrying Nocona and a young girl who was riding behind the Comanche leader. After Ross fought and wounded him, Nocona sang a death song, and then Ross's Mexican servant killed the warrior.[20]

But DeShields's account, although the one most often cited in historical literature, is not the first to identify Peta Nocona as Ross's foe. Victor M. Rose in his 1881 book *Ross' Texas Brigade* first identified Nocona as the person Ross fought. The Rose book contains a biographical sketch of Sul Ross and describes the fight with Nocona. In the spring of 1881, in a letter concerning the sketch, Ross told Rose, "I can only promise to supply you with the merest outlines by way of suggestions and trust the embellishment thereof to yourself." In his own book, De Shields acknowledged he received "valued narratives from Rose."[21]

Nonetheless, DeShields's story of the encounter between Ross and an Indian adversary differs from the one in Rose's book. In *Ross' Texas Brigade*, Rose does not mention a one-and-one-half-mile chase, a girl riding behind a fleeing Peta Nocona, a death song, or a Mexican servant. Indeed, the only common claim in the Rose and DeShields accounts of the brief fight is that the Comanche warrior was Nocona. Was the change from Mohee to Peta Nocona nothing more than one of

Quanah, or Quanah Parker, taken after he had settled on the reservation near Fort Sill in Indian Territory

Rose's "embellishments," one that DeShields adopted? After all, Ross himself said he fought Mohee.

Notwithstanding the Rose and DeShields reports that Nocona died at Pease River, considerable evidence exists that Peta Nocona was not even at Mule Creek. Certainly, no one killed him there. At least two people reported they had seen Peta Nocona after the battle. One of these persons was Nocona's son Quanah Parker who said on several occasions that not only was his father not killed at Mule Creek but also that he was not there and thus could not have participated in the fight.[22] Rather, at the time of the battle, Nocona rode with Quanah, Pecos, and Nocona's favorite Comanche wife toward the Texas Panhandle. Quanah said, "two year, three year maybe (after the battle), my father sick. I see him die."[23] A number of writers exhibit no knowledge of Ross's Mohee claim, and thus dismiss Quanah's statements as simply lies designed, they say, to protect the family's good name.[24]

Another person who reported to having seen Peta Nocona after the battle is the famous scout and interpreter, Horace P. Jones. Jones served the government as interpreter at Camp Cooper when, after her capture, federal troops brought Cynthia Ann Parker to the post. Jones later said that in the fall of 1861 or 1862, while serving as interpreter at Fort Cobb in Indian Territory (present Oklahoma), Peta Nocona, having heard that Jones had seen and talked to Cynthia Ann, came to ask Jones about her capture and what became of her. The two men sat in the shade of a large walnut tree and talked.[25] No one has claimed Jones lied.

On at least one occasion Quanah Parker said the warrior Sul Ross fought near Mule Creek was Peta Nocona's brother.[26] Considering the ways in which pre-reservation Comanches identified their kin relationships, however, the "brother" could have been a blood brother or a half-brother or a cousin. Who knows?

The nature of the Sul Ross fight with a Comanche warrior, whoever he might have been, is another subject of conflicting accounts and subsequent controversy. As Ross and his rangers struck the little village, Comanches who survived the first volley scattered and fled. According to Ross, he and M. W. Somerville, a member of the Texas Rangers, chased two riders on a single horse. After a mile into the pursuit, Ross, apparently having left the large and heavy Somerville behind, remained the only person still in the chase. Another half mile brought him nearly even with his fleeing rivals, and he shot the back riding person. According to Ross, the rider proved to be a fifteen-year-old girl, and when she fell from the horse, she also pulled the front rider from the animal. At this point, the "fight," such as it was, between the warrior on foot and Ross on horseback began.[27]

During the fight, Ross claimed to have used his firearms and the Comanche used his bow with arrows and then a spear. Ross managed to wound the man in the arm, but his horse was hit near the base of its tail. After a few moments, Ross's Mexican servant rode up, shot, and killed the warrior. No one questions that Ross fought with someone on December 19 and after he had wounded his adversary, someone else killed the man. But the Ross version of what happened is not consistent with accounts other eyewitnesses gave to describe the incident.

Ben Dragoo, a seasoned Texas Ranger from McLennan County, wrote that the Ross-Comanche encounter took place right in the village. No long chase occurred and there was no double riding girl. Dragoo admits that Ross's servant shot the Comanche fighter, but the shot did not kill him. According to Dragoo, after the servant fired upon the wounded warrior, another ranger struck the man in the head with his gun and scalped him—while he was still alive. Dragoo mistakenly said that Ross received a wound during the struggle, a statement that is not true, and therefore, Dragoo's capacity for recalling events or possibly even his veracity may be called into question.[28]

Peter Robertson, a militiaman who may have acted as an expedition scout, added to the confusion. If, in fact, he served as a scout as both he and Dragoo reported, Robertson was with the rangers and cavalrymen and participated in the attack. He said he was and did. He also claimed that, when Ross thought a warrior was attempting to get other Comanches to make a defensive stand in the village, Ross charged him and the fight followed. According to Robertson, there was no long chase, and no double riding girl. Rather, as Robertson reported, the Comanche leader died when "some of the boys" shot him from a distance of fifty to seventy-five yards away, a shot Ross supposedly acknowledged as being a "splendid shot." The fight Robertson described could have happened in the village, as Dragoo claimed, but it could not have happened after a chase of one and one-half miles, as Ross claimed.[29]

Tom Padgitt was Ross's brother-in-law, having married Ross's sister Kate in 1878. Padgitt was not at Mule Creek, but claimed Ross told him about the fight "both at home and around the camp fire." Either Ross gave Padgitt a different account of his chase than he gave at other times, or Padgitt badly misunderstood what his brother-in-law was telling him, for according to Padgitt, Ross told him the girl and man were riding double and Ross shot the girl. According to Padgitt's version, the girl did not fall off the horse and therefore did not pull the man off the horse. Rather, the man jumped off the horse and the girl remained on the horse, and as he rode past the girl, Ross noticed she was shot and he allowed her to go on. Padgitt does not tell us if Ross thought the girl was mortally wounded or that she would survive. In any event, what he claims Ross told him is very different from what Ross reported on other occasions.[30]

Of course, it is possible, and maybe probable, that Padgitt invented the story that his wife's brother did not kill a girl. In such a scenario, Padgitt can say that when he found out he had shot her, Ross allowed the young woman to ride away. If he made up the story to further the family's reputation, Pagitt forgot to comment on whether the girl was left to die an agonizing death alone on the prairie or rode wounded but happy to her friends and family in the Texas Panhandle. In any event his rendition of the event is in stark contrast to that of his brother-in-law. In his 1870's "correct history" letter to the *Galveston News*, when describing his chase of Mohee, Ross did not mention a girl riding behind Mohee.[31]

Was there a double riding girl? Did Ross kill a young woman somewhere else on the battlefield? It is not likely Ross simply fabricated a story about killing a fifteen-year-old girl by shooting her in the back. Although it first appeared at or near the time Ross was trying to get elected governor of Texas, it was not the kind of story that would garner a lot of votes, even in 1886 Texas. Obviously, it did not hurt him politically—he won by a large margin—but it could not have helped him either. What probably mitigated any potential damage to his political fortunes was his claim that when he shot her, he did not realize she was a young female. Because four women were found "almost in a pile," the girl Ross chased and shot was not one of them, for her body, if Ross is correct, would have been found a mile and one-half away, and not part of "a pile" in the camp.[32]

Yet, the location of the girl's body remains something of a mystery. Ross could have killed the girl during the initial charge or after a chase somewhere away from the other four females. If so, Jonathan Baker, the school teacher who kept a diary and wrote about four women and three men having died, was mistaken about the sex of the seven dead Comanches and simply mistook a female for a male. Then, in that case five of the seven dead were female. They were all scalped and wrapped in buffalo robes, which would have made sexual identification somewhat difficult.[33]

Still another matter of conflict is the claim that the warrior Ross fought sang "a wild, weird song," before dying. The account first appeared in James DeShields's 1886 book, *Cynthia Ann Parker*. Ben Dragoo, one of the rangers, must have read the book, for some years later he stated, "If that chief sang a death song that day it was after we left him—dead." Then, in 1894, while serving as president of Texas A & M College, Ross told Susan Parker St. John, Cynthia Ann's cousin from Kansas who had come to meet with him about the Pease River fight, the dying man "did not sing, as [DeShields] says."[34]

While there is no dispute Cynthia Ann Parker was one of three Comanches taken in the fight, there are disagreements as to who first identified her as a white woman and who, in fact captured her. The men claiming to be the first to identify her as Anglo included Ross; Charles Goodnight, a scout for the militiamen and later a famed rancher in the Texas Panhandle; and Ben Dragoo. The actual person, whoever he was, seems unimportant.

The identity of the person who captured her remains another matter. Ross from a time soon after the fight in 1860 until the 1894 interview with St. John always claimed Lieutenant Tom Killiher of the rangers captured Cynthia Ann. But, again in 1894, Ross admitted to St. John that Sergeant John Spangler of the U. S. Second Cavalry captured the mother of three.[35] Although it came after the fact, the surprising shift in

Naduah, or Cynthia Ann Parker, and her daughter Topsannah, taken about 1862 not long after they had been sent to their Anglo family and friends.

identification agrees with what others always said about the abduction. That is, information provided in the Ross-St. John interview is consistent with what Sergeant Spangler wrote in his 1861 report of the battle and capture of Cynthia Ann, and a statement Horace P. Jones, the highly competent army interpreter, made about 1887. Likewise, it is similar to what Texas Ranger Captain John M. Elkins said a fellow ranger who participated in the battle told him. In other words, the Spangler and Jones accounts and the Elkins comment agree with what Ross at long last confessed to St. John: it was, indeed, John Spangler who on December 19, 1860, seized Cynthia Ann Parker away from her Comanche friends and family.

A couple of other men, Peter Robertson and Ben Dragoo, who also were at Mule Creek, saw the abduction in different ways. About 1920 or 1921, Robertson stated: "I don't consider that any one man could lay claim to the honor of having captured Cynthia Ann Parker. If there was any particular honor connected with her capture [,] it belonged as much to one as another in the company." Then he added, "Every man in the outfit saw her movement, and we all considered that she surrendered to the command, and not to any one individual." Dragoo, also in the 1920s, concluded: "I want to say that no particular individual is entitled to more honor in the capture of Cynthia Ann Parker than any other who was engaged in the battle of Pease river [*sic*]."[36]

Sul Ross gave conflicting accounts on just about every incident of the fight and abduction, and discrepancies between his statements and the reports of other participants remain numerous. Moreover, to meet his political needs, details in his various accounts changed over time, creating serious dissonance in his own reporting. Did he, for example, fight Mohee or Peta Nocona?[37] Were there "not more than twenty" rangers with Ross in his charge through the Comanche camp or were there forty? Did Tom Killiher or Sergeant John Spangler capture

Cynthia Ann Parker? Did the warrior he fought sing, or not sing, a death song before he died?

Nonetheless, in histories of the battle of Pease River and the abduction Cynthia Ann Parker, Ross remains the person most often cited and quoted. Many such citations note the 1886 DeShields biography of Cynthia Ann, particularly the short section where the author presumably quotes Ross, who at the time was running for governor of Texas. Were the forty rangers and death song stories a product of DeShields's imagination and not something Ross told the popular writer? Both stories and the identification of the person Ross fought as being Peta Nocona first appeared in the little book, which in the ways it describes the battle of Pease River proved an effective piece of campaign literature.[38] Ross told Susan Parker St. John that DeShields's "account is almost correct" except "Nocona did not sing as he says, and it was [John] Spangler who caught Cynthia Ann's pony." The comment implies that Ross did not tell DeShields the person he fought sang a death song and DeShields simply added it for effect. Although Ross did not refute him about it, DeShields to enhance the story may also have simply changed the number of rangers to forty. Also, in 1894 Ross was still telling St. John that the warrior he fought was Nocona.[39]

In the end, the story of the battle of Pease River and the abduction of Naudah or Cynthia Ann Parker remains full of contradictions, characterized by all manner of disagreement and disputation. If Cynthia Ann had not been one of the captives, the Mule Creek fight would be relegated to little more than footnotes. Her capture, however, elevated the whole sorry episode to a place of minor prominence in the history of Texas Indian wars, and concomitantly created a significant number of falsehoods that will not go away.

With their varied eyewitness accounts, differing official reports, and contrasting testimony, events along Mule Creek that cold, windy morning hunger for greater clarity and resolution. Even today, over 150 years later, specific details of those disorganized moments remain as disputed and as marked by confusion as they were in the aftermath of December 19, 1860.

———————◆◆×◆◆◆———————

It is hard to kill a myth. Some years ago an article appeared in the *Dallas Morning News* explaining how Cynthia Ann Parker (Naudah) in 1860 was taken from Comanches, after having lived among them for nearly twenty-five years. We did not think the description could be correct and determined to investigate. Our research uncovered a number of inconsistencies and errors in the reporting, and we found that too many writers, in describing the event, had used unreliable and even fraudulent sources. Despite our protestations, the errors and mistakes, the myths if you will, will not go away.

In an effort "to set the record straight," we have endeavored to come to grips with the contrasting reports from federal soldiers, Texas Rangers, and civilian militiamen. At the same time, we have tried to show how the errors—the myths—appeared, reasons they will not go away, and why the story of Cynthia Ann's capture is instructive as historiography and an important "fly on the wall" moment in Texas history we would have liked to have witnessed.

SELECTED BIBLIOGRAPHY

Betty, Gerald. *Comanche Society: Before the Reservation*. College Station: Texas A&M University Press, 2002.

Brenner, Judith Ann. *Sul Ross: Soldier, Statesman, Educator*. College Station: Texas A&M University Press, 1983.

Carlson, Paul H., and Tom Crum. "The 'Battle' at Pease River and the Question of Reliable Sources in the Recapture of Cynthia Ann Parker." *Southwestern Historical Quarterly* 113, no. 1 (July 2009): 32-52.

————. *Myth, Memory, and Massacre: The 1860 Capture of Cynthia Ann Parker.* Lubbock: Texas Tech University Press, 2010.

Crum, Tom. "Folklorization of the Battle of Pease River." *West Texas Historical Association Year Book* 72 (1996): 69-85.

Crum, Tom, and Paul H. Carlson. "Did Quanah Parker Lie?" *Chronicles of Oklahoma* 93, no. 3 (fall, 2015)

Hacker, Margaret Schmidt. *Cynthia Ann Parker: The Life and the Legend.* Southwestern Studies No. 92. El Paso: Texas Western Press, 1990.

Hagan, William T. *Quanah Parker, Comanche Chief.* Norman: University of Oklahoma Press, 1993.

Kavanagh, Thomas W. *Comanche Political History: An Ethnohistorical Perspective, 1706-1875.* Lincoln: University of Nebraska Press, 1996.

Selden, Jack K. *Return: The Parker Story.* Palestine, TX: Clacton Press.

NOTES

1 Robertson quote in J. Marvin Hunter, ed., "The Capture of Cynthia Ann Parker," *Frontier Times* 16, no. 8 (May 1939): 365.

2 For a larger view, see Paul H. Carlson and Tom Crum, *Myth, Memory, and Massacre: The Pease River Capture of Cynthia Ann Parker* (Lubbock: Texas Tech University Press, 2010), 29-60; Paul H. Carlson and Tom Crum, "The 'Battle' at Pease River and the Question of Reliable Sources in the Recapture of Cynthia Ann Parker," *Southwestern Historical Quarterly* 113, no. 1 (July 2009): 32-52; and Tom Crum, "Folklorization of the Battle of Pease River," *West Texas Historical Association Year Book* 79 (1996):69-85.

3 There is little documentary evidence to suggest the existence of a person by the name of Peta Nocona. See Gerald Betty, *Comanche Society Before the Reservation* (College Station: Texas A & M University Press, 2002), 4. Sul Ross, who some argue killed Nocona in 1860, called the man "a noted warrior of great repute," but in the mid-1870s he said the person he killed was named Mohee.

4 "Quanah Parker Sets History Straight," *Semi-Weekly Farm News* (Dallas), October 29, 1909; "Straightens Out History," *Dallas Morning News,* October 25, 1910. See also "Quanah Route Day Draws Large Crowd," *Dallas Morning News,* October 25, 1910; and J. Evetts Haley, ed., "Charles Goodnights Indian Recollections," *Panhandle-Plains Historical Review* 1 (1928): 3-29.

5 Doyle Marshall, *A Cry Unheard: The Story of Indian Attacks in and around Parker County, Texas, 1858-1872* (Aledo, TX: Annetta Valley Farm Press, 1990), 29-35, 39-45; Ida Lasater Huckabay, *Ninety-four Years in Jack County* (Waco: Texian Press, 1974), 60-64; John Carroll McConnell, *West Texas Frontier,* 2 Vols. (Palo Pinto: Texas Legal Bank & Book Co, 1939),

I: 26-32; and Rupert Norval Richardson, *The Frontier of Northwest Texas, 1846-1872* (Glendale, CA: Arthur H. Clark Co., 1963), 210-11.

6 Marshall, *A Cry Unheard*, 39-45; John W. Spangler, First Sergeant, Company H, to Nathan G. Evans, Captain, Second Cavalry, Camp Cooper, December 24, 1860, National Archives (NA), photocopy in possession of authors (hereafter Spangler to Evans, December 24, 1860); Captain L. S. Ross to Governor Sam Houston, January 4, 1861, as it appeared in "More about the Capture of Woman Prisoner," *San Antonio Express*, February 23, 1908 (hereafter Ross to Governor Houston, January 4, 1861).

7 Ross to Governor Houston, January 4, 1861; Spangler to Evans, December 24, 1860; "From the Frontier," *Dallas Herald*, January 2, 1861; and "Indian News," *Galveston Civilian*, January 15, 1861. See also, John W. Spangler to Nathan Evans, January 16, 1861, in the *San Antonio Ledger*, February 2, 1861, as cited in Jack K. Selden, *Return: The Parker Story* (Palestine, TX: Clacton Press, 2006), 292-94 (hereafter Spangler to Evans, January 15, 1861).

8 Spangler to Evans, December 24, 1860; and Spangler to Evans, January 15, 1861.

9 Ross to Governor Houston, January 4, 1861; Spangler to Evans, December 24, 1860; Peter Robertson, interview (1920 or 1921), in Hunter, ed., "The Capture of Cynthia Ann Parker," 364-65 (hereafter Robertson, interview).

10 Hiram B. Rogers, "Recollections of Ranger H. B. Rogers of the Capture of Cynthia Ann Parker," as told to J. A. Rickard, n.d. filed with Benjamin F. Gholson, "Recollections of B. F. Gholson," as told to J. A. Rickard, August 1928, typescript, Dolph Briscoe Center for American History, University of Texas at Austin.

11 See and compare, for example, "Ben Dragoo Tells of the Capture of Cynthia Ann Parker," *Frontier Times* 1, no. 3 (December 1923): 25-27 (Dragoo's story appears in several places, including in different issues of *Frontier Times*.); Robertson interview; Francis M. Peveler, "Reminiscences" (notes to J. Evetts Haley), October 14, 1932, in Nita Stewart Haley Memorial Library and J. Evetts Haley History Center, Midland; "The Parker Captives," *Galveston News*, June 3, 1875; "The Parker Captives," *Dallas Weekly Herald*, June 19, 1875; Robert H. Williams, The Case for Peta Nocona," *Texana* 10, no 1 (1972): 55-72; Carlson and Crum, *Myth, Memory, and Massacre*, 105-130; S. C. Gwynne, *Empire of the Summer Moon: Quanah Parker and the Rise and Fall of the Comanches, the Most Powerful Indian Tribe in American History* (New York Scribner, 2010), 175-79; and Selden, *Return*, 167-76.

12 A few Comanche comments about the Pease River fight can be found in Paul I. Wellman, "Cynthia Ann Parker," *Chronicles of Oklahoma* 12, no. 2 (June 1934): 163-74.

13 "From the Frontier," *Dallas Herald*, January 2, 1861; Ross to Governor Houston, January 4, 1861; "Indian News," *Galveston Civilian*, January 15, 1861; Spangler to Evans, December 24, 1860, and January 16, 1861; Benjamin F. Gholson interview with Felix Williams and Harvey Chelsey, August 26, 1931, in Rupert N. Richardson, ed., "The Death of Nocona

and the Recovery of Cynthia Ann Parker," *Southwestern Historical Quarterly* 46 (July 1942): 15-21 (hereafter Gholson interview, 1931); Benjamin F. Gholson, "Recollections of B. F. Gholson," as told to J. A. Rickard, August 1928, typescript, Dolph Briscoe Center for American History, University of Texas at Austin (hereafter Gholson, "Recollections," 1928).

14 Gholson interview, 1931; Gholson, "Recollections," 1928.

15 Johnathan Hamilton Baker, Diary of Jonathan Hamilton Baker, manuscript, entry for December 20, 1860, private collection, Tarrant County Historical Commission, Fort Worth (hereafter Baker, Diary—first, manuscript), entries for December 19-20, 1860. See also Jonathan Hamilton Baker, Diary of Jonathan [James] Hamilton Baker, 1858-1918, typescript, Dolph Briscoe Center for American History, University of Texas Austin.

16 Ross to Governor Houston, January 4, 1861.

17 "The Parker Captives," *Galveston News*, June 3, 1875; "The Parker Captives," *Dallas Weekly Herald*, June 19, 1875.

18 Spangler to Evans, December 24, 1860.

19 Spangler to Evans, January 16, 1861.

20 "The Parker Captives," *Galveston News*, June 3, 1875; James T. DeShields, *Cynthia Ann Parker* (Saint Louis: n.p., 1886; reprint, with foreword by John Graves, Dallas: Chama Press, 1991), 41-44. See also J. W. Wilbarger, *Indian Depredations in Texas* (Austin: Hutchings Printing House 1889; facsimile reprint, Austin: The Steck Company, 1935), 335-38.

21 Sul Ross to Victor M. Rose, June 1878 and April 21, 1881, in Perry Wayne Shelton, comp., *Personal Civil War Letters of General Lawrence Sullivan Ross with Other Letters* (Austin: Shelly and Richard Morrison, 1994), 85; Victor M. Rose, ed., *Ross' Texas Brigade: Being a Narrative of Events Connected with its Service in the Late War Between the States* (Louisville: Courier-Journal, 1881), 160.

22 Haley, ed., "Charles Goodnight's Indian Recollections," 3-29; "Quanah Parker Sets History Straight," *Semi-Weekly Farm News* (Dallas), October 29, 1910; "Straightens Out History," *Dallas Morning News*, October 25, 1910; Marion T. Brown, letter to her Mother, January 27, 1887, in C. Richard King, ed., *Marion T. Brown: Letters from Fort Sill, 1886-1887* (Austin: Encino Press, 1970) , 63.

23 "Straightens Out History," *Dallas Morning News*, October 25, 1910; "Quanah Parker Sets History Straight," *Semi-Weekly Farm News* (Dallas), October 29, 1910. See also Carlson and Crum, *Myth, Memory, and Massacre*, 106-107.

24 See, for example, Williams, "The Case for Peta Nocona," 55-72; Gwynn, *Empire of the Summer Moon*, 194-95. See also Tom Crum and Paul H. Carlson, "Did Quanah Parker Lie?" manuscript in possession of authors.

25 The Horace Jones quotes are in "Marion's Indian Notes from Interpreter H. P. Jones, Jany, 1887," and Marion T. Brown, letter to her father, December 20, 1886, both in King, ed., *Marion T. Brown*, 78 and 35 respectively.

26 Haley, ed., "Charles Goodnight's Indian Recollections," 3-29; "Quanah Parker Sets History Straight," *Semi-Weekly Farm News* (Dallas), October

29, 1909; "Straightens Out History, *Dallas Morning News*, October 25, 1910.

27 DeShields, *Cynthia Ann Parker*, 41-44.

28 "Ben Dragoo Tells of the Capture of Cynthia Ann Parker," *Frontier Times* 1, no. 3 (December 1923): 25-27.

29 Hunter, ed., "The Capture of Cynthia Ann Parker," 364-365

30 "Padgitt Replies to Quanah Parker," *Dallas Morning News*, November 21, 1909.

31 "The Parker Captives," *Galveston News*, June 3, 1875.

32 Quote is from Charles Goodnight in J. Evetts Haley, *Charles Goodnight: Cowman and Plainsman* (Norman: University of Oklahoma Press, 1935), 55.

33 Baker, Diary—first, manuscript, entries for December 19-25, 1860.

34 DeShields, *Cynthia Ann Parker*, 41-44; "Ben Dragoo Tells of the Capture of Cynthia Ann Parker," (December 1923): 25-27; Susan Parker St. John, 1894, notes of Ross interview in the Joseph Taulman Papers at the Dolph Briscoe Center for American History, the University of Texas at Austin.

35 St. John, 1894, notes of Ross interview in Taulman Papers.

36 Robertson, interview; "Ben Dragoo Tells of the Capture of Cynthia Ann Parker," *Frontier Times* 6, no. 7 (April 1929): 291.

37 "The Parker Captives," *Galveston News*, June 3, 1875; DeShields, *Cynthia Ann Parker*, 41-45.

38 Granted, the stories also appear in the Ross Family Papers at Baylor University, but there is good reason to believe the Ross Family Papers borrowed from DeShields rather than DeShields borrowed from the Family Papers. If this is not true, then the forty ranger and death song accounts originated with Ross and not DeShields.

39 St. John, 1894, notes of Ross interview in Taulman Papers.

CHAPTER FIVE

"Margaret, Texas Is Lost": Sam Houston Refuses to Take a Loyalty Oath to the Confederacy, March 16, 1861

Mary L. Scheer

ON MARCH 15, 1861, THE delegates to the Texas secession convention meeting in Austin, after earlier declaring Texas an "independent sovereignty," took an oath of allegiance to the Confederacy. Subsequently, they ordered all public officials to follow suit. The events leading up to that pivotal moment in Texas history pitted the secession convention against the executive: Texas Governor Sam Houston, an avowed Unionist. Caught in the snare of history, Houston had received various petitions, editorials, and letters, urging him to convene the legislature or call a convention on the matter. When Houston refused to do either, the radicals therefore acted on their own, drawing up an ordinance of secession and declaring the instrument of 1845 by which Texas entered the Union as "hereby repealed and annulled." As the showdown between the secessionists and the Unionists approached, many wondered what

Houston would do: Accede to the secessionists? Uphold the Union? Resign his position? Lead a pro-Union army? Go into exile? Answers to those questions would soon unfold at the appointed moment for Houston to give his answer: high noon on March 16, 1861.[1]

The events of this crucial moment in Texas history are entwined with the life and times of Sam Houston. Born ironically on March 2, 1793—a day to be celebrated as Texas Independence Day—he and his family had trekked westward from Virginia to eastern Tennessee to embark upon a new beginning. After a brief career as a school teacher, he joined the U.S. Army and saw action in the War of 1812 against the Creek Indians in Alabama. Returning to Nashville, he studied law and was admitted to the bar, setting up a legal practice in Lebanon, thirty miles east of Nashville. But his "personal qualities—proven courage, oratorical ability, and a commanding physical presence—made a move into electoral politics virtually inevitable." Thereafter, his star rose quickly from a two-term member of the House of Representatives to Tennessee governor, Republic of Texas president, U.S. senator, and Texas governor.[2]

During that time Houston developed a lasting friendship with President Andrew Jackson (Old Hickory), who would influence his young protégé. While the lines between federal and state power were unclear at the time, Jackson sympathized with the various regions on specific issues such as the tariff and the bank question. But the nullification crisis of 1832 transformed the question from regional interests to the national union. In his Nullification Proclamation of December 10, 1832, Jackson argued that states' rights did not include nullification or secession. "To say that any State may at pleasure secede from the Union is to say that the United States are not a nation."

Sam Houston, circa 1859

COURTESY THE LIBRARY OF CONGRESS

Houston took that message to heart and carried it with him the rest of his life.

Between the annexation of Texas in 1845 and the secession crisis, a total of fifteen years, Texas was the twenty-eighth state in the Union. During that time it fought a war with Mexico, fixed its northern and western boundaries as they exist today, settled its public debt, established a chain of frontier forts, endowed its public schools, and attracted immigrants to help populate Texas. As a slave state, however, the question of slavery was more serious and less easily solved. The census of 1847 had reported that 38,753 slaves, or approximately 27 percent of the total population, resided in the state. Over the years annexation had the effect of rapidly increasing the number of slaves from 58,161 in 1850 to 182,566 slaves on the eve of the Civil War, representing about 30.2 percent of the Texas population. How Texas and the nation would solve this seemingly intractable problem lay in the months ahead.[3]

Developments on the national stage that led to secession and Civil War affected Texas and Texans. The most immediate concern faced by both the United States and Texas was the outbreak of war with Mexico in 1846. Still bristling over the loss of an independent Texas, Mexico had never extended official recognition and openly planned to reclaim Texas at its earliest opportunity. With annexation, the war broke out almost immediately. Mexico deemed the action as an illegal land grab under the banner of Manifest Destiny. It rejected any further attempts to negotiate with the United States over the purchase of additional Mexican lands in California or to settle boundary disputes over the region known as the "Nueces Strip." Soon thereafter President Polk dispatched General Zachary Taylor and his troops to the Rio Grande where Mexican troops were also massing. Declaring a defensive war against the United States, Mexico then ordered its troops across the river and attacked a detachment of U.S. dragoons. Responding to Polk's claim that Mexico had "shed American blood on American soil," Congress declared war on May 13, 1846.

With lingering hatred against the Mexican government, Texas public sentiment was decidedly pro-war. Margaret

Houston wrote her husband on May 16 that there was "great excitement through our county about the war." Approximately 5,000 to 7,000 Texans enthusiastically volunteered to serve in the U.S. army, mainly with Taylor's army in northern Mexico. Even Governor J. Pinckney Henderson requested that the legislature release him from his duties to command the Second Texas Regiment that attacked and seized Monterrey. Senator Sam Houston, who had favored "the immediate annexation to the U States," however, remained ambivalent about the current situation. Believing that "other territory could be obtained by the old Jacksonian plan of purchase" he refused to accept a military commission to take part in the war. On July 17 he wrote: "I am not committed, and nothing but an emergency of great need, will induce me to renew the toils of camp. . . ." But when Mexico severed relations with the United States, Houston supported the war in the Senate and later voted to ratify the treaty that secured its victory.[4]

The Texas-New Mexico border controversy also kept Texas in the national spotlight. The end of the War with Mexico had settled the southern border dispute, but opened another on Texas's western frontier. The disputed lands included a vast amount of territory never a part of Texas, which held many of the principal settlements of New Mexico and a strip of land reaching north into Colorado and Wyoming. At the same time the controversy also concerned the extension of slavery into the territories with pro- and antislavery forces aligning themselves on opposite sides of the issue. If Texas claims to the region were upheld, then slave soil could extend to the farthest western reach of the Rio Grande. But if slavery was prohibited from any territory acquired as a result of the war with Mexico, as introduced in Congress by the Wilmot Proviso, then slavery could be contained.

With the failure of the Wilmot Proviso, Congress remained divided over the boundary controversy. In a May 8, 1848, speech before the U.S. Senate, Houston addressed the question of jurisdiction over the territory from Santa Fe to the Rio Grande. Inhabited by bands of Indians and "some half-civilized Mexicans," he emphatically insisted that Texas considered the region as a part of the Republic. Moreover, overtures had been made by those residents living there "to have the benefit of our laws and institutions." In a special session of the legislature on August 12, 1850, Governor Bell declared that Texas must assert its rights "at all hazards and to the last extremity."[5]

While Texans tenaciously pressed their claims, in 1850 an advantageous compromise by Congressman Henry Clay of Kentucky resolved the problem, albeit temporarily. During the negotiations, Houston delivered a lengthy speech. Through a series of resolutions Congress settled the border dispute by setting the boundary of Texas at its modern limits. In return Texas received $10 million to pay off its debt and endow a public school fund. Other parts of the Compromise of 1850, however, addressed the growing sectional crisis. Houston supported the compromise as "a reconciliation, an adjustment of all the cause of differences which now agitate the Union." He then specifically advocated extending the Missouri Compromise line of 36° 30', expressing a willingness to make necessary compromises, rather than jeopardize "the peace and harmony of the Union." Ending his speech, he beseeched those present that "if this Union must be dissolved, that its ruins may be the monument of my grave, and the graves of my family. I wish no epitaph to be written to tell that I survive the ruin of this glorious Union."[6]

Houston's second term as senator began in December 1853, just prior to the shattering of the sectional calm that the compromise had secured. The next year Senator Stephen

A. Douglas of Illinois, chairman of the Senate Committee on Territories, introduced the Kansas-Nebraska bill, which would effectively overturn the Missouri Compromise and allow slavery to extend into northern territories through "popular sovereignty." Southern Democrats enthusiastically supported the measure and most Texans assumed Houston would too. Over two days, February 14-15, 1854, Houston explained his opposition to the bill by defending the Missouri Compromise as "a *solemn* compact between the States," one in which the "vital interests of all the States, and *especially of the South*, are dependent, in a great degree, upon the preservation and sacred observance of that compact." The abandonment of the compromise, he concluded, would be "anarchy, discord, and civil broil." On January 6, 1854, Houston wrote Margaret: "I will vote alone if it is my conviction of right. I am right, and feel firm in my purpose." Two months later the bill became law with Houston as the only southern Democrat to vote against it.[7]

The outcry against Houston spread across the South and into Texas. A correspondent to the *Richmond Enquirer* lashed out at Houston's negative vote: "Nothing can justify this treachery; nor can anything save the traitor from the deep damnation which such treason may merit." Several newspapers called for his immediate resignation. On November 26, 1855, the Texas legislature passed a resolution "that the Legislature approves the course of [Senator] Thomas J. Rusk in voting for the Kansas-Nebraska Act and disapproves the course of Sam Houston in voting against it." Later, the Democratic State Convention, meeting in January 1856, also condemned his vote on the Kansas-Nebraska bill, noting that it was not in accord with "the sentiments of the Democracy of Texas." Clearly, Houston was out of step with other Texans who believed in slavery's right to expand into the territories. He was, according to many at the time, fast becoming "a senator without a party," one whose political career, by all accounts, would soon be over.[8]

Houston returned to the Senate in January of 1854 to confront the results of the Kansas-Nebraska Act. Under the law's provisions, elections for the territorial legislature would be held in March to determine whether Kansas would be free or slave. Proslavery ruffians from Missouri crossed the border to cast their votes, bringing the legitimacy of the election into question. Free Soil settlers repudiated the proslavery government and elected a governor and legislature of their own. Violence soon erupted between the two partisans and the events in "Bleeding Kansas" led to the "sack of Lawrence" and the raid by John Brown at Pottawatomie Creek. Sectional fights also erupted on the floor of Congress when Senator Andrew Butler of South Carolina brutally attacked Senator Charles Sumner of Massachusetts with a cane.

Although Houston did not participate in the debates over the Kansas crisis, he foresaw the consequences. He wrote to Margaret on December 25, 1857, that the problems in Kansas were "the offspring of the Repeal of the Missouri Compromise." It was, he said, "fraught with danger to the whole section from which I come. . . ." One of those problems was the Lecompton constitution, a proslavery document, which was never given a fair chance under the concept of popular sovereignty. When the vote came up for approval of the constitution in the Senate, Houston voted in the affirmative, claiming that it was "in accordance with the views of three-fourths, at least, of the Legislature of Texas." This action was uncharacteristic of Houston, but in any case, the House blocked its passage and the constitution was sent back to Kansas for a true referendum.[9]

In the five critical years prior to the Civil War, national developments increasingly influenced many Texans, including

Houston. Most immediately was the election of 1856 where the two major parties divided over slavery. The Democrats pledged "non-interference with slavery" while the new sectional Republican Party promised to interfere by preventing its expansion. At the same time, the election stirred up agitation between those advocating the Union and those supporting disunion. Finding neither the Democrat James Buchanan nor the Republican John C. Frémont acceptable, Houston favored the candidate of the Know Nothing Party, Millard Fillmore. He told the Senate that the Know Nothings "go for the union out and out, or I would not act with them." Further, "Fillmore, and the Union," he asserted, were synonymous and he flatly rejected any "sentiment in favor of disunion."[10]

With a Democratic presidential victory in 1856, Houston returned home the next year and announced as an independent candidate for governor of Texas. Houston, however, was "on the 'wrong' side of the most emotional issue in Southern history—expansion and the long-range future of slavery." As a slave owner, he viewed the institution as a "necessity of their [southerners'] condition," but one that would have to be sorted out "within the parameter of keeping the Union together." Conflicting interests, he firmly believed, could be resolved: "This can be done, and let us not despair and break up the Union." But the Democratic Party, which controlled politics and the press in the state, united behind Hardin R. Runnels, a disciple of John C. Calhoun and the extension of slavery. Houston, who ran as an independent, lost by a vote of 32,552 to 28,678. He received the news of his defeat while sitting with Margaret on their porch in Huntsville. Disappointed, but not downtrodden, he turned to his wife and said: "Margaret, wait until 1859."[11]

Despite his defeat, Houston continued to serve in the Senate for another two years. During that time the state legislators, in an attempt to discredit Houston, voted his replacement, Judge John Hemphill, who would replace him in 1859. Nevertheless, Houston continued to represent Texas on a range of issues from a southern route for the transcontinental railroad to a boundary bill to mark lines between the territories and Texas. In all instances, particularly on sectional questions, he proclaimed his "patriotic devotion" to his country, the Union, and the Constitution. He also announced his intention to run for governor of Texas again. In a letter to his friend George W. Paschal of the Austin *Southern Intelligencer,* he wrote: "The Constitution and the Union embrace the principles by which I will be governed if elected."[12]

Houston's gubernatorial victory on August 1, 1859, was a tribute both to his continued popularity and "the vitality of unionism in Texas." On December 21, after taking the oath of office as the only man to serve as governor of two states—Texas and Tennessee—Houston delivered his inaugural address. He began his speech by relating the economic, intellectual, and moral conditions of the state. Then, in his concluding remarks, he "irresistibly" reminded Texans that Texas "entered not into the North, nor into the South, but into the Union." Further, Houston cautioned against the "ravings of fanatics" whose "aim is to array sectionalism upon their side, and thus promote strife and confusion." Elected by the people, Houston pledged to "pursue the course which will best conduce to the prosperity of Texas." But if "national abstractions" intruded on state matters, he would "look to the people to sustain me."[13]

It was not long before "national abstractions" encroached on the affairs of state government. Even before Houston's inauguration, abolitionist John Brown had attacked the arsenal at Harpers' Ferry in Virginia, presumably to arm the slaves and lead an insurrection. Although no direct comments by Houston on the failed raid exist, he did refer in his January 13, 1860, message to the Texas legislature to "the triumph of conservatism" by northerners "to put down the fanatical efforts of misguided abolitionists, who would endanger the safety of the Union to advance their vapid schemes." He pointed out that nowhere does the "love of our common country" burn with more fervor than "in the hearts of the conservative people of Texas." Texas, he insisted, "will maintain the Constitution, and stand by the Union. It is all that can save us as a nation. Destroy it, and anarchy awaits."[14]

Amid rumors of a possible draft for a presidential bid in 1860, Houston could only watch as the nation moved closer to dissolution. On January 21, 1860, after transmitting resolutions advocating the right to secession from South Carolina to the Texas legislature, as required by his office, Houston sent an impassioned message condemning disunion, using Jackson's words: "The Union—it must and shall be preserved." In a speech in Austin that same year he warned that "civil war would surely follow secession" and mean the end of slavery. Then, in his Thanksgiving Day Proclamation of October 27 he offered a prayer that God might "shield us still in the time of peril, that we may be preserved a United people, free, independent, and prosperous."[15]

As the thunder of approaching secession grew louder, Houston tried to calm those who feared a possible Republican victory in 1860. In an address to a Union mass meeting in Austin, he answered those who opposed the election of Abraham Lincoln, an event that many Southerners promised would lead to immediate secession. Although also opposed to Lincoln and his party, Houston declared that "we have no excuse for dissolving the Union. The Union is worth more than Mr. Lincoln." He then advised constitutional means to correct any encroachment upon southern rights. If Mr. Lincoln failed to protect its citizens in accordance with the Constitution, Houston advised, then it "provides a remedy."[16]

The presidential election was held on November 6, 1860. Houston voted that day, but refused to make public his candidate. The next day, still uncertain of the outcome, Houston wrote his son: "How the State will go, I can't say, but 'The Union must be preserved.'" He then predicted that "if an attempt is made to destroy our Union, or violate our Constitution, there will be blood shed to maintain them. The Demons of anarchy must be put down and destroyed."[17]

With news of Lincoln's election, the drum beat for secession grew louder. An "excited state of public feeling" spread across the state. Public meetings approved resolutions calling for a secession convention. Petitions circulated, urging a special session of the legislature. And civic leaders in Austin met to consider the secession process. However, only the legislature had the legal authority to assemble a convention, and only Governor Houston could call a special session to consider the matter. In an emotional address to the people of Texas, he pleaded that "the election of a President in the mode pointed out by the Constitution, is no just cause for a revolution and a dissolution of the Union."[18]

Faced with overwhelming support for a special legislative session, Houston yielded. He set January 21, 1861, as the date for the legislature to meet and consider a "convention of delegates fresh from the people." In his message to the pro-secession legislature he recommended that "the people be the tribunal of last resort," and that "no action be considered final until it has been submitted to them." The same day that the legislature met,

Margaret wrote a letter to her mother, Nancy Lea. She observed that the town had "filled up fast" in anticipation of the important meeting. She further noted that "the present appearance of things is gloomy enough." But with her staunch religious faith she believed that "the Lord can bring lights out of darkness and beauty out of chaos." Houston, she continued, "seems cheerful and hopeful . . . but in the still watches of the night I see him agonizing in prayers for our distracted country."[19]

Despite Houston's opposition, the legislature approved a secession convention to meet on January 28, 1861. By an overwhelming vote of 152 to 6, it approved removing Texas from the Union. This was followed on February 1 by a formal ordinance of secession. Houston recognized the powers of the legislature, but subtly reminded the convention members that its authority rested only "within the scope of the call under which its delegates were elected." In other words, the convention could only address the issue of secession, not whether to join the Confederacy. He then reminded them that their action must be "submitted to the vote of the ballot box, for their ratification or rejection." Once the people declared their will, Houston said: "No citizen will be more ready to yield obedience to its will, or to risk his all in its defence, than myself. . . . I am with my country [Texas]."[20]

Houston pinned his hopes for Texas on a referendum to be held on February 23, 1861, or at least that the state would not join the Confederacy. Earlier he had suggested that if the voters approved secession, then the state should remain independent. Rather than join the Southern confederacy, he wrote J. M. Calhoun of Alabama, it should unfurl once again "her Lone Star Banner, and maintaining her position among the independent peoples of the earth." Thus, if the Union were dissolved and civil war followed, Texas could "tread the wine press alone."[21]

On election day the voters of Texas endorsed secession by over three to one with a vote of 46,153 to 14,747. News spread like a prairie fire throughout the capital. There was cheering and ringing of bells in Austin, followed by the firing of cannons. A messenger arrived at the Governor's Mansion to deliver the results to Houston, who was sitting on the front porch. According to his daughter Maggie, his face turned ashen and his head dropped to his chest. He then turned to Margaret and said: "Texas is lost. My heart is broken."[22]

As Houston had recognized, the referendum question put to the people of Texas was whether it should secede from the Union only, not to join the Confederacy. Nevertheless, on March 5, by a vote of 109 to 2, the convention adopted an ordinance to no longer be a "sovereign State," but to join the new Southern nation and send delegates to the convention of the seceding states in Montgomery, Alabama. Houston, denying its authority to do so, stated: "The people alone have any right to say what form of Government they will have." On March 14 the convention rejected Houston's challenge by requiring all state officials to take an oath of loyalty to the Confederacy. Houston's secretary replied that the governor "did not acknowledge the existence of the Convention and should not regard its action as binding upon him."[23]

On March 15, 1861, the convention dispatched George Chilton, a member of that body, to the Governor's Mansion to inform Sam Houston that he would have to swear his allegiance as well. An avowed Unionist, Houston requested additional time to consider this important decision and Chilton allowed him until noon the following day to provide his answer. What transpired during the next twenty-four hours provides a compelling moment in the history of Texas and in the life of one man. Governor Houston, who commanded the troops at

San Jacinto, served as the first president of the Republic, was elected senator from Texas, and was rumored to be a possible presidential candidate, retired to his quarters to consider the future of Texas—and his own.[24]

Nancy (Nannie) Houston, the oldest daughter of Sam and Margaret, recalled the events that unfolded at the Governor's Mansion. Following dinner, Margaret placed the two-volume family Bible before her husband. Houston read from it, and then retired to an upstairs bedroom. Fifteen-year-old Nannie told her father not to be worried. Removing his shoes so that his pacing would not disturb his wife and family, Houston burned his lamp "until daybreak." Later, he came downstairs and told his wife: "Margaret, I will not do it."[25]

On March 16 Houston went to the capitol before the appointed hour—but not to his office or the legislative chamber. Instead, he sat in the capitol basement and whittled while the roll call took place. Three times his name was called and three times he refused to answer or take a loyalty oath to the Confederacy. The convention therefore declared the governor's office vacant and appointed Lieutenant Governor Edward Clark to fill that position.[26]

The night before, as Houston contemplated his decision, he penned a farewell statement that was later printed in the *Southern Intelligencer* of March 20. Realizing that he would be removed as governor, he wrote that he was "worn out with the cares of office," and now chose to spend his remaining days in the "bosom of my family." On many past occasions, he reminded his fellow citizens, he had yielded to their solicitations to serve his party and discharge his duties as the governor of Texas. But the legislature had obstructed his "efforts to reform abuses and effect measures calculated to promote the public good." Only his oath as chief executive under the Constitution prevented him from

Margaret Lea Houston, circa 1840

yielding to the "excitement and passion." He continued that he
loved Texas too much "to bring civil strife and bloodshed upon
her," and therefore would "make no endeavor to maintain my
authority as Chief Executive of this State."[27]

Throughout the secession crisis, Houston often turned to his wife Margaret for comfort and support. Slender with deep blue eyes, Margaret was described as "a simple beauty, quiet and serene." Her frequent letters to her husband during the crisis contained news from home about their growing family and religious notes, intended to encourage him to attend church services and convert to Christianity someday. Centered on her rural domestic life, the Bible, and her children, Margaret shunned publicity, content to remain in the shadows of her famous husband. Nevertheless, she took a private interest in his political career, especially since it took him away from her so much. She understood that Houston could not refuse those who called him to public service. Proclaiming his intention to defer to her wishes if she opposed his remaining in public life, Houston assured her that it was not "the splendor of the station," but a sense of duty to the country that induced him to serve. So in his darkest hour, when Houston faced the greatest decision of his career—one that would also affect his wife and children—he turned to his "best adviser," Margaret. She consoled him, telling him to ask God for guidance, and reassured him that she would abide by his decision.[28]

Returning to the Mansion following his dismissal, Houston, his family, and a loyal servant began to pack their belongings for a return to Independence. Three days later, however, messengers arrived and informed Houston that a group of his friends were "armed and ready" to return him to office. Horrified, he asked if "all the people are gone mad?" He thanked them, but emphatically condemned such action that would "deluge the capital of Texas with the blood of Texans, merely to keep one poor old man in a position for a few days longer, in a position that belongs to the people." Even President Lincoln's offer of 70,000 men to help keep Texas in the Union did not sway him saying, "this I rejected. . . ." He would not take up arms against Texas.[29]

The next month, April 12, 1861, Confederate batteries opened up on Fort Sumter in Charleston Harbor and the Civil War began. Houston's steps to prevent secession and keep Texas in the Union had failed. In an April 19 speech at Galveston he prophesized: "Let me tell you what is coming. Your fathers and husbands, your sons and brothers, will be herded at the point of the bayonet. You may, after the sacrifice of countless millions of treasure and hundreds of thousands of lives, as a bare possibility, win Southern independence, if God be not against you, but I doubt it." The next month Houston addressed a crowd in Independence. He again warned of the coming troubles upon Texas. But the sixty-eight-year old Houston could not abandon the South or Texas. Despite the strength of his Unionism, he was now "a conservative citizen of the Southern Confederacy." He intoned: "The time has come when a man's section is his country. I stand by mine."[30]

While there were many pivotal, often dramatic moments in the life and career of Sam Houston—signer of the Texas Declaration of Independence, victorious hero at San Jacinto, and first president of the new Republic of Texas—there were also moments when he was not uniformly heroic and principled. Like most individuals, he was a figure of complexity and contradictions. He was a gambler and heavy drinker, who earned the nickname "The Big Drunk," but also late in life embraced temperance and religion. In 1832 he came to Texas to engage in questionable land speculation schemes, yet he stepped forward to lead a small Texian army against a larger Mexican force, thus securing independence for Texas. It is exactly because of his public/

private personas, his conflicts and triumphs, his virtues and human foibles, that I find him fascinating.

Although Sam Houston failed to prevent the rush to secession in 1860-61, he provided leadership, courage, and wisdom at a critical moment in Texas history. As governor of Texas he cautioned calm and reason in the face of agitation and emotion. He possessed enormous courage by taking an unpopular position and standing by his beliefs and principles, regardless of the consequences. Houston also wisely and correctly predicted the dangers of disunion: civil strife and bloodshed. Houston's faith in the Constitution and the Union was unwavering. By refusing to take a loyalty oath to the Confederacy, he chose not to "sacrifice his conscience," or his self-respect. Rather than involve Texas in the tragedy of the Civil War, Houston ended his career.

As both a historical figure and iconic symbol, Sam Houston's stand against disunion was his finest hour. When Houston refused to pledge his allegiance to the Confederacy on March 16, 1861, he stood virtually alone. To have acted any other way would have betrayed his long-standing beliefs. True to his principles and single-minded in his devotion to the Union, he displayed uncommon courage in the face of overwhelming opposition and constituent pressure. As the celebrated "fly on the wall," I would have liked to have eavesdropped on this crucial moment in Texas history when one man placed principle above self-interest.

Selected Bibliography

Buenger, Walter L. *Secession and the Union in Texas.* Austin: University of Texas Press, 1984.

Campbell, Randolph. *Sam Houston and the American Southwest.* New York: Harper Collins, Publ., 1993.

Haley, James. *Sam Houston.* Norman: University of Oklahoma Press, 2002.

James, Marquis. *The Raven.* Austin: University of Texas Press, 1929, 1989.

Meyer, Edward R., Jr. "Sam Houston and Secession." *Southwestern Historical Quarterly* 55, no. 4 (April 1952): 448-458.

Roberts, Madge Thornall, ed. *The Personal Correspondence of Sam Houston.* 4 vols. Denton:University of North Texas, 1998-2001.

———. *Star of Destiny: The Private Life of Sam and Margaret Houston.* Denton: University of North Texas Press, 1993.

Seale, William. *Sam Houston's Wife: A Biography of Margaret Lee Houston.* Norman:University of Oklahoma Press, 1970.

Williams, Amelia, and Eugene C. Barker, eds. *The Writings of Sam Houston, 1813-1863.* Austin: Jenkins Publishing Co., 1970.

NOTES

1 Marquis James, *The Raven* (Austin: University of Texas Press, 1929; 1989), 411.

2 Randolph Campbell, *Sam Houston and the American Southwest* (New York: Harper Collins, Publ., 1993), 12.

3 Ron Tyler, et al., eds., *The New Handbook of Texas*, 6 vols. (Austin: Texas State Historical Association Press) 5: 1081-1083; Randolph B. Campbell, *Empire for Slavery: The Peculiar Institution in Texas, 1821-1865* (Baton Rouge: Louisiana State University Press, 1989), 55-56, 68-69; James D. B. DeBow, comp., *Statistical View of the United States . . . Being a Compendium of the Seventh Census*, Washington D. C., 1854, 95.

4 James, *The Raven*, 346, 360-361; Madge Thornall Roberts, ed., *The Personal Correspondence of Sam Houston* (Denton: University of North Texas Press, 1999), 2: 73, 140; Madge Thornall Roberts, *Star of Destiny: The Private Life of Sam and Margaret Houston* (Denton: University of North Texas Press, 1993), 131-135.

5 Amelia W. Williams and Eugene C. Barker, eds., *The Writings of Sam Houston, 1813-1863* (Austin: Jenkins Publishing Co., 1970), 5: 51.

6 The Compromise of 1850 was a series of resolutions suggested by Henry Clay of Kentucky. He proposed that California be admitted as a free state and that the Mexican Cession be organized as two territories—New Mexico and Utah. It further set the Texas boundary to what it is today. Texas would also have to pay off its public debt. The slave trade would be outlawed in the District of Columbia and a stronger fugitive slave law would be passed. Williams and Barker, eds., *The Writings of Sam Houston*, 5: 119-144; Edward R. Mayer, Jr., "Sam Houston and Secession," *Southwestern Historical Quarterly* 55, no. 4 (April 1952): 449.

7 Williams and Barker, eds., *Writings of Sam Houston*, 5: 492, 502; Roberts, *The Personal Correspondence of Sam Houston*, 4: 94, 122; Anna Irene Sandbo, "Beginnings of the Secession Movement in Texas," *Southwestern Historical Quarterly* 17 (July 1914-April 1915): 50-56.

8 Williams and Barker, eds., *Writings of Sam Houston*, 5: 469-523; Campbell, *Sam Houston and the American Southwest*, 128, 133; Marquis, *The Raven*, 382-384.

9 The Lecompton Constitution was eventually turned down by the people of the territory and statehood would be postponed for some years. Williams and Barker, eds., *Writings of Sam Houston*, 5: 494-502, 7:42; Roberts, ed., *The Personal Correspondence of Sam Houston*, 4: 266, 284; Campbell, *Sam Houston and the American Southwest*, 127-138; 46-49; Sandbo, "Beginnings of the Secession Movement in Texas," 46-49.

10 Roberts, ed., *The Personal Correspondence of Sam Houston*, 4:234; Williams and Barker, eds., *The Writings of Sam Houston*, 6: 388.

11 Williams and Barker, eds., *The Writings of Sam Houston*, 6:167-177; Campbell, *Sam Houston and the American Southwest*, 136; James L. Haley, *Sam Houston* (Norman: University of Oklahoma Press, 2002), 336-337; Madge T. Roberts, *Star of Destiny: The Private Life of Sam and Margaret Houston* (Denton: University of North Texas Press, 1993), 264.

12 Williams and Barker, eds., *The Writings of Sam Houston*, 7:110-112, 340.

13 Ibid., 7:383-385.

14 Ibid., 7:421; A. W. Terrell, "Recollections of General Sam Houston," *Southwestern Historical Quarterly* (October 1912), 16:133.

15 Williams and Barker, eds., *The Writings of Sam Houston*, 7: 439; 8: 173; Roberts, ed., The *Personal Correspondence of Sam Houston*, 206.

16 Williams and Barker, eds., *The Writings of Sam Houston*, 8:151; A. W. Terrell, "Recollections of General Sam Houston," *Southwestern Historical Quarterly* 16, no. 2 (October 1912): 133. See also Ralph A. Wooster, *Texas and Texans in the Civil War* (Austin: Eakin Press, 1995), 1-24.

17 Williams and Barker, eds., *The Writings of Sam Houston*, 8:184-185; Roberts, *Star of Destiny*, 294.

18 Williams and Barker, *The Writings of Sam Houston*, 8: 206; Campbell, *Sam Houston and the American Southwest*, 151.

19 Williams and Barker, *The Writings of Sam Houston*, 8:250; Roberts, ed., *The Personal Correspondence of Sam Houston*, 4: 380-382.

20 Williams and Barker, *The Writings of Sam Houston*, 8: 253-254.

21 Ibid., 8: 228-229.

22 *Journal of the Secession Convention of Texas*, 1861 (Austin: Austin Printing Co., 1912), 88; Roberts, *Star of Destiny*, 296.

23 Williams and Barker, *The Writings of Sam Houston*, 8: 268-271; *Journal of the Secession Convention*, 91; Maher, "Sam Houston and Secession," 455-456; John F. Kennedy, *Profiles in Courage* (N.Y.: Harper and Brothers, Publ., 1955/1956), 115.

24 *Journal of the Convention*, 178-179.

25 *Journal of the Convention*, 183-184; William Seale, *Sam Houston's Wife: A Biography of Margaret Lea Houston* (Norman: University of Oklahoma Press, 1970), 206-207; Campbell, *Sam Houston and the American Southwest*, 155-156; James, *The Raven*, 411-412; Kennedy, *Profiles in Courage*, 100-117.

26 *Journal of the Convention*, 183-184.

27 Williams and Barker, *The Writings of Sam Houston*, 8:271-278.
28 Seale, *Sam Houston's Wife*, 136-137; Roberts, *Star of Destiny*, 195, 298, 346; George W. Paschal, "Last Years of Sam Houston," *Harper's New Monthly Magazine* (April 1866): 630-635.
29 Williams and Barker, *The Writings of Sam Houston*, 8:293.
30 Ibid., 8:293, 301-305.

CHAPTER SIX

"...and Then the Ball Opened": A Violent Incident at Scabtown, Menard County, Texas, on New Year's Eve, 1877

Chuck Parsons

*F*ROM THE EARLIEST DAYS IN Texas there has been conflict between three races: Native Americans, mainly Comanche, Kiowa and Apache; Mexicans, who once owned the land as part of their country; and the invading Anglos from the United States. When the United States acquired the land in 1845, it became necessary to protect the settlers who insisted on moving further and further west, always onward toward the ocean. The government therefore constructed a string of forts at critical points in order to protect these settlers and their homes. With a military presence, the threat to the settlers became minimal and gradually the number of soldiers was reduced.

Often once-busy frontier forts became bustling communities. The inhabitants were former soldiers, hotel managers, restaurant owners, barkeeps, saloon owners, laundresses, blacksmiths, post office workers, prostitutes, and occasionally a photographer. Such a settlement arose in what became Menard County in the Texas Hill Country. The protection for the settlers came from Fort McKavett, today a historical site with some of the fort's buildings restored.[1]

In 1852 Fort McKavett had been established to provide protection for the daring settlers who attempted to establish a farm or ranch far from the frontier line. But when the Civil War broke out in 1861, the post was abandoned and the settlers were left to fend for themselves. At war's end, with the threat of raiding parties now common, the post was re-activated. At its peak 400 troops were stationed there.

About a mile north of the actual fort was a civilian establishment. Reporter Hans Mickle from the *San Antonio Daily Express* described the place as having an "air of comfort and convenience" everywhere. The civilian settlement was known to some as Lewisville, ostensibly after W.W. Lewis who had befriended Mickle. Others called the place "Scabtown," which consisted of two general merchandise stores, at least three saloons and places which "allowed the widest latitude and characteristic of a frontier town and post." For the readers in San Antonio or elsewhere, most everyone understood that in Lewisville or Scabtown one could find whatever one wanted: a game of cards, whiskey, or a woman.[2]

In 1871 Menard County was organized and the next year erected a courthouse to provide a secure place for deeds, marriage licenses, and other vital records. As a result, law, order, and business began to thrive. Clerks and lawyers now became community members. A sheriff was appointed to maintain order, especially in the places where the potential for disturbances was great. And businessmen such William W. Lewis, a former Texas Ranger in Company D of the Frontier Battalion, operated a saloon in Menardville (as the county seat was then called), and advertised his establishment. In 1877 Hans Mickle visited Menard (as it is known today) and observed the large advertisement for Lewis's saloon: a painting of a steamboat going up the Salt River in Arizona, with Mickle riding in the boat.[3]

Among the civilian population in Scabtown (Lewisville) were Charles and Ida Miller and their family. On New Year's Eve of 1877 the Millers decided to host a dance for friends, all former United States soldiers of the 10th Cavalry, universally known as "Buffalo Soldiers." They had been part of an all-black unit and had faced adversity together. How many ex-soldiers the Millers invited, and how many actually attended, is unknown. From subsequent reports it appears they held the dance in their home, which could not have permitted too many to attend at any one time. In late afternoon or early evening of New Year's Eve 1877, the stage was set to send out the old year and enjoyably bring in the new year of 1878.

One individual who did not receive an invitation to the dance at Miller's place was the commander of Frontier Battalion Company E, Texas Ranger Lieut. Nelson Orcelus Reynolds, known as "N.O." or "Major" Reynolds. He had joined Company D in mid-1874 along with W.W. Lewis and had shown such efficiency in dealing with outlaws and leading various scouts that on September 1, 1877, he was made Lieutenant Commander of Company E. His lack of obtaining the rank of captain at the time was due only to the limited funding from the state legislature. At this point of his career in Menard County, he had had four months of experience as commander of Company E. With darkness approaching, Reynolds chose to make camp to rest the horses and men. Their general hunting after fugitives from justice would continue the next day.[4]

Lieutenant N. O. Reynolds, from image made in 1875

Lieutenant Reynolds had several other Rangers on this scout: Sergeant Henry McGhee, Privates Thomas Gillespie, Richard Harrison, and Tim McCarty, the latter on detached service from Capt. Neal Coldwell's Company A, as well as

George Stevenson, the camp cook, and Ben Johnson, the company's teamster. Under normal circumstances these two black men, Stevenson and Johnson, would remain in camp while the Rangers were away on patrol. Although always on duty due to their position as Texas Rangers, on this day, December 31, 1877, they no doubt hoped for some relaxation to celebrate the New Year. Once camp was set up, Lieutenant Reynolds left to relax at the mercantile store of the widow Lehne; he knew that he could depend on Sergeant McGhee to manage things in his absence. At first all seemed peaceful enough, but that would soon change.[5]

Much of what we know about the incident at Scabtown comes from Reynolds's official reports as well as from the memoirs of another Texas Ranger who served under Lieutenant Reynolds, James B. Gillett, but who at the time was on duty elsewhere. He learned what happened that New Year's Eve from fellow Rangers, and years later recorded the events at Scabtown on that tragic eve. In addition, Menard County Sheriff James B. Comstock provided details in his official report.[6]

Former members of the 10th Cavalry hosted the dance at Scabtown that night. As soldiers many of these men had drilled, marched, and faced danger together. Somehow the Rangers learned of the dance, but being white, Reynolds and his squad chose to ignore it. After all, as all soldiers know, one must take the opportunity to rest when it presents itself. Others of his squad were not so inclined to rest, such as the cook, George Stevenson, nor the teamster Ben Johnson. Stevenson was actually black, but looked like a light mulatto. "Almost white, but well thought of by all the boys in the company" as Gillett recalled, never suspecting that his racial prejudice was evident in that one statement. Teamster Ben Johnson was a mulatto also, but apparently was not "almost white" as was Stevenson.[7]

How George Stevenson learned about the dance is unknown, but most likely from word of mouth, or from signs posted around Scabtown. He wanted to go to the dance and invited Ben Johnson to go along with him. They obtained Reynolds's permission to attend and after cleaning themselves up they left camp, each armed with a pistol. This was not unusual in the 1870s and 1880s since a man without his pistol was not considered fully dressed. Not expecting any trouble they left camp together, ready to usher in the New Year. The Rangers at the camp planned to catch up on their rest while Lieutenant Reynolds, who frequently suffered from arthritic aches and pains, chose to go to the Lehne Mercantile store for a good night's sleep in more comfortable quarters. Reynolds therefore left Sergeant McGhee in charge of the camp.[8]

Stevenson and Johnson were both admitted to the dance with no trouble, but almost immediately a disturbance broke out. They were part of the Rangers who, as Gillett recalled, were "despised" by some of the ex-soldiers in attendance. Maybe Miller and his friends had previous trouble with the Rangers or white lawmen in the past, and now the opportunity presented itself to even a score at the expense of two of Reynolds's men. Whether for simple racial or for more personal reasons, Miller and his friends quickly "jumped on" the pair, including a little beating, and then to add insult to injury, they took their pistols. Once kicked out of the dance, Stevenson and Johnson had but one recourse: go back to camp and explain what had happened, without their pistols. The embarrassment, of course, could be laughed off and whatever bruises they had received would quickly heal, but they were responsible for the pistols. There was no good way to explain away that loss. Stevenson had actually borrowed the pistol he had lost from Private McCarty who was ultimately responsible for the weapon; now he had to report it missing.[9]

After learning of the incident and the loss of the pistols, McCarty went to Lieutenant Reynolds and explained what had happened. How much detail they discussed is unknown. But to the lieutenant, all that mattered was that the two pistols had to be recovered. After all, they were the property of the State of Texas. It was all quite simple: the pistols had to be recovered, no matter what.

Lieutenant Reynolds therefore left his comfortable sleeping quarters, went back to camp and gathered everyone for the mission. Stevenson, Johnson, McGhee, Gillespie, Harrison and, of course, McCarty were quickly ready to go and retrieve those pistols—"or else." Although Reynolds may not have explained what the "or else" meant, it was clear to all and well understood by those with him that New Year's Eve. No one questioned that the pistols would be recovered by whatever means necessary.

At Charles Miller's "dance hall" —nothing more elaborate than his own living quarters—Lieutenant Reynolds called out a "Hello, the house" to alert the occupants within. He identified himself and—now having their attention—simply demanded the return of the two pistols. Charles Miller knew why the Rangers were there, but had no appreciation of who he was dealing with; he could not have realized the potential for a violent confrontation with armed white men who would have no hesitation to shoot a black man for no reason or any reason, such as the recovery of the stolen pistols. Miller then threw down the challenge: "Stand your ground you white livered sons of bitches!" and shouted further insults at the Rangers. Reynolds, showing great patience, again demanded their surrender so they could search the house.

Charles Miller must have anticipated gunplay and may have even wanted a fight. He called out: "If we die we will die right in this house!" Reynolds, of course, had no way of knowing if Miller really wanted a gunfight or was just expressing drunken bravado. Ida Miller, Charles Miller's wife, by now had heard and seen enough and told her husband to give the pistols back to the Rangers. Obviously trying to calm the situation before it escalated beyond hurling insults, she took one of the pistols and approached the door as if to return the weapon. But Charles grabbed it from her yelling: "Here, take your damned old pistol" and fired, intending to shoot the nearest Ranger, who happened to be Private Tim McCarty. Miller missed with that first shot.

Ranger McCarty returned fire. Reynolds now ordered his men to shoot, resulting in a deadly gunfight. The Rangers did not need a second command and the firing became general. Both the Rangers and those within the house joined in the exchange of gunfire. Miller again fired at McCarty, but this time did not miss as the bullet plowed its way through his chest, just below the left nipple. McCarty had the strength to call out to his commander, "Lieutenant, I am killed!"[10]

Every Ranger heard that scream from the lips of young Tim McCarty, causing their blood to boil. Now it became a matter of *killing*, not simply recovering pistols. Each Ranger contributed to the fusillade. While the size of the Miller house is unknown, the fact that it was large enough to host a dance suggests that the building could hold a dozen or so individuals. Since it was still fairly early in the evening, not more than half a dozen individuals were inside, including Charles Miller, his wife Ida, their little girl, name unknown, and ex-soldiers Steve Saunders and Henry Clay, as well as a few others.

Two men of Reynolds's company as they appeared in the early 1870s. Seated is Tom Gillespie and standing is James B. Gillett.

COURTESY PANSY GILLETT ESPY

Reynolds and his men poured volleys of shots from their Winchesters into the house with deadly results. When there was no more fire from inside the Rangers cautiously entered. As the smoke cleared, the scene was revealed: Charles Miller, Steve Saunders, Henry Clay, all former "Buffalo Soldiers," who at one time had served their country, lay dead on the floor. But there was also another victim, the nameless and innocent little girl. Ida Miller later claimed to have been wounded in the melee as well. Ranger James B. Gillett later wrote that one black man had escaped, having hidden under the bed when the trouble started. He then jumped through a window when the Rangers entered, disappearing into the darkness.[11]

Lieutenant Reynolds's first concern was to determine the condition of the wounded Tim McCarty. He was alive, yet with a serious wound in his chest. Lieutenant Reynolds did what he could for Private McCarty. Certainly there was a doctor in that settlement, but the available record does not indicate who may have been called. In 1880 Dr. W. E. Waters served Menard County, but there is no evidence that he was summoned there in January of 1878 to try and minimize McCarty's suffering.[12]

The shooting, sounding like a barrage of gunfire for several minutes, alerted the entire community of Scabtown. Menard County Sheriff James H. Comstock approached to investigate. He had been appointed county sheriff in October of 1876, and had scarcely a year's worth of experience in that frontier county. Sheriff Comstock conducted an investigation and called a coroner's jury. It came to the conclusion that the blacks "came to their death while resisting officers in the discharge of their duty." No inquest was recorded on the little girl.[13]

On January 2, 1878, Lieutenant Reynolds telegraphed Adjutant General William Steele the news about the Scabtown incident. He reported that during his attempt to arrest Saunders,

Miller and Clay "charged with appropriating State arms they resisted arrest and all killed. Our loss one man wounded Tim McCarty." Reynolds made no reference as to race in this communication.[14]

The next day Reynolds sent a second telegram to Steele. It simply and briefly stated: "Timothy McCarty Company A died last night from the wounds received on [January] first." Reynolds also took the time to write a lengthy letter to his superior, Frontier Battalion Major John B. Jones, providing greater detail. His explanation concluded with this comment: "The citizens are Jubilent [sic] over the Killing of the Negroes and I think this Place will be quiet for some time to Come." He also wrote a letter to an unidentified acquaintance in which he expressed "sympathy with the relatives and friends of McCarty."[15]

On January 8, 1878, Sergeant Henry McGhee wrote a letter to his brother John W., explaining what had happened. McGhee certainly knew that news of the killing would receive publicity and he wanted his brother to know the facts of this Scabtown affray, at least as Henry McGhee knew them. He explained that the squad had arrived at Fort McKavett on December 31 and had "first-rate winter quarters, good tents and everything in good shape." He then began his account of how Fort McKavett was "a pretty rough place and the negroes here need killing." McGhee further explained that upon learning that Stevenson and Johnson had been disarmed, Reynolds and the others started to arrest the blacks and recover the pistols. After locating them, Reynolds demanded the return of the pistols and their surrender. They refused to do either. McGhee then explained in full what happened, saying that they:

> would kill every white man in town first. The Lieutenant insisted, however, and finally they agreed to give up

their pistols, but just as a Ranger reached out his hand to receive one of them, the negro shot him, and then the ball opened. We killed all that were in the house except one, who ran and got away, though. I think he is wounded. The negroes emptied their six-shooters—it was right lively for a little while. I got in ten shots with my Winchester rifle, and I would not be surprised if it did some damage. [McCarty] was seriously wounded. I don't think he will live. He is one of the best men in our command and is brave as a lion.

McGhee included a postscript before sealing the envelope, adding that McCarty had died at 1:20 p.m. on January 2, 1878. This was the first and only man Lieutenant Reynolds ever lost in action. McCarty was buried at the post, but the location of his grave has been lost.[16]

Major Jones discussed the Scabtown incident with Adjutant General William Steele and Governor Richard Hubbard. Of course Reynolds's action was approved by them, but Steele was aware of some newspaper editors who expressed disapproval of what he had done. To prevent additional negative reactions, Jones ordered Reynolds to obtain a copy of the coroner's report and get it to Steele so if any further bad press occurred, he could publish it. Jones believed that if the facts as expressed by the coroner were known, there would be no further criticism of the Rangers. He also notified Captain Coldwell that Private McCarty had been killed in action. At that point Jones, Steele, and Hubbard, as well as Reynolds, considered the matter closed.[17]

But the killing of Miller, Saunders, Clay, and the little girl did not remain closed. Did race play a role in the incident? Since most whites at that time considered themselves superior to other races, some writers have suggested that if the ex-soldiers had been white instead of black, Reynolds would not have been so quick to give the order to fire. Evidence of racial bias and hatred surely existed among some of the participants and observers. For example Ranger James B. Gillett expressed the general prejudice so common among whites when he wrote that those dead ex-soldiers had associated with "white gamblers and lewd women" so much that they considered themselves "the equals of white men." Further, Reynolds found that the local citizenry was "jubilant" over the killings. But was it because those three dead men were bullies and ruffians and had been troublesome to the community, or was it because they were black? Ranger Henry McGhee, in writing to his brother, believed that his Winchester had "done some work" and that the "the negroes here need killing." This statement was intended as a reminder that killing Negroes would keep them "in their place," inferior and subservient to the dominant white society.

But the Scabtown affray was not so easily forgotten by state officials. Ida Miller, widow of Charles Miller who was mourning the loss of her daughter and her husband, decided she wanted and needed justice. On January 3, with the bodies of the three men and her little girl barely settled in their graves, she wrote a note that was printed in the *San Antonio Daily Express*, later reprinted by the *Galveston Daily News*, giving great publicity to her plight. Whether she actually wrote it or had a friend who did is unknown, but in it she explained what happened: "My little child's head was shot to pieces and my husband was shot in four places. The other two were shot and fell in the fire." How long she stayed at Fort McKavett is unknown, but by March 1878 she was at Fort Concho, a distance of over 200 miles. On March 21 she wrote to Fritz Tegener, then justice of the peace in Travis County, that she felt justified in writing him since she knew him from when they were at Fredericksburg and she did his laundry. "I hope you will assist me by explaining [examining?] this letter when you receive it and help by your in fluence [*sic*] to bring the Murderers of my husband and child to summary justice." In her mind the term "justice" meant placing Reynolds and his men on trial, issuing a quick verdict of guilty and then immediate death by hanging. But that was not all.

> Since they Killed my people all Save four little children they have robbed me of my property in Menard County and left me helpless, with one arm broken to pieces to Support myself and little ones, [and] they threatened my life if I should go back to McKavett to look after my effects or to make complaint, as the Lieutenant of the Rangers fears the consequences of his bloody work.[18]

Justice Tegener must have wondered why he should become involved in the incident. In an effort to hurry it out of his mind, he referred the letter to Governor Hubbard, who in turn referred it to Adjutant General Steele "with instructions as hereafter—to have this completely examined." One might suspect that the terms "with instructions as hereafter" was code to let the matter quietly drop and fade away. Apparently, this is what happened as there are no further documents regarding the tragedy in the available records.[19]

In the aftermath of the violent incident, the various parties returned to their daily lives. The friends and relatives of Timothy McCarty mourned his passing and then continued their lives. Reynolds and his Rangers ultimately forgot about the shooting in Scabtown as they returned to hunting down fugitives with the potential for a gunfight that could cost another Ranger's life. Hubbard, Jones, and Steele pursued their administrative matters and worries about legislative funding and the realities of Texas politics in the 1870s and 1880s. They could not concern themselves with such matters as Ida Miller's hunt for summary justice or what would happen to her other children.

The loss of a small child during the Scabtown incident received little or no notice. In a January 5, 1878, memo by Sergeant C.L. Nevill, Reynolds's future brother-in-law, he recorded that only one Ranger and three blacks were killed. He noted:

> Lt. Reynolds returned from Menard Co. having marched to McK Dec 31st 77 where some negroes robbed Ben Johnson and George Steveson [sic] Teamsters of the Batt[alion] of their Pistols[.] when ordered to surrender by Lt. Reynolds they said they would die first and fired but doing no damage and then a fight took place between the rangers and negros [sic] which resulted in the killing of 3 Negros our loss was one man Tim McCarty wounded from which he died[.]

It is not surprising then, that while Ida Miller yearned for summary justice, it never came.[20]

—————◆◆►◄◆◆—————

Although never involved in law enforcement, but being a long-time student of the Wild West—the Rangers, outlaws, and other lawmen—as well as a father and grandfather, to me there is much more to the violent incident at Scabtown than the killing of men as they resisted arrest. I see it as a callous act, believing there must have been another way to recover those pistols. But to the Rangers, the facts of the case seemed simple enough: they had to recover the pistols and if the three blacks were killed resisting arrest, well such things do happen. I wonder, however, if any of them even thought about the little girl, the "collateral damage" as it would be called today. I also wonder if before the first shot was fired, were the Rangers anxious for some action, wanting some type of resistance so that they could experience a little excitement? After all, scouting for fugitives or "Indian signs" was often boring and unproductive, traveling mile after mile on horseback searching, but finding nothing. It appears that once Lieutenant Reynolds gave the order to fire, McGhee, Harrison, Gillespie, and Reynolds continued to empty their Winchesters, while McCarty bled. McGhee's letter indicated that he took some pleasure in blasting away. But did not the others feel the same? What they said about shooting the black men would be unacceptable today, but if a similar situation existed in today's society between law officers and riotous citizens, the same racial terminology, uttered in anger, would be no different. Lieutenant Reynolds later had two daughters. When they were little girls, I wonder if he ever thought of the little black girl who was unintentionally killed along with the three ex-soldiers. I cannot help but think he did.

If I could have been a "fly on the wall" and eavesdropped in on the conversation immediately before the two visitors— Johnson and Stevenson—entered Miller's "dance hall," their words may have been just as racially motivated against the white Rangers who had stopped so close to Scabtown. Would that have been no less racially charged? Looking back at the entire tragic incident, I conclude that both sides allowed their prejudicial feelings to dominate rather than sound judgment. Miller and his friends gained nothing in their treatment of Stevenson and Johnson; if sober they could have returned the weapons on Reynolds's demand. In this situation Reynolds, perhaps feeling somewhat belligerent because his peaceful sleep had been disturbed, may have overreacted. Could he not have demanded Miller to exit the house with the pistols, rather than simply blasting into the building's interior—not knowing, or apparently caring, who or what was hit? Looking back at this incident with the available evidence, I think that it could have been handled differently. But Reynolds only knew he had to recover the pistols, and acted without giving it a great deal of thought.

Pondering this moment and the frontier society of nineteenth-century Texas, I find the affray at Fort McKavett fascinating. I wish the historical record told us more. I also wish we knew such things as: What actions had these men experienced as soldiers? Had they ever fought Comanche or Kiowa or Apache together, fighting for their lives? Where did Charles and Ida Miller meet? What experiences did Ida Miller have that placed her in that Scabtown dwelling that particular night? What happened to her? Did she remarry or did she continue her unhappy life raising her remaining children? If I had been "a fly on the wall," hovering above both groups—the Miller residence and the Rangers' camp—I'd see and hear what happened on New Year's Eve 1877 in Scabtown, Menard County, Texas. I'd also find answers to my questions, which now must remain for future research.

SELECTED READINGS

Cunningham, Sharon, and Mark Boardman. *Revenge! And Other True Tales of the Old West*. Lafayette, IN: Scarlet Mask Publishers, 2004.

Gillett, James B. *Six Years with the Texas Rangers: 1875-1881*. Chicago: R.R. Donnelley & Sons, Co., 1943.

Glasrud, Bruce A., and Harold J. Weiss Jr., eds., *Tracking the Texas Rangers: The Nineteenth Century*. Denton: University of North Texas Press, 2012.

Miller, Rick. *Texas Ranger John B. Jones and the Frontier Battalion, 1874-1881*. Denton: University of North Texas Press, 2012.

Nevill, Charles L. "Minutes of Co, E. Scouts etc. by C.L. Nevill 1st Sergt." Unpublished manuscript in Texas State Library and Archives.

Parsons, Chuck, and Donaly E. Brice. *Texas Ranger N.O. Reynolds: The Intrepid*. Denton: University of North Texas Press, 2014.

Rose, Peter R. *The Reckoning: The Triumph of Order on the Texas Outlaw Frontier*. Lubbock: Texas Tech University Press, 2012.

Sullivan, Jerry M. *Fort McKavett: A Texas Frontier Post*. Lubbock: Texas Tech University Press, 1981.

Utley, Robert M. *Lone Star Justice: The First Century of Texas Rangers*. New York: Oxford University Press, 2002.

NOTES

1 See Jerry M. Sullivan, *Fort McKavett: A Texas Frontier Post* for a brief history, originally published as Vol. XX, 1981, *The Museum Journal*, under the editorship of Gale Richardson, by the West Texas Museum Association, Texas Tech University, Lubbock. Also informative is "Fort McKavett: State Historical Park" brochure P WD BR, P4503-092 (7/94) in author's collection.

2 *San Antonio Daily Express*, November 27, 1878. Mickle correspondence from Fort McKavett.

3 Claudia Hazelwood, "Menard, Texas" in *The New Handbook of Texas*, Vol. 4, page 614. William W. Lewis served in the Frontier Battalion from May 25, 1874, to November 30, 1876, under Capt. Daniel W. Roberts and then Capt. Frank M. Moore. Texas Ranger Service records, Adjutant General Papers, Texas State Library and Archives. By 1880 he resided in Menardville with occupation listed as "Merchandise." He was then 24 years old with a wife, 19-year-old Minie H. and a two-month-old daughter. 1880 Menard County Federal Census, 135. *San Antonio Daily Express*, November 27, 1878. Mickle correspondence from Fort McKavett. Charles L. Nevill kept a "minute book" consisting of notes of each scout while with Reynolds. The December 31, 1877, entry reads simply: "Lt. Reynolds and scout went to Menard Co in search of fugitives." The memo book, now at the Texas State Library and Archives, measures 3-1/2 x 6 inches in size. He identified it as "Minutes of Co E Scouts and etc. by C.L. Nevill 1st Sergt." Nevill's small ledger covers the period from September 1, 1877, to April 17, 1879. Nevill numbered the pages up to 39 and then discontinued the pagination.

4 For a complete biography of Reynolds see Chuck Parsons and Donaly E. Brice, *Texas Ranger N.O. Reynolds: The Intrepid*, 2nd ed. (Denton: University of North Texas Press, 2014).

5 Timothy J. McCarty was mustered into the Frontier Battalion on September 10, 1877, by Maj. John B. Jones. He was 27 years old, five-feet-nine-and-one-half inches tall, had black hair, blue eyes, and dark complexion. He was a native of Virginia. At his death the State owed him $42.66. McCarty's service record. The Texas Peace Officer's Memorial, located at 1601 South Interstate 35 in Austin, places his name on column 9, row C, line 17. He is also honored on the National Law Enforcement Officers memorial in Washington, D.C. McCarty's name is located on the east wall, panel 56, line 26.

6 James B. Gillett, *Six Years with the Texas Rangers, 1875-1881* (Chicago: R. R. Donnelley & Sons, Co., 1943), 130, 132. Sheriff James B. Comstock to editor of Austin's *Daily Democratic Statesman*, written January 7 and printed in the issue of January 12, 1878; and Reynolds to Major Jones, January 3, 1878.

7 Gillett, *Six Years with the Texas Rangers*, 130.

8 The Lehne Mercantile store had been the business of William Lehne, but by 1877 apparently he had passed and the store was operated by his widow, Theresa. The letter Reynolds wrote informing Major Jones about the fight was on the letterhead of Mrs. William Lehne. Francis Clark was the commanding officer of the 184 individuals enumerated at the fort. Besides the soldiers, there was one barber, three cooks, a blacksmith, a dress maker, numerous laundresses, and one photographer—McArthur Cullen Ragsdale—whose photographs of Texas Rangers have been preserved, although apparently his preference was for Company D subjects. "Inhabitants in Fort McKavett, enumerated June 7, 1880, by N.Q. Patterson," 125.

9 Gillett, *Six Years with the Texas Rangers*, 130.

10 Sheriff James H. Comstock to Editor of *Daily Democratic Statesman*, written January 2 and printed January 12 issue; and Lieutenant N.O. Reynolds to Major Jones, January 3, 1878.

11 Gillett, *Six Years with the Texas Rangers*, 132.

12 The 1880 Menard County Federal Census lists the occupants of Fort McKavett showing name, age, sex, marital status, where from, and occupation. The only physician identified was 48-year-old Dr. W.E. Waters, born in Washington, D.C. with a 35-year-old wife, Annie E., born in Maine. They had one daughter, Chese E., seventeen. Dr. William Elkanah Waters (1835-1903) exhibited a distinguished talent during the Civil War, ultimately rising to the rank of Assistant Surgeon General. At his death on October 26, 1903, he was buried in Arlington National Cemetery.1880 Menard County Federal Census, 125 and Find A Grave.

13 As yet no newspaper article has been discovered that criticized Reynolds's action, resulting in the death of the ex-soldiers, a little girl, and the Ranger. Although Adjutant General Steele may have been aware of such criticism by certain editors, that criticism never reached publication. Could Steele or Jones have been aware of Sergeant McGhee's version of the incident and were fearful that might have a negative effect on future appropriations? Sergeant Henry Warren McGhee was the son of Henry Anderson and Jane (Warren) McGhee, born January 1, 1854. He came to Texas from Alabama after the Civil War. Ranger McGhee wrote his brother John W., then residing in McLennan County, about the gunfight, providing historians with additional information about the affray. Henry W. McGhee died May 31, 1891, of Bright's disease. McGhee's letter to his brother was printed in the *Waco Weekly Examiner and Patron*, dated January 1 but not printed until the issue of January 11, 1878.

14 Discussion of the coroner's report appears within the Comstock letter printed in the *Daily Democratic Statesman* of January 12, 1878. Little is known of James H. Comstock, not even his full name. He was born in Illinois on April 1, 1845, but the 1900 Census shows his birthplace as Connecticut. He was appointed sheriff of Menard County on October 14, 1876, and elected on November 5, 1878, and served until November 2, 1880. Sammy Tise, *Texas County Sheriffs*, 371. By 1900 he served as a deputy sheriff of El Paso County, Texas. Comstock died in El Paso on August 1, 1917, of cir-

rhosis of the liver according to attending physician Dr. L.L. Schwab. He is buried in Concordia Cemetery, El Paso. Official Texas death certificate # 21784.

15 We can only wish we knew who the acquaintance was. The letter may have been to Irene Temperance Nevill whom Reynolds would marry on September 13, 1882. Her brother Charles was a sergeant in Company E and Reynolds may well have wished his future in-law family to know he was all right.

16 Kimble County historian Frederica Burt Wyatt compiled a listing of the individuals buried at Fort McKavett, based on her "on the ground" inventory, as well as other sources. Although we suspect the four victims of the Scabtown gunfight are buried there, no markers remain to mark their graves. "The Cemetery at Fort McKavett, Texas," Junction, Texas: Kimble County Historical Museum, 1999.

17 Major John B. Jones to Lieutenant Reynolds, January 8, 1878; and letter to Capt. Neal Coldwell, January 7, 1878.

18 Ida Miller to Fritz Tegener, written at Fort Concho, March 21, 1878. This letter appeared in the *Galveston Weekly News* of January 21, 1878, as news from Menard County.

19 The notation by Tegener is on the original letter of Ida Miller in the Texas State Library and Archives.

20 Charles L. Nevill, "Minutes of Company E Scouts," 28-29.

CHAPTER SEVEN

With the Yalies in the Deep Woods, May 10-13, 1909

Dan K. Utley

IN THE FIRST DECADE OF the twentieth century, what would soon become known as the conservation movement began to coalesce around a small number of key factors then growing in acceptance on a broader societal scale. They included some acknowledgment of the limited supply of natural resources and thus the need for a measure of preservation, but also the pragmatic use of those resources, where possible, to sustain yields for future generations and the inevitable growth they would require. With philosophical roots reaching well back into the previous century and the writings of individuals such as Henry David Thoreau, George Perkins Marsh, Ernest Thompson Seton, John Muir, and others, conservation took on a more activist demeanor in the early 1900s. No issue better exemplifies that than the landmark environmental battle Muir enjoined over the proposed inundation of the Hetch Hetchy Valley within California's Yosemite National Park. Fighting to preserve the wilderness area for its own sake in light of increasing demands for water by rapidly expanding urban areas, Muir ultimately lost the battle but won the war, and conservation was forever changed at that point.

Despite the national publicity surrounding such landmark locales as Hetch Hetchy, changes in conservation activism played out more commonly along the ragged edge of everyday life wherever the pressures of development and resource exploitation threatened the status quo of the natural landscape. The Progressive reforms of the early twentieth century, fueled in large part by technology and science, sought a new paradigm of social pragmatism away from the perceived excesses of the Gilded Age. Along that edge of change were the nation's forests, particularly in the South, where vast stands of timber began to give way to capital investments that quickly converted the stumpage into money. With the earlier depletion of forests in the Northeast and Midwest, the yellow pines of the Southern forests were next in line, given the "cut out and get out" mentality that had prevailed in timber production for generations. As environmental historian Curt Meine wrote, "From New England to New York and Pennsylvania, up through Michigan and across Wisconsin and Minnesota, a trail of slash and ash had followed the lumber baron's exploitation. The bawl and din of emerging nationhood drummed out the isolated voices of protest." The East Texas Piney Woods, representing the practical western limits of the great Southern forest and predominated in the southeast part of the state by highly prized growths of longleaf pine (*Pinus palustris*), or swamp pine, were thus a timely focal point for implementation of—or at least viable consideration of—new scientific forestry reforms. In the era of open exploitation of natural resources, even talk of sustained yield forestry was a radical departure.[1]

The period from the 1880s to the 1920s was a boom era for timber production in East Texas. It began in earnest when

Yale Forest School, class of 1909. Aldo Leopold is seated on the floor in the light-colored suit. The second individual to his right is Percy J. "Paxie" Paxton, his friend and tent mate at Mooney's Lake.
IMAGE COURTESY OF THE UNIVERSITY OF WISCONSIN
DIGITAL COLLECTION CENTER, IDENTIFIER S01508

rail lines first pierced the forest core, bringing true market viability, then declined sharply when, despite the best efforts of conservationists, the moneyed lumber interests began looking westward from the largely cutover land. In just forty years, the industry had depleted an area roughly the size of Indiana—and it had been done primarily with two-man crosscut saws, double-bit axes, narrow-gauge railroads, mule teams, and steam-powered rehaul skidders.[2] Although there were limited efforts at selective cutting, clear cutting prevailed, and there was no systematic plan for forest reserves or replanting. For some the result was to open land prized by agriculturalists—the lumberman's bequest to the farmer. Economically, Texas and the other states of the Old South remained part of the cotton culture. As historian David L. Chapman observed in his administrative study of the Texas Forest Service, "the whole agrarian tradition in the South was based on exploiting the land to its fullest, using it up, and then moving on to virgin tracts where the process would begin again." It was, he noted, "the legacy of the cotton economy."[3]

Against the odds in Texas and elsewhere, those promoting forest conservation nevertheless had reason for hope in the first decade of the twentieth century. By 1908, there were clear indications that change was imminent. The reasons are myriad, but first and foremost was a promising team of leadership at the national level, beginning with Theodore Roosevelt, a true conservationist at heart who became president upon the death of William McKinley in 1901. Equally significant was his close advisor, Gifford Pinchot, the head of the newly formed U.S. Forest Service (USFS) who, despite his commitment to conservation, nevertheless found himself at odds with Muir over Hetch Hetchy. Born to a well-heeled family and raised in eastern Pennsylvania, schooled at Yale University, and inspired by time spent observing cutting-edge scientific forestry programs in France, Germany, and Switzerland, Pinchot seemed destined to develop a new conservation ethic for the fledgling profession of forestry in the U.S. Sympathetic to the naturalist tenets of George Perkins Marsh, who drew historical connections between resource depletion and the fall of societies, he was also a Progressive follower of the utilitarian concepts espoused much earlier by British philosopher Jeremy Bentham. Borrowing heavily from the latter in particular, Pinchot penned the words that served as the guiding principle of his mission and that of his agency. With reference to the need for forest reserves, he noted, "where conflicting interests must be reconciled the question will always be decided from the standpoint of the greatest good of the greatest number in the long run."[4]

Working in close partnership on innovative conservation measures, Roosevelt and Pinchot in 1908 promoted broad public education measures that also engendered a sense of promise. In May of that year, Roosevelt convened a White House Conference of Governors—the first gathering of its kind— to discuss specifically the conservation of natural resources. Governor Thomas Campbell of Texas chose not to attend, but instead sent three advisors: W. Goodrich Jones of Temple; Richard Fenner Burges of El Paso; and Jeff D. Montgomery of Palo Pinto.[5] In opening remarks to the conference, Roosevelt stated, "[Conservation] is the chief material question that confronts us, second only—and second always—to the great fundamental question of morality." After several days of meetings and deliberations, conference attendees issued a joint declaration that called for, among other things, the establishment of state conservation commissions, further urging "the continuation and extension of forest policies adopted to secure the husbanding and renewal of our diminishing timber supply, the prevention of soil erosion, the protection of headwaters, and the maintenance of the purity and navigability of our streams." It concluded with the sweeping admonition, "Let us conserve the foundations of our prosperity." The conference had the immediate effect of positioning conservation higher up the list of national concerns and called on states to cooperate in solutions. As Pinchot later wrote, "Conservation became the commonplace of the time."[6]

On the industrial side of the equation, the years 1907 and 1908 represented a time of production reassessment and market readjustment. The Panic of 1907 led to a slowdown of excessive manufacturing across the spectrum, but timber seemed particularly hard hit by the economic slowdown. As it turned out, 1907 marked the peak year of the bonanza era in Texas, a year in which 673 sawmills operated in the state. With increased calls for conservation, the inevitability of lower prices driven by overproduction, and the reality that the industry in Texas was fast approaching a point of no return in terms of available stock, the end seemed only a short distance in the future. There were a few companies that heeded the call for forest conservation, at least on a limited trial basis, including the Thompson Brothers enterprise headquartered in Houston. It would be the leadership of that company, together with the expressed interest of Chief Forester Pinchot that led to a remarkable Lone Star moment in the deep woods of East Texas centered on Tyler County in 1909.[7]

To understand the significance of the event and how it occurred in such a remote locale, it is necessary to return to the story of Pinchot's professional education. When he entered Yale in 1899, there was no credible forestry program and indeed no forestry profession in the nation. Pinchot remained focused on his goals, however, and following a lengthy sojourn in Europe at such prestigious schools as L'Ecole Nationale Forestière in Nancy, France, he returned to the U.S. determined to promote the establishment of similar institutions. Given his family's wealth, longstanding interests in land management, commitment to public service, and ties to Yale University, the solution was for the Pinchot family, headed by his parents James W. and Mary Eno Pinchot, to fund the creation of the Yale Forest School (now the Yale School of Forestry and Environmental Science). It opened in 1900 with seven students. The first chairman of the school was Gifford Pinchot's close friend and USFS colleague, Henry Solon Graves, who would gain

widespread credibility in his own rights as a forester and conservationist. While Pinchot professed to distance himself from
the school, his influences as a founder, U.S. Chief Forester,
and occasional professor were unmistakable. As a result, the
school closely followed his utilitarian model, and the majority
of its graduates quickly joined the ranks of the USFS. Others
became early leaders of fledgling state forestry programs (the
forerunner of the Texas Forest Service began in 1915), thereby
spreading the influence of both Yale and Pinchot in the emerging realm of professional forestry.[8]

One of the basic programs of the Yale Forest School curriculum for the Master of Forestry degree involved the use of
field schools in the nation's "lumber woods" outside the New
England area. Designed to enrich the students' classroom
learning through real world experiences, the field schools
served as practicums that allowed them to work alongside their
professors and other seasoned timber workers on such aspects
of forestry as surveying, timber cruising (estimating the volume of standing timber), lumbering, millwork, and even the
construction of tram roads. For those students preparing to
graduate, the spring field schools represented the last part of
the curriculum, and frequently students moved from the lumber woods training directly to positions in forestry. While some
of the regular field schools were understandably held at the
Pinchot family estate, Grey Towers, at Milford, Pennsylvania,
school officials also sought out cooperative agreements with
lumber companies along timber fronts in Missouri, Louisiana,
Alabama, and, in the spring of 1909, Tyler County in East
Texas. The Texas host was the Thompson Brothers Lumber
Company, whose holdings included a sizeable mill operation at
Doucette, then a thriving community of approximately 1,200
individuals just three miles north of the county seat, Woodville.

The company's frontline camps included an active operation about five miles southwest of Woodville. There, attorney John Allen Mooney made a lakeside site available to the Yalies where they could camp for their three months of training. Although the students would work at the mill in Doucette, in tracts near Colmesneil in the north part of the county, and at other sites, Mooney's Lake served as the official home base that spring.[9]

The choice of the Thompson Brothers operation was an important one for officials of the Yale Forest School, in large part because it was a stable company headed by J. Lewis Thompson, a somewhat sympathetic supporter of conservation efforts. A 1908 edition of the trade journal *American Lumberman*, noted as much in a special feature on the company. "If conservation of the forests as an idea should advance as rapidly in the next ten years as it has during the past ten," the article predicted, "the Thompson lumbering interest might be made perpetual." Because company management represented a marked change from past operations, it added, "Wanton destruction of forests cannot be laid at their door."[10]

The Thompson operation also proved a good choice because of the transitional status of the Doucette mill run by Alexander Thompson. Already an operating mill in 1906 when the Thompsons bought out the Sunset Lumber Company, it suffered a devastating fire on August 4, 1908, causing the company to redesign and modernize the plant. The investments in that regard proved considerable and even included replacement of the outmoded narrow gauge rail lines. The students would essentially be working at a state-of-the-art mill. Interestingly, too, was the fact that Canadian-born Peter A. Doucette, considered to be "the best logging man in Texas and probably one of the best qualified loggers in the United States," was an employee of the company.[11]

In the spring of 1909, students of the Yale Forest School master's program made their way from New Haven to the Woodville camp via boat and rail, with stopovers in New Orleans and Beaumont. They included young men of great promise who would figure prominently in both state and national forestry programs through the following decades. The best known, particularly with regard to his future impact on the national conservation movement, was Aldo Leopold of Burlington, Iowa. Born into a wealthy family that greatly valued the outdoors, Leopold had an acute inquisitive nature about the world around him, whether it was in the farm fields of Iowa or in the remote wilderness of Les Cheneaux Islands of Michigan's Upper Peninsula along Lake Huron, where the family annually took extended vacations in the late summer months. He carefully observed birds and other animals within his environments and kept meticulous records of their activities during his regular "tramps" off the beaten path. His attention to detail and his ability to record his own abiding reflections about nature became the touchstones of his upbringing. Somewhere along that personal journey of his youth, Leopold began to focus on the new science of forestry and so set his sights on studies at Yale.[12]

It is largely through Leopold's writings, particularly his letters home to his family in the spring of 1909 that the student perspective of the camp experiences in the Texas woods have survived in the historical record. The related correspondence began even before the end of classes at Yale that spring and detailed the journey southward, including a note on the New Orleans layover, where "one A. Leopold fell from the high estate of the tee-totaler and the nichtraucher."[13]

Taking the Texas and New Orleans (T&NO) train north out of Beaumont, the students debarked at Doucette, from which they took a tram line part of the way southwest toward Mooney's Lake before walking the remaining distance. At the camp, Leopold made his home in an eight-foot by ten-foot wall tent with his roommate, Percy J. "Paxie" Paxton, who would later have a long and distinguished career with the USFS. One of Leopold's first outings away from camp was to the south, where he and two other students participated in a sawmill survey and lodged overnight with the Tolar family, likely in the vicinity of Hillister. Leopold's letter about the event provides a glimpse of East Texas rural life at the time: "It was mighty interesting, with the numerous hounds, the immaculate cabin under the giant magnolias, the open hearth and dutch oven cooking, the Pine Knot fire, the feather-beds, etc."[14] A few weeks later, he also provided a detailed account of the thickets in which he conducted topographic work, observing, "when it comes to running a line across a Bay-Gall (baygall, or swampy area), an airship would really be preferable. They are absolutely the thickest places I have ever seen, and are chuck full of Wood-Ticks and Sand Flies and all other varmints."[15]

Leopold's letters, replete with similar detailed descriptions of the East Texas environment, reveal the same type of literary approach to his naturalist observations that would be the defining element of his numerous essays in later years. Consumed by his studies at New Haven and at the finishing school in Lawrenceville, New Jersey, before that, the young scholar had drifted from the routine of the woodland tramps that were so much a part of his early life. That began to change, however, as he adapted to his new surroundings in the woods. As his biographer Curt Meine observed, "The naturalist in Leopold reemerged during these weeks in Texas. Both at work and in his free time, Aldo began to explore the woods with the old-time enjoyment and newfound enthusiasm."[16] That reemergence is clearly evident in his letter to his mother, Clara Starker Leopold, on April 10:

> I have had quite an amusing day. Was sent on topo-graphic work way down to Big Cypress Creek. It is six miles to down there. I ran lines through the big Cypress Swamp all day, and had a very interesting time with the mud, the flies, an ungodly number of catbri-ers, and a cotton-mouth moccasin,—who by the way got under a log and escaped. Also saw a pileated wood-pecker, and had a conversation with a Great Horned Owl. Also saw my first Black Squirrel.[17]

A few days later, on April 13, Paxie and Aldo took the log train to Doucette and then caught the main rail line south to Woodville, where they boarded at the Stewart Hotel, a ram-bling, multi-story frame establishment only a short walk south of the depot. The county seat with a population numbering less than a thousand did not escape Leopold's careful scrutiny. "This is a funny little town," he wrote his father, Carl Leopold. "I never saw so many dogs. Counted nine at one street-con-sultation this evening. Also were Prize-taking Razorbacks. It is quite a nice little place though." In Woodville, the two stu-dents, joined by others, took the U.S. Civil Service exams for forestry administered by the town's postmaster. As Leopold told, "The Exam began at nine o'clock this morning [April 14] and lasted seven hours. . . . It was a good deal of strain, but I certainly did murder it."[18] The following day, they took the second phase of the exam, which covered dendrology and lumbering. Following the examinations, which he later learned he passed, qualifying him for federal work, Leopold proceeded on to the mill at Doucette, where, after finding the local ho-tel too full of "varmints" for his liking, he returned to the Stewart. Writing of the local cuisine, he noted, "In Woodville everything is fried except the biscuits. They are just slightly singed on the outside."[19]

Back in camp by the end of the month with stress of the federal exams well over, Leopold became more contemplative and began to allow himself the time to put his new experiences in a personal perspective. Writing to his mother, he recorded: "I am all alone here with my candle, and the rain pattering gently on the tent. . . . I could sit here all night and tell you all about the delights of 'snooping around' in the woods, of how everything I see there puts me in mind of the old days, and of how I would like this minute to begin again on my birds and flowers if only I had the time." Somehow, he found the time and thus wrote of observing anhingas (water turkeys), coots, gallinules, bitterns, blue herons, and a snowy egret, which he described as "one of the rarest, and certainly the most beautiful, of all our water birds."[20] A few weeks later he wrote again to his mother of the broader natural landscape he enjoyed. "It really is a beautiful region. If you could see the full moon tonight, sailing high over the towering pine-trees, you would like it too. I have decided, again and again, that it is worth all the trouble of the mosquitoes, and fleas and snakes and pigs, and more too."[21] The wilderness aspect of forestry that appealed the most to Leopold and which would become a hallmark of his innovative work in the USFS, and far beyond, was clearly evident in his writings from the Woodville camp, even at the age of twenty-two.

On Saturday, May 8, Leopold first mentioned what would be a memorable Lone Star moment with significance far beyond the front line camp at Mooney's Lake. "We have quite an event coming off here next Monday and Tuesday," he wrote to his mother. "The Conservation Committee of the Southern [Yellow] Pine Manufacturers Association holds its annual meeting here at the camp. Mr. Pinchot is also to be here, and Prof. Graves too. Tuesday we get a holiday to listen to the Proceedings." And, he added, "The men are to be lodged all about camp."[22] Three days later, in a letter to his father, Leopold wrote, "The last couple of days have been pretty busy ones for me. I have been acting as chairman of the committee which has charge of taking care of our distinguished guests." The professional magnitude of the moment was not lost on him, as he added, "I for one am having an interesting time. It is an opportunity of considerable value to us, to meet all these prominent men." One of those individuals Leopold was able to visit with closely was the president of the host company, J. Lewis Thompson, who the Yalie described as "a most interesting man."[23] Other leading lumbermen present for the committee meeting included John Barber White of Kansas City, Missouri, and John C. Kaul of Birmingham, Alabama. All of the industrial representatives at the meeting were considered key individuals, both regionally and nationally, who might carry forward the message that the time had come for new conservation measures in the lumber woods. Pinchot, Graves, and others were there to keep the dialogue going from the scientific and scholarly viewpoints.[24]

Unfortunately, if Leopold wrote of his observations of the committee proceedings or his conversations with Pinchot and Graves, those records do not survive. What remains, however, are a number of perspectives, including those of Pinchot and Yale professor Henry Haupt "Chappie" Chapman about the committee deliberations. Newspaper accounts of the meeting leave no doubt that Pinchot viewed the gathering as a landmark in the evolution of conservation. As reported on May 12 in the *Dallas Morning News*:

> In the dense pine woods of East Texas, in Tyler County,
> near the beautiful little city of Woodville, took place
> today a conference which is the most important step
> which has ever been taken in forestry and the conser-
> vation of the resources furnished by nature. This is the
> opinion enthusiastically expressed by Gifford Pinchot,
> Chief of the United States Forestry Service. . . . This is
> the first conference of the kind ever held. . . .[25]

Writing later that year in *Forest Quarterly*, Professor Chapman
recorded that the conservation committee significantly "decided to recommend the cutting of yellow pine in two operations separated by a period of years, instead of removing the
entire stand in the first cut as at present." The results of the
action, he believed, would leave behind trees of considerable
size to warrant the investment of time. According to his cal-
culations, a span of twenty years could result in an increased
valuation of 100 percent, "of which 56 per cent is growth on
merchantable trees and 44 per cent maturing in the interval."
But, as Chapman's article concluded, this was an argument
in theory and not yet the reality of practice. Attributing the
statistical information to the findings produced by the Yale
Forest School in Tyler County through cooperation with the
Thompson Lumber Company, he revealed: "The company
does not own the land and the marking was made for purposes
of instruction only. The timber will be cut clear."[26] The model
plan itself gave way to the cut out and get out mentality that
continued to prevail along the timber front, despite talks to
the contrary. Ultimately, too, the USFS side of the equation
changed dramatically when Pinchot, long touted as a revered
advisor to Roosevelt, failed to enjoy the same standing with the
new president, William Howard Taft. A number of factors, but
most notably a particularly volatile political stalemate known
as the Pinchot-Ballinger Controversy, led to the chief forester's

departure in 1909 and eventually to a devastating split in the Republican Party. Although his successor at the USFS was his close friend, Henry Solon Graves, the tone of the service soon began to reflect the more cautionary and less political leadership of the new chief.[27]

Pinchot, commonly referred to as the Chief and later recognized as the "father of U.S. forestry," eventually chose to enter politics as a means of continuing his fight for reforms, serving as the governor of Pennsylvania in two separate terms. Aldo Leopold, the young man who welcomed him to Mooney's Lake in 1909, joined the USFS as planned upon completion of the spring field school. Earlier, passing on an opportunity to work in a forest products program, he stated that he had no intention of being "a Tie-pickler or Timber-tester,"[28] choosing instead to be a forest ranger. His first assignment was the Apache National Forest in what was then the Arizona Territory. While at the USFS, he pioneered the concept of wilderness preservation within the forest reserves, in effect arguing that the common good espoused by Pinchot should be expanded to include places preserved for their overarching sentimental and natural value to the general public. He also worked to promote game management, or wildlife management as it came to be known, within the service. In both regards early on, he remained a follower of Pinchot's philosophy, as did most early graduates of the Yale Forestry School. As Meine observed, though, "Leopold did not so much absorb the Pinchot doctrine as adopt it by default. In his professional attitudes, the utilitarian idea dominated because he found confirmation there for his own notions of conservation." Those independent views coalesced famously in Leopold's land ethic, in which he noted, "A thing is right when it tends to preserve the integrity, stability, and beauty of the biotic community. It is wrong when it tends otherwise."[29] Jack Ward Thomas, USFS Chief in the mid-1990s, cogently summed up the evident philosophical connections between the two giants of conservation when he reflected, "I think if you look at the greatest good for the greatest number in the long term and then you turn and you look at [Leopold's] land ethic, that looks to be an evolutionary process, not a dramatic breakthrough."[30]

Over the years, the professional trails of Pinchot and Leopold that at times seemed divergent, in reality crossed many times. Leopold eventually left the USFS after twenty-eight years of service and eventually settled in as a beloved professor at the University of Wisconsin, from which he made regular visits to his nearby retreat northeast of Baraboo that he called the Shack. There, he put his conservation practices to good use in managing the land, while continuing to write his essays and articles, and developing a wide following. Sadly, he died there in 1948, two years after the death of Pinchot, while helping a neighbor fight a brush fire. The following year, his most famous work, a collection of essays entitled *A Sand County Almanac*, was published, bringing him even greater notoriety and acclaim. The book is now considered a landmark in conservation literature and has sold more than two million copies. Although Pinchot and Leopold traveled extensively in their work and even returned to Texas, there is no evidence that either revisited Tyler County. Their encounter in the deep woods near Woodville—the meeting of two of the greatest leaders of the conservation movement, the father of forestry and the father of wildlife conservation—remains little known and often overlooked, despite the promise it represented on so many levels at a pivotal time.

The story of the meeting at Mooney's Lake gained important public attention in 1986, when through the work of former

Texas Forest Service (TFS) Chief Forester Arthur David Folweiler, himself a Yale forestry graduate, class of 1931, the Texas Historical Commission placed a marker at the agency's regional headquarters two miles east of the camp. The text acknowledges the significance of the gathering, not only to conservation measures of the time and to future legislation, but also to the later creation of the TFS and its ongoing programs.[31] The marker records a Lone Star moment that perhaps Aldo Leopold summed up best in the closing of his last letter from the Woodville camp. While he wrote about the relentless heat of the deep East Texas woods in May 1909, his words are hauntingly prophetic when taken in the context of the broader story: "A *breeze* has begun to blow—isn't that fine?[32]

In many respects, the Lone Star moment of the Yalies in the deep woods represents a personal journey for me. As a native Texan long interested in conservation history, I value greatly the remarkable contributions both Aldo Leopold and Gifford Pinchot made to the movement. Along with such individuals as Rachel Carson, John Muir, Ernest Thompson Seton, Edward Abbey, and many others, they represent important landmarks along my course of study and understanding. More importantly to me, though, is the land represented by the story. I grew up in Woodville and, like Leopold, came to appreciate both the environmental wildness and the awe-inspiring natural beauty of the surrounding area. Although the landscape I knew was largely cultural, representing multiple waves of growth and successive plantings wherein loblolly and shortleaf pines long ago replaced the native longleaf stands, I have an abiding sense of the hills and the stream valleys that still define the land. As a boy, I hunted and fished that area, even, if memory serves, dropping a line or two in Twin Lakes at some point. At Camp Urland, the Boy Scout camp just a few short miles north of where the Yalies made home, I spent countless hours as a young man and later as an adult leader walking what I thought was every square inch of those grounds. After I left Woodville to enter the University of Texas, I returned one summer and raised tuition money by working on a culled hardwood removal crew south of town on land on or near that surveyed by the Yalies almost sixty years before. As I read Leopold's letters about the wildlife and the terrain, I can visually understand the meaning of his words. They touch my unmistakable sense of place, even though I left East Texas decades ago. In my memory, though, I know the land well. In the severe heat of that East Texas summer of 1968, I worked in the swamps and baygalls Leopold described, and regularly joined my fellow crew members in building small pine straw smoke fires (always properly extinguished) in a futile attempt to fend off the ever-present mosquitoes that would even swarm in your mouth if you dared to talk. Following graduation, I once again returned to my hometown, where I augmented my meager teaching salary at Wheat Junior High by driving a school bus, which included a side route along the road down toward Twin Lakes and ended with a turnaround at the entryway to the private estate.

If I could have been a "fly on the wall"—or maybe more appropriately a wall tent—I would have found much to eavesdrop on during the time of the Yale Forest School. If I could have been there in person, I would no doubt have found it compelling when Pinchot and Leopold exchanged greetings, and when John Barber White, J. Lewis Thompson, and other lumber barons talked openly—maybe for the first time with government officials and university professors—about the need for conservation and the promise of renewed forests for the cutover

South. But, above all, I would have enjoyed tramping the woods with Aldo Leopold, seeing my home country as he saw it and experiencing his take on the wildlife and the landscape I now share with him through his writings. I would have wanted to travel with him to Woodville to view how my hometown looked at the turn of the last century and maybe to give him a glimpse into the future. The depot and the Stewart Hotel on East Bluff Street are gone, as are the T&NO rail lines they once adjoined, but I remember when they were still there. In my mind's eye, little has changed in some respects about my hometown, but in reality I know it is a far different world. Still, I have no doubt that Leopold and I could share a meal that he would recall—like something fried with singed biscuits on the side.

SELECTED BIBLIOGRAPHY

Earley, Lawrence S. *Looking for Longleaf: The Fall and Rise of an American Forest*. Chapel Hill: University of North Carolina Press, 2004.

Leopold, Aldo. *A Sand County Almanac and Sketches Here and There*. New York: Oxford University Press, 1949.

Lewis, James G. *The Forest Service and the Greatest Good: A Centennial History*. Durham, NC: Forest History Society, 2005.

MacMullen, Edith Nye. "Planting the Seed: The Origins of the Yale Forest School," *Forest History Today* (Spring 1999): 11-16.

Maxwell, Robert S., and Robert D. Baker. *Sawdust Empire: The Texas Lumber Industry, 1830-1940*. College Station: Texas A&M University Press, 1983.

Meine, Curt. *Aldo Leopold: His Life and Work*. Madison: University of Wisconsin Press, 1988.

Miller, Char. *Gifford Pinchot and the Making of Modern Environmentalism*. Washington: Island Press, 2001.

Pinchot, Gifford. *Breaking New Ground*. New York: Harcourt, Brace, and Co., 1947.

NOTES

1 Curt Meine, *Aldo Leopold: His Life and Work* (Madison: University of Wisconsin Press, 1988), 75; Lawrence S. Early, *Looking for Longleaf: The Fall and Rise of an American Forest* (Chapel Hill: University of North Carolina Press, 2004), 44.

2 Robert S. Maxwell and Robert D. Baker, *Sawdust Empire: The Texas Lumber Industry, 1830-1940* (College Station: Texas A&M University Press, 1983), 3-4; Earley, *Looking for Longleaf*, 161-162.

3 David Lane Chapman, "An Administrative History of the Texas Forest Service, 1915-1975," PhD dissertation, Texas A&M University, August 1971, 51.

4 Char Miller, *Gifford Pinchot and the Making of Modern Environmentalism* (Washington: Island Press, 2001), 55-56 and 155; Gifford Pinchot, *Breaking New Ground* (Washington: Island Press, 1947), 261.

5 Chapman, "An Administrative History of the Texas Forest Service," 47.

6 Pinchot, *Breaking New Ground*, 351-353.

7 Chapman, "An Administrative History of the Texas Forest Service;" J.C. Dionne, "The Lumber History of Texas for 1909," in *Year Book 1909*, Texas Department of Agriculture Bulletin, May-June, 1910, No. 13, 337-347.

8 Miller, *Gifford Pinchot*, pp. 83-88; Pinchot, *Breaking New Ground*, 152-153; Edith Nye MacMullen, "Planting the Seed: The Origins of the Yale Forest School," *Forest History Today*, Spring 1999, 11-14.

9 Miller, *Gifford Pinchot*, 71-83; A.D. Folweiler, "Information Pertinent to a 1909 Historical Event in Tyler County, Texas," historical narrative for "The Yale Summer Forestry Camp and Gifford Pinchot" marker application, Tyler County marker files, Texas Historical Commission, Austin, Texas; *Yale Forest School, Biographical Record of the Graduates and Former Students of the Yale Forest School, with Introductory Papers on Yale in the Forest Movement and the History of the Yale Forest School* (New Haven: Yale Forest School, 1913), 22-23.

10 "Lone Star Pine," in *American Lumberman*, September 26, 1908, 150. Reprint.

11 "Lone Star Pine," 148; W.T. Block, *East Texas Mill Towns & Ghost Towns*, Volume I (Lufkin: Best of East Texas Publishers, 1994), 357-362; Lou Ella Moseley, *Pioneer Days of Tyler County* (Fort Worth: Miran Publishers, 1975), 193-194. Sources differ on the Doucette namesake, with some crediting Peter A. Doucette and others his brother, Fred, who was killed in a tram engine explosion in 1898. It is also possible, as at least one source speculates, the town name honored both men.

12 Meine, *Aldo Leopold*, 22-29.

13 Aldo Leopold letter to his mother, Clara Starker Leopold, March 19, 1909. This and other letters between Leopold and his mother and father cited in this chapter came from the Aldo Leopold Archives, accessible through the University of Wisconsin Digital Collection, http://digital.library.wisc.edu/1711.dl/AldoLeopold [hereafter cited LP for Leopold Papers].

14 Megan Biesele, "Hillister, Texas," in Ron Tyler, ed. *The New Handbook of Texas*, Volume 3 (Austin: Texas State Historical Association, 1996), 622; Aldo Leopold letter to Clara Starker Leopold, March 19, 1909, LP.

15 Aldo Leopold letter to Clara Starker Leopold, April 3, 1909, LP.

16 Meine, *Aldo Leopold*, 82.

17 Aldo Leopold letter to Clara Starker Leopold, April 10, 1909, LP.

18 Aldo Leopold letter to his father, Carl Leopold, April 14, 1909, LP.
19 Aldo Leopold letter to Clara Starker Leopold, April 25, 1909, LP.
20 Aldo Leopold letter to Clara Starker Leopold, April 25, 1909, LP.
21 Aldo Leopold letter to Clara Starker Leopold, May 4, 1909, LP.
22 Aldo Leopold letter to Clara Starker Leopold, May 8, 1909, LP.
23 Aldo Leopold letter to Clara Starker Leopold, May 11, 1909, LP.
24 "Conservation of Timber Resources Is Discussed; Gifford Pinchot Meets with Lumbermen in East Texas," *Dallas Morning News*, May 12, 1909, 14; "Mr. Pinchot in Texas," *Southern Industrial and Lumber Review* (May 1909): 60.
25 "Conservation of Timber Resources is Discussed," *Dallas Morning News*, May 12, 1909, 14.
26 Henry H. Chapman, "An Experiment in Logging Longleaf Pine," *Forest Quarterly* 7, no. 1 (March 1909): 385 and 393-395.
27 James G. Lewis, *The Forest Service and the Greatest Good: A Centennial History* (Durham: NC: Forest History Society, 2005), 66-68.
28 Aldo Leopold letter to Clara Starker Leopold, February 12, 1909, LP.
29 Meine, *Aldo Leopold*, 503.
30 Lewis, *The Forest Service and the Greatest Good*, epigram, xiii.
31 "The Yale Summer Forestry Camp and Gifford Pinchot" historical marker file.
32 Aldo Leopold letter to Clara Starker Leopold, May 29, 1909, LP.

CHAPTER EIGHT

"So Long, It's Been Good to Know You": Black Sunday, April 14, 1935

Heather Green Wooten

*E*VERYONE WHO WAS THERE REMEMBERS it, Palm Sunday, April 14, 1935. A pristine, warm and sunny afternoon in the Texas Panhandle was suddenly interrupted by a dust storm of biblical proportions. Rising up from the north, a tremendous tidal wave of swirling black earth bore down on the land, engulfing everything within its path. "It was a terrible thing to see, I'll tell you right now. That thing just rolled. It just rolled coming in," exclaimed one observer.[1] "We were too scared to pray and too scared to run," recalled another.[2] No one had seen anything like it. Was this phenomenon a manifestation of God's wrath? Was the world coming to an end?

The epic dust storm remembered as "Black Sunday" signaled the apex of an unprecedented environmental disaster that threatened to destroy the agricultural breadbasket of America. The storm's magnitude remained permanently etched in the memories of those who witnessed it. While the Japanese attack on Pearl Harbor was the turning point for Texans coming of age during the 1930s and early 1940s, others who spent their youth in the Texas Panhandle give Black Sunday precedence as the landmark event of their lives. More importantly, Black Sunday became a defining moment in the culture and identity of the Texas Plains. The physical and psychological trauma imparted by the storm strongly influenced circumstances and attitudes that continue to shape the realities of the Texas Panhandle region. It also gave rise to one of the most famous anthems of the era:

> So long, it's been good to know you,
> So long, it's been good to know you,
> So long, it's been good to know you,
> This dusty old dust is a gettin' my home,
> I've got to be drifting along.

The causes of Black Sunday took root years before when the Great Plains grasslands seized the capitalist vision. Once the domain of wandering buffalo herds, the vast prairie grassland became an unfenced grazing range owned by corporate livestock interests. The farmers arrived next. Supported throughout the 1920s by an international demand for wheat and equipped with powerful new machinery, plains farmers devoted large holdings to single-crop agriculture. Spurred by new, "scientific" dryland farming techniques and the popular belief that "rain follows the plow," farmers engaged in the swiftest and most extensive plow-up in world history. One-way disc plows pulled by muscular tractors pulverized the topsoil for fall planting. Farmers planted wheat in the pasture during the winter months, harvested the crop with steam-powered combines in late spring and recommenced plowing in the summer.[3]

It worked nicely for a time. A decade-long series of wet springs and autumns produced bountiful harvests and lush profits. By the end of the 1920s, over thirty-three million acres of Great Plains prairie sod had been turned—over two million in the Texas Panhandle alone—and converted to wheat fields.[4] But farmers were courting disaster. The plains grasslands were not suited to a full-scale agricultural system. Agricultural historian Garry L. Nall observed, "Too frequently, farmers ignored or did not understand such basic elements as types of soil, climatic factors, and slope of the terrain." It was a mistake to cultivate the grassland. As tractors stripped bare the topsoil of the southern plains, they peeled away the native grasses that, for millennia, had held the soil in place. The result, according to Nall, "not only created extensive wind damage, but also hampered conservation of moisture left in the soil."[5] As the ecological balance of the plains fell under threat, Mother Nature began to deliver a wrenching rebuke.

In 1932 plains farmers confronted a crisis. The nation was three years into the Great Depression. Although the wheat harvest the previous year bore a historically high yield, Europe was no longer interested, and the United States already had more wheat than it could use.[6] Then the rains stopped. A nation-wide drought, originating in the East moved westward, growing deadlier as it infiltrated the arid plains. High temperatures seared the Texas Panhandle. Water supplies dwindled and crops wilted in the fields. Initially, Panhandle residents were unruffled by the climatic turn. Like financial downturns, droughts are cyclical and they had experienced dry spells often enough. While some were far more serious than others, for instance, the combined drought and ferocious winters of 1885-1887 that devastated the cattle industry, the pattern was often the same. Livestock died, claims were abandoned, immigration stopped, and many people vacated the Great Plains region. Then within a few short years, rains returned, crops grew lush, and the dry times became a distant memory.[7]

Black Sunday dust storm approaching the outskirts of Amarillo.
COURTESY OF AMARILLO PUBLIC LIBRARY,
PHOTO ARCHIVE #358, VOL 3.

This drought would be different. The lack of rainfall combined with years of extensive overgrazing and plowing up the earth produced a tremendous calamity. For almost a decade, rainfall amounts throughout the Texas Panhandle dipped far below local norms. For twelve years, between 1929 and 1940, "rainfall failed to reach the normal 19.67 inches at Amarillo" nine times. Farmers in the vicinities of Canyon and Dalhart reported less than thirteen inches between 1933 and 1936.[8] Fierce winds bearing gusts of thirty to sixty miles per hour repeatedly raked the sun-blistered land. "That drought," one plains farmer noted, "put the fixin's on us."[9]

The worst part was the dust. Whirlwind gusts sucked up the loosened topsoil, flung it aloft, and blew it for miles across the Panhandle and into other states. "Dusters" or "Black Blizzards" they were called—tons of accumulated topsoil swept from barren fields that regularly pummeled the land. Each duster brought a fine, blinding grit that stung the skin, scratched the paint off of surfaces, and piled inches deep wherever it fell. The never-ending task of clearing dirt from homes, gardens, and flowerbeds burdened housewives in the region. Olin E. Hinkle recalled track meets held on the West Texas State University campus on days so laden with dust "that the officials had difficulty determining which competitors won . . . Hurdles topped over just as the starter's pistol was about to fire. Records remained unofficial, of course, and were doomed to stay that way."[10]

The color of the dirt varied according to its origin. Red dust came from Oklahoma, a grayish tan from New Mexico, and a yellow-orange from elsewhere in the Texas Panhandle. Sometimes the dirt from several regions invaded all at once. While many dusters blew in from the southeast or southwest, the most dreaded storms arrived from the north. Blowing off the rich farmlands of Kansas, these dust clouds boiled up with thick, black dirt, and kept lower to the ground, as they silently rolled along the earth's surface. The blizzards left in their wake a thick layer of black, greasy dirt, finer than flour that floated on the surface of water, and congregated in every nook and cranny.[11]

By 1935 the Texas Panhandle was choking on dust with the dirtiest spring on record. Twenty-eight storms pummeled the region in March followed by another twenty-six in April. Almost daily, bleak weather reports carried promises of high wind, blowing dust and limited visibility.[12] People thought they had seen it all at the beginning of March when a towering black cloud resembling "a vast mass of smoke from a giant oil fire," rolled across the southern Plains. The heaviness of it broke windows, damaged railroad communication lines, and caused a woman to faint in the lobby of a downtown Amarillo hotel.[13]

"Bad, oh, bad" veteran Panhandle farmer William DeLoach described the storm in his diary. Of his thirty-seven years on the Plains and western Oklahoma, DeLoach had never witnessed a duster of that magnitude, and, he wrote, "I have seen lots of them."[14] Surely, Panhandlers concluded, nothing could top the smothering, grit-filled "freak of nature" endured that day. Unfortunately, an eyewitness later observed, "We didn't realize that we hadn't seen the feature, just a preview of coming attractions."[15] Indeed, the worst was yet to come.

The morning of April 14 dawned lustrously clear. Panhandle residents awoke to a vivid, pink sunrise that softly melted into a translucent mid-morning sky of rich blue. A soft, silky breeze had replaced the commanding winds of the previous day. Local weather reports promised moderate temperatures, with highs in the low eighties. On this Palm Sunday, a dust-weary people considered the blessed weather an answer to prayers. Many started the day tackling the dirt: mopping down floors, scrubbing caked dust off of windows, and hanging laundry. Others took a trip to church to praise the Almighty, singing hymns with windows opened wide to the springtime air. The radiant early afternoon provided long-deferred opportunities for picnicking, taking a Sunday drive, and visiting friends.[16] However, far to the north, a high-pressure system sitting over the Dakotas was wrestling with a cold front sweeping down from Canada. Journalist Timothy Egan wrote, "With the clash of warm and cold currents, the air turned violent. Winds screamed over the grasslands, carrying dust so heavy that visibility was less than a hundred yards."[17] A mammoth wall of dust marched southward, gaining in intensity as it moved. Twirling clods of earth, twigs, and specks of sand joined the advancing dust. The soils of Colorado and Kansas collided with Oklahoma and then headed straight for Texas.[18]

By mid-afternoon people in the Panhandle detected a change. In the distance a thin, black cloud appeared on the horizon. As it grew, temperatures began to drop. The air cracked and barbed wire fences glowed with static electricity. Animals became agitated. Rabbits frantically skittered across open fields. Horses pawed and sniffed the ground. Outside of Dalhart, a young Melt White noticed birds flying low, in a straight line, parallel with the insects. Another observer saw flocks "twirling and swooping" as they fled south.[19]

Then it hit, an enormous wall of virulent, black swirling earth, rolling from the north, pounding upon the land. Rising fifteen thousand feet in the air, and bearing three hundred thousand tons of topsoil, the land-based tsunami twisted and churned as it surged forward at "express train speed."[20] The magnitude of the storm, recalled an eyewitness, was "both beautiful and terrifying."[21] Clyde "Bud" Hodges of Miami, Texas, remembered a neighbor who was ferrying a truckload of cattle that afternoon. "This guy cussed every breath." Hodges noted, but when he beheld the mammoth black duster surging toward him, "he quit cussing."[22] The eerie part was the quiet. This storm did not ride on a gale of wind. It spun forward in ominous silence as it quickly blocked out the sun and engulfed the land in inky blackness.[23]

Everyone ran for cover. They scurried into homes, churches, businesses, and underground tornado shelters. In an effort to manage the invading dirt, people frantically wetted down bed sheets and covered windows, stuffed rags in-between doors and fumbled for lamps. Families gathered together in rooms, placed damp cloths over mouths and noses as the cloud consumed everything in a chilling, cloying darkness. "It was just black, black, black," said Wanita Brown. "You could not see your hand in front of your face."[24] Canyon resident Ben Guill recalled that the sensation felt like "entering the mouth of a cave."[25] Rivulets of black dust slithered down walls and permeated every inch of air space. Grit sandwiched between teeth, invaded eyes and ears, settled on the surfaces of skin and turned faces and exposed areas black. People fought for breath as they inhaled the heavy pungent dust.[26] It was a terrifying feeling, Chester Thompson of Amarillo remembered, "There was no sound, no wind, it was just as if you were suddenly covered with a blanket, tight." It was the only time in Thompson's life that he harbored "the fear of being smothered."[27]

The storm caught hundreds of individuals out in the open. Blinded by dust, people became disoriented, often just a short distance from their homes. Some stayed put while others anxiously fought their way forward. As they clutched at barbed wire fences to navigate, the static electricity sent a jolt that propelled them backward.[28] A group of Girl Scouts overtaken by the dust cloud while on an exploratory venture in the canyons outside of Amarillo became stranded for almost twelve hours before being rescued in the early hours of the following day.[29] Motorists lured to the highways earlier in the afternoon pulled off the road or drove into ditches to wait out the storm. Not everyone exhibited such caution. Jesse Bennett was enjoying a carefree afternoon carousing in his old Model A Ford when the black blizzard approached outside of Dumas. Feeling courageous under the influence, Bennett sped north to meet the phenomenon—and quickly regretted it. "I like to choked to death before I got back to town," he later professed.[30]

The heavy assault of dirt knocked out phone lines and paralyzed transportation systems. Trains on Fort Worth and Denver Railroad lines slowly advanced in the darkness, then stalled, unable to push through the accumulating drifts.[31] Airplanes were coerced from the sky, including that of daredevil aviatrix Laura Ingalls during an attempt to break the world record for non-transcontinental flight. As her plane crossed over the Panhandle, Ingalls encountered the "most appalling thing I ever saw in all my years of flying." Unable to fly above the gigantic dust cloud, Ingalls emergency landed in Amarillo, thus postponing her ambitious mission until the following summer.[32]

The storm was wretched for animals. Chickens mistook the dusty darkness for nightfall and went inside to roost. Cattle bellowed and horses snorted incessantly as thick clouds of dust rained down in barnyard stalls. Resident Frank Vanderberg recalled the terror of "Old Pete," a family mule. Left out in a nearby field, he remembered the mule let out "the loudest bray," a "cry of anguish" Vanderberg clearly recalled decades later.[33]

It all resembled a scene from the biblical plagues. "My Gosh," declared the eight-year-old Fred Vanderberg to his father, "Is the world coming to an end?"[34] Violet Pipes of Pampa

Black Sunday storm approaching a community in the Texas Panhandle
COURTESY THE PANHANDLE PLAINS
HISTORICAL MUSEUM, CANYON, TEXAS

recalled an elderly woman caught in the center of town as the storm bore down. In a desperate attempt to seek shelter, the woman tottered into the first lighted open doorway she could find. It turned out to be the Empire Café and Bar, operated by "pretty raunchy" waitresses. Once the woman realized where she was, she fell to her knees in horror. "Don't let me die here," she prayed, "I'm a devout old lady." Pipes added, "She thought the duster was the end of time."[35] Many Panhandle residents shared a similar thought. Grassroots fundamentalism, prominent throughout the Texas Panhandle and southern plains, saw uncommon trials and natural disasters as both evidence of God's displeasure and a sign of the final judgment.[36] "There is no such thing as chance," a southern Baptist minister declared in March of 1935. "Everything is test, or punishment, or reward, or prevision."[37]

Throughout the 1930s, traveling evangelists bearing fire and brimstone messages chock full of biblical literalism, regularly admonished audiences. "Wicked and perverse ways"—the recent repeal of Prohibition and "riotous spending" to name a couple—accounted for the economic crisis and dusty chaos that had consumed communities.[38] Biblical references of Judgment Day reinforced these evangelical appeals, including Deuteronomy 28:24: "The Lord shall make the rain of thy land powder and dust; from heaven shall it come down on thee, until thou be destroyed." Two days before Black Sunday a minister delivered a strong warning to the editor of the *Amarillo Globe-News*: "Only a complete turning to God can prevent the complete collapse of this portion of Texas in which we live . . . Turn your paper over to God."[39] Of course, not everyone accepted this perspective. "I can't believe [God] would select the very best people for punishment when there are others so much deserving of his wrath," wrote a local columnist in the *Amarillo Globe-News*.[40] As the angry and perplexing dust cloud darkened the sky, many people could not help but recall the oft-quoted prophetic symbols and scripture. The fact that the storm arrived at the start of the Easter Season provided further resonance.[41]

The most famous articulation of Doomsday sentiment came out of Pampa. Twenty-three-year-old folk singer and songwriter, Woodrow Wilson ("Woody") Guthrie, and his wife Mary were dressing for evening church services when the storm hit. Employing vivid religious symbolism, Guthrie described the overwhelming black cloud "like the Red Sea closing in on the Israel children."[42] Suddenly, the day turned to night "so dark you can't see a dime in your pocket, a shirt on your back, a meal on your table or a dadgum thing."[43] A burning light bulb shone dimmer than a lighted cigarette. Guthrie continued, "A lot of people that was religious minded and up pretty well on their scriptures said, 'Well, boys, girls, friends, and relatives, this is the end. This is the end of the world.'"[44] In 1939, Guthrie immortalized the episode when he penned the song, "So Long It's Been Good to Know You." Throughout the seven verses, Guthrie captured the foreboding and calamitous nature of the day. Three are as follows:

> A dust storm hit and it hit like thunder,
> It dusted us over, it dusted us under,
> It blocked out the traffic, it blocked out the sun,
> And straight for home all the people did run.
>
> The telephone rang and it jumped off the wall
> And that was the preacher a making his call.
> He said, "Kind friend, this might be the end,
> You got your last chance at salvation of sin!"
>
> The churches was jammed, the churches was packed,
> That old dust storm blowed so black
> That the preacher could not read a word of his text,

So he folded his specs, and he took up collection, said:
"So long it's been good to know you."[45]

The colorful descriptions Guthrie provided in his ballad are not reflective of his actual Black Sunday experience. In an interview with Sylvia Grider, Mary Guthrie maintained that the couple sat out the storm in their small rented shack alone, instead of with a roomful of friends and relatives. Nor did they receive a telephone call from a minister.[46] Published four years after Black Sunday, the song is a composite of the genuine accounts and exaggerated tales people shared with each other in the aftermath of the storm. The ballad fit seamlessly into the "Cyclone Tales" repertoire Guthrie presented to audiences via radio broadcast and live performances.

The black duster, thought by some to signal the "end of the world," lasted less than an hour. As the storm subsided, people emerged from homes, stranded cars, and other shelters to encounter a sobering landscape. Layers of powdery, greasy dust blanketed fields and grasslands, created high drifts against barnyards, and submerged fences. Cattle, having bunched together for protection, lay suffocated in heaps against fences, their lungs teeming with dust.[47] Outside of Spearman, Fay Christian returned home to discover the storm had killed all 250 of the fryer chickens accidentally left out in the yard.[48] Housewives faced a massive clean-up. Thick coats of dirt saturated rugs, scratched furniture, soiled curtains and linens, seeped into closets, and permeated refrigerators. The women scooped dirt by the bucketful out of their homes, swept down porches, sidewalks, even lawns. Local business owners also suffered. The storm pushed mounds of dust against doorways and storefronts, nicked windows, and sifted over merchandise. All clothing in apparel shops bore a dull brown tint.[49]

The day after Black Sunday, the region surrounding the Texas Panhandle was given a name. Robert Geiger, an Associated Press reporter caught in the midst of the storm issued a series of dispatches, the first for a newspaper in the nation's capital, the *Washington Evening Star*. In his story, Geiger lightly used the term, "dust bowl" to refer to the windblown, drought-stricken area that included parts of Kansas, New Mexico, Eastern Colorado, and the Panhandles of Oklahoma and Texas. The expression caught on, quickly infiltrated the national vocabulary and manipulated contemporary American perceptions of the southwestern Great Plains.[50]

Another regrettable result of Black Sunday involved the increase of serious health issues. "The dust was inescapable," news reporter Frank McNaughton declared two days after the storm, "My lungs still ache."[51] Severe respiratory ailments including influenza, emphysema and bronchitis plagued Panhandle communities, killing the very young and very old. Particularly dreadful was dust pneumonia. The extremely fine dust that blew across the plains contained high silica content that had a poisonous effect very similar to the black lung disease experienced by coal miners. The Lubbock Hospital and Sanitarium reported a noted upsurge of dust pneumonia cases.[52] On April 19, the *Ralls Banner* published two front-page stories reporting the deaths of local citizens struck down by the excessive dust the previous Sunday. J. Perry Hendrix recalled the farming community of less than 1,000 persons held "at least a funeral a day" for "those who contracted pneumonia from the dust."[53] Responding to the increasing incidence of dust pneumonia, the Red Cross opened six emergency hospitals in Colorado, Kansas, and Texas during the spring of 1935 and issued an urgent call for 10,000 dust masks to be distributed among the five Dust Bowl states.[54]

"I give up," proclaimed Judge H. E. Hoover. A seasoned Canadian, Texas banker, and stockman, Hoover had habitually scoffed at the duster-related distress of local Panhandle citizens. He had seen storms much worse, he assured them, as a young man living on the plains in the 1880s. The Black Blizzard of April 14, 1935, changed the old critic's perspective. That storm and its results were, he admitted, "the worst I've ever seen."[55]

Life in the Texas Panhandle resumed after Black Sunday. The sun emerged, the sky cleared and people carried on as they continued prayers for a conclusion to the miserable drought and profusion of dirt. By 1939 they received an answer. The rains gradually returned, and the worst of the drought ended. However, in retrospect, the ferocity of Black Sunday had a monumental impact. It became more than the storm everyone remembered. The episode brought sickness, death, and an unflattering name for the region. Through songs penned after Black Sunday, folk balladeer Woody Guthrie brought the plight of the Dust Bowl to a worldwide audience. Yet, the effects of Black Sunday also set in motion three historical trends that helped redefine the Panhandle region. It influenced the adaptation of new techniques and methods of caring for the land, encouraged the migration of thousands of individuals from the Panhandle, and reinforced the grit and character of the thousands more that remained.

The dust from the epic storm did not stay on the western plains. Winds blew the gigantic dust cloud two thousand miles eastward toward the Atlantic Coast. On April 19, the storm approached Washington D.C. The timing was perfect for a young New Dealer named Hugh Hammond Bennett, who believed that the ecological damage on the Great Plains could be reversed. Many farmers in the Texas Panhandle agreed, but federal relief and recovery measures implemented before 1935 addressed the symptoms of the Dust Bowl rather than the cause. Bennett, later known as the "father of soil conservation," sought a comprehensive federal conservation program to help local farmers heal and revitalize the land. Yet, congressional enthusiasm remained tepid. Employing a talent for showmanship, Bennett strode into Room 333 of the Senate Office Building and began a lengthy testimony before a Senate subcommittee. In early afternoon, the storm rolled in, darkening the room and filling the air with thick, heavy, choking dust. "This gentlemen," Bennett said with a flourish, "is what I'm talking about." By April 27, 1935, Congress declared soil erosion a "national menace," and enacted Public Law 46, creating the Soil Conservation Service within the U. S. Department of Agriculture. Thus, new agricultural techniques, including crop rotation, terracing, and contour plowing, proceeded throughout the Texas Panhandle.[56]

Despite these efforts, the storm of Black Sunday marked a season of lost hopes and opportunity. Depressed agricultural conditions compelled many "next year" people, those who waited for a reprieve the following year, to abandon their farms. Between 1935 and 1940 the Texas Panhandle lost 15,000 residents and the number of farms declined by nearly 25 percent.[57] Numerous families joined the exodus of tenants from eastern Oklahoma and Arkansas as they followed Route 66 west in search of a better future in Arizona or California. However, most Panhandle residents stayed behind, reluctant to leave their homes and determined to salvage some fruits of their labor. "It was always nip and tuck with everything," said Dolly Longhaufer of Claude, Texas. "You [had] to do with what you got."[58] Sustained by a resilient spirit and community bonds, these "nesters" withstood the unsettling hardships of the era. Over three-quarters of a century after Black Sunday, a steady self-reliance and pride in survival continues to color the regional temperament of the Texas plains. More importantly is the effect on us all—the necessity to listen closely to the land, and pay heed to the tenor of its voice.

Why would I want to be a "fly on the wall" and eavesdrop on such a tumultuous event as Black Sunday? In truth, my fascination for Black Sunday and the Dust Bowl in general is longstanding. It began over four decades ago when my father took me to view a photographic exhibition featuring the work of Dorothea Lange, Arthur Rothstein of the Farm Security Administration (FSA), and other contributors. In a world long before the internet, it was my first exposure to the sobering realities of the Dust Bowl and its effect upon the human condition. The collective destitution and personal resilience emanating from those images quieted my light-hearted teenage sensibilities like very few things could in those days. They affect me still.

Economic depression, hunger, drought, and constant dirt-filled winds tested the endurance of every soul that resided on the Panhandle Plains. The dusty pandemonium of Black Sunday was the ultimate symbol of this hardscrabble existence. Perhaps if I stepped back in time, and intimately observed the many experiences of Black Sunday, I could understand how this storm shaped the individual lives and decisions of those who stayed and those who eventually left the Texas Panhandle. Today, extensive drought and over usage of natural resources keeps the land on the edge of vulnerability. The rapid depletion of the Ogallala Aquifer, a vast underground reservoir that sustains life on the plains, amplifies the danger of another ecological crisis. It remains to be seen whether fundamental lessons of the Dust Bowl were in fact learned. It is my fervent hope that we are spared another such terrifying moment—a twenty-first century version of "So Long It's Been Good to Know You."

SELECTED BIBLIOGRAPHY

Carlson, Paul H. "Black Sunday—The South Plains Dust Blizzard of April 14, 1935." *West Texas Historical Association Year Book* 67 (1991): 5-17.

Cray, Ed. *Ramblin' Man: The Life and Times of Woody Guthrie.* New York: W. W. Norton, 2004.

Egan, Timothy. *The Worst Hard Time: The Untold Story of Those Who Survived the Great American Dust Bowl.* Boston: Houghton-Mifflin, 2006.

Lookingbill, Brad D. "'A God Forsaken Place': Folk Eschatology and the Dust Bowl." In *Americans View Their Dust Bowl Experience,* edited by John R. Wunder, Frances W. Kaye and Vernon Cartensen. Boulder: University Press of Colorado, 1999.

———. *Dust Bowl USA: Depression America and the Ecological Imagination, 1929-1940.* Athens: Ohio University Press, 2006.

Nail, David L. *One Short Sleep Past: A Profile of Amarillo in the Thirties.* Canyon: Staked Plains Press, 1973.

Nall, Garry. "The Struggle to Save the Land: The Soil Conservation Effort in the Dust Bowl." In *The Depression in the Southwest,* edited by Donald W. Whisenhunt. Port Washington, NY: Kennikat Press. 1980.

Stallings, Frank Jr. *Black Sunday: The Great Dust Storm of April 14, 1935.* Fort Worth: Eakin Press, 2001.

Turner, Alvin O., ed. *Caroline Henderson: Letters from the Dust Bowl.* Norman: University of Oklahoma Press, 2001.

NOTES

1 Fred Vanderberg, Sr., Pampa, Texas in Frank Stallings, Jr., *Black Sunday: The Great Dust Storm of April 14, 1935* (Fort Worth: Eakin Press, 2001), 58.

2 Sylvia, "Black Easter," 63 in Wilson M. Hudson, ed., *Diamond Bessie and the Shepherds* (Austin: Encino Press, 1972).

3 Dryland farming called for the fallowing of fields to allow moisture to accumulate underneath the packed soil. This technique, combined with the "listing" method, which destroyed weeds and pulverized the soil, prepared the seed bed for October planting. Chris Magoc, *Environmental Issues in American History: A Reference Guide to Primary Documents* (Westport, CT: Greenwood Press, 2006), 189-190; Paul Bonnifield, *The Dust Bowl: Men, Dirt, and Depression* (Albuquerque: University of New Mexico Press,

1979), 40-44, 50; Garry L. Nall, "The Struggle to Save the Land: The Soil Conservation Effort in the Dust Bowl," in Donald W. Whisenhunt, ed., *The Depression in the Southwest* (Port Washington, NY: Kennikat Press, 1980), 26-27. The "rain follows the plow" theory was devised in 1881 by land speculator Charles Dana Wilber. See Henry Nash Smith, *Virgin Land: The American West as Symbol and Myth* (Cambridge, MA: Harvard University Press, 1950), 182.

4 R. Douglas Hurt, *The Dust Bowl: An Agricultural and Social History* (Chicago: Nelson-Hall, 1981), 25; Timothy Egan, *The Worst Hard Time: The Untold Story of Those Who Survived the Great American Dust Bowl* (Boston: Houghton-Mifflin, 2006), 101.

5 Garry Nall, "Dust Bowl Days: Panhandle Farming in the 1930s," *Panhandle Plains Historical Review* 48 (1975): 53.

6 Brad D. Lookingbill, *Dust Bowl USA: Depression America and the Ecological Imagination, 1929-1941* (Athens: Ohio University Press, 2001), 21-22.

7 William C. Holden, *Alkali Trails* (Southwest Press, 1930), 147; Magoc, *Environmental Issues in American History*, 189.

8 Jim W. Kuhlman, *The Block Pasture* (Self-published manuscript, 1998), 177; "Rainfall at Canyon, Texas: 1880-1954," typewritten manuscript, W. H. Upchurch Papers, Panhandle Plains Historical Museum Archive (hereafter cited as PPHM); Nall, "Dust Bowl Days," 42-43.

9 Magoc, *Environmental Issues in American History*, 190; Paul H. Carlson, *Amarillo: The Story of a Western Town* (Lubbock: Texas Tech University Press, 2006), 134.

10 Ruth Lowes and W. Mitchell Jones, *We'll Remember Thee: An Informal History of West Texas State University, The Early Years* (Canyon: West Texas State University Alumni Association, 1984), 54-55.

11 Margaret Bourke White, "Dust Changes America," *Nation* 140 (May 22, 1935): 597 (597-98); Egan, *The Worst Hard Time*, 175; Hurt, *The Dust Bowl*, 31; Renshaw Bailey, interview, April 21, 1971, transcript in PPHM; Caroline Henderson, *Letters from the Dust Bowl*, ed. Alvin O. Turner (Norman: University of Oklahoma Press, 2001), 141.

12 H. T. Collman, "Dust Storm of the Vicinity of Amarillo, Texas: Data Taken from Records of United States Weather Bureau, Amarillo, Texas," May 10, 1936, John C. McCarty Collection, Amarillo Public Library.

13 Hurt, *Dust Bowl*, 36-37.

14 William G. DeLoach, March 4, 1935 in *Diary of William G. DeLoach, 1914-1964*, Volume 6, Southwest Collection, Texas Tech University.

15 George Turner, "Black Spring: Beginning of the Dust Bowl," *Amarillo Globe-News*, April 13, 1975.

16 Egan, *Worst Hard Time*, 198-199; Grider, "Black Easter," 62.

17 Egan, *Worst Hard Time*, 202.

18 David L. Nail, *One Short Sleep Past: A Profile of Amarillo in the Thirties* (Canyon: Staked Plains Press, 1973), 102.

19 Lookingbill, *Dust Bowl USA*, 60; Egan, *Worst Hard Time*, 209, 219; Ben Guill in Stallings, *Black Sunday*, 42.

20 Robert Geiger, "Writer Caught in Dust," *Amarillo Daily News*, April 15, 1935; Frank McNaughton, "Black Blizzard Is Described by News Writer Caught in It," *Amarillo Daily News*, April 16, 1935; Hurt, *Dust Bowl*, 38.

21 Jesse Rose Benton in Stallings, *Black Sunday*, 27.

22 Clyde (Bud) Hodges in Stallings, *Black Sunday*, 67.

23 *Amarillo Daily News*, April 16, 1935.

24 Wanita Brown, interview, April 2, 1989, transcript in PPHM.

25 Lowes and Jones, *We'll Remember Thee*, 56.

26 Nail, *One Short Sleep Past*, 106-107.

27 "Chester Clinton Thompson, My Story, 1909-1971," Stephanie Su Thompson Vance, Unpublished manuscript, PPHM.

28 Fay Christian, interview, November 12, 1990, transcript in PPHM.

29 "Another Dust Storm Likely," *Amarillo Daily News*, April 16, 1935.

30 Jesse Bennett, interview, February 21 1978, transcript in PPHM.

31 Hurt, *Dust Bowl*, 39.

32 *Amarillo Daily News*, April 17, 1935; Paul H. Carlson, Black Sunday— The South Plains Dust Blizzard of April 14, 1935," *West Texas Historical Association Year Book* 67 (1991): 8.

33 Frank Vanderberg in Stallings, *Black Sunday*, 56; *Amarillo Daily News*, April 16, 1935.

34 Fred Vanderberg, Sr., Pampa, Texas, Stallings, *Black Sunday*, 58.

35 Ed Cray, *Ramblin' Man: The Life and Times of Woody Guthrie* (New York: W. W. Norton, 2004), 70.

36 Brad D. Lookingbill, "'A God Forsaken Place': Folk Eschatology and the Dust Bowl," in John R. Wunder, Frances W. Kaye and Vernon Cartensen, eds., *Americans View Their Dust Bowl Experience* (Boulder: University Press of Colorado, 1999), 151.

37 Anderson M. Baten, "Faith in Yourself," in Lookingbill, "A God Forsaken Place,"160.

38 Ruby Winona Adams, "Social Behavior in a Drought Stricken Texas Panhandle Community," Master's thesis, University of Texas, 1939, 73, 80; B. Byron and Frederick W. Rathjen, *The Golden Spread: An Illustrated History of Amarillo and the Texas Panhandle* (Northridge, CA: Windsor, 1986), 97; Lookingbill, *Dust Bowl USA*, 25.

39 *Amarillo Globe-News*, April 12, 1935. See also David Nail, *One Short Sleep Past*, 114.

40 *Amarillo Globe-News*, April 10, 1935.

41 Grider, "Black Easter," 66.

42 Woody Guthrie, Library of Congress Recordings, Elektra Records, Rounder 1041/42/43 cited in *Cray, Ramblin' Man*, 69; Grider, "Black Easter," 69.

43 Cray, *Ramblin' Man*, 69.

44 Guthrie, Library of Congress Recordings, Rounder 1041/42/43.

45 Alan Lomax, *Hard Hitting Songs for Hard-Hit People* (New York: Oak Publications, 1967), 226-227.

46 Grider, "Black Sunday," 69.

47 Wanita Brown, interview; *Amarillo Daily News,* April 16, 1935

48 Fay Christian, interview.

49 Nail, *One Short Sleep Past,* 106-108; Carlson, "Black Sunday," 10: Bourke-White, "Dust Changes America," 598.

50 Donald Worster, *Dust Bowl: The Southern Plains in the 1930s* (New York: Oxford University Press, 1979), 28; Hurt, *Dust Bowl,* 3: An earlier effort led by the *Dalhart Texan* to locate the origin of the phrase is discussed in Nall, *One Short Sleep Past,* 124. See also, "Hunt for Dust Bowl Culprit Near End—Suspect Is Found," *Amarillo Daily News,* November 5, 1941.

51 *Amarillo Daily News,* April 16, 1935.

52 *Lubbock Avalanche-Journal,* April 14, 1935.

53 Carlson, "Black Sunday," 10-11.

54 Hurt, *The Dust Bowl,* 52; Lookingbill, *Dust Bowl USA,* 22.

55 "Black Blizzard Declared 'Worst' by Judge Hoover," *Amarillo Daily News,* April 20, 1935, 10.

56 Wellington Brink, *Big Hugh: The Father of Soil Conservation* (New York: Macmillan, 1951), 6-7; Egan, *Worst Hard Time,* 227-228; Lookingbill, *Depression USA,* 22; Garry Nall, "The Struggle to Save the Land," 32.

57 Pryce and Rathgen, *The Golden Spread,* 99; R. Douglas Hurt, "Letters from the Dust Bowl," *Panhandle Plains Historical Review,* 52 (1979): 1.

58 Dolly Longhaufer, interview, September 30, 1990, transcript in PPHM.

CHAPTER NINE

"The Game of the Century," November 30, 1935

Bill O'Neal

THE ATMOSPHERE AROUND THE TEXAS Christian University
(TCU) football stadium in Fort Worth pulsated with energy
and excitement on the last Saturday of November 1935. The
TCU Horned Frogs and the Southern Methodist University
(SMU) Mustangs readied themselves to play the most important football game in the history of Texas sports. Archrivals
TCU and SMU boasted identical 10-0 records, and were nationally ranked first and fourth respectively. The winner of
this "Game of the Century" would be named champions of
the Southwest Conference, and even more importantly, would
play in the Rose Bowl—which had never hosted a Texas team.

This exceptional late-season matchup generated the first
national broadcast of a college football game from Texas.
Grantland Rice, acknowledged as the "Dean of American
Sports Writers," came to Fort Worth to cover the game, and so
did such other prominent journalists from the northeast as Paul
Gallico of the *New York News*, Bill Cunningham of the *Boston
Post*, and Joe Williams of the *New York World-Telegram*.[1] Such

national media coverage was unprecedented for a Texas sporting event, and promoted the status of the Southwest Conference.

TCU's concrete stadium opened on the campus in 1930. The seating capacity was 24,000, and for the historic game with SMU, 3,500 temporary bleacher seats were built. But several thousand more fans came with every intention of seeing the game, even after all of the $1.65 tickets were sold. Many determined spectators climbed onto the tops of automobiles and jumped over the fence, or stood on someone's shoulder and clambered onto the field.[2] Grantland Rice enjoyed the spectacle as "over 37,000 wildly excited Texans and visitors from every corner of the map packed, jammed and fought their way into every square foot of standing and seating space to see one of the greatest football games ever played in the sixty-year history of the Nation's finest college sport."[3] There was barely room even for a "fly on the wall."

SMU's coach in 1935 was William Madison "Matty" Bell. At thirty-five years he was one year younger than second-year TCU coach Dutch Meyer, but Bell had been a head coach since his graduation from Centre College in Danville, Kentucky. Bell was born in Fort Worth, and he was a student athlete at North Fort Worth High School. He matriculated at little Centre College in Danville, playing football during the World War I era for the Praying Colonels.

After receiving a B.S. degree in 1920, he went to Haskell Institute, coaching at Jim Thorpe's alma mater for two seasons. The young head coach then spent a year at Carroll College in Wisconsin, before returning to TCU in 1923 as head coach of the Horned Frogs. His freshman coach and scout was Dutch Meyer. That same year TCU joined the Southwest Conference, and Coach Bell propelled the Frogs to a strong start in the SWC, compiling a 33-17-5 record in six years. Bell also coached basketball, and he amassed a 71-41 record on the court. Following an 8-2 football season in 1928, Bell left TCU for Texas A&M University. During the next five years, Bell had only one losing season. But he suffered a losing record in Southwest Conference games, and he was fired after a 6-3-1 season in 1933. For 1934 he was hired as SMU's line coach by Ray Morrison. It was Bell's first—and only—season as an assistant coach. The Mustangs enjoyed an 8-2-2 record, and Morrison left Dallas to coach at Vanderbilt University.

Matty Bell was promoted to lead SMU's football team, becoming the only man ever to be head football coach at three Southwest Conference schools. He inherited a talented squad rich in returning starters. There were ten senior starters and one junior. The 1935 Mustangs would have experience, size, and speed—and a veteran head coach who knew how to handle such a team. "When I was coaching at Texas A & M we played Tulane's 1931 Rose Bowl team," he related, "and I never forgot the ice-water poise they had in the unexcited way they went about their business. I told myself if I ever had a great team I'd try to keep them in the same frame of mind."[6]

In 1935 he *had* a great team. Among ten senior starters, the most famous player was 147-pound Bobby Wilson, a fleet, elusive back who led the Southwest Conference in scoring in 1934 and 1935 and was an All American selection in both seasons. Wilson was a two-time All-State back at Corsicana High School, one of five CHS Tigers who were recruited by SMU, just fifty-five miles away. Former Tiger Bob Finley, a fine runner and passer, stated that although Wilson was popular with his Mustang teammates, "he was a nervous type before games. He just couldn't sit still. But in the game, when we needed yards, we gave it to Wilson. He could stop and start quicker than anybody I've ever seen."

Another former Corsicana star was Maco Stewart, a tall, 190-pound end who was chosen a Mustang tri-captain in 1935. Rugged guard Billy Stamps, regarded at the time as one of the best linemen ever to play Texas high school football, anchored SMU's line. Like their Corsicana teammate Bobby Wilson, Maco Stewart and Billy Stamps were all-time All State players, and all three would be voted into the Texas High School Sports Hall of Fame.

Fullback Harry Shuford, a native of Tyler, was SMU's most reliable power runner throughout 1935. Tackle Truman "Big Dog" Spain and guard J.C. "Iron Man" Wetsel both were big, stellar linemen. So was tackle Maurice Orr, who also kicked extra points. Harry Shuford, J.C. Wetsel, and Maco Stewart were tri-captains of the Mustang squad.

The Mustangs were strong at every position: size, talent, experience. At a time when most starters went both ways, SMU thus was strong on both offense and defense. Matty Bell had a reputation as an excellent defensive coach, and on offense he taught a wide-open attack that featured speed and twenty to twenty-five passes per game (an exceptional number for the era). The team's only weakness was depth. There were only five or six players that were good enough to replace the starters in a close game. Otherwise, Coach Bell acknowledged that his "boys" were ambitious and had confidence in themselves and their team.

The gifted Mustangs opened the season on September 21 by trouncing North Texas State University, 39-0. The next week SMU rolled over Austin College, 60-0, before blanking visiting Tulsa, 14-0. The first three games were shutouts. Indeed, in a twelve-game schedule, eight SMU opponents were held scoreless by the rock-ribbed Mustang defense. Aside from TCU, the best opponents on the SMU schedule were Rice (which finished with an 8-3 season mark), Baylor (8-3), and UCLA (8-2). Each of these fine teams was shut out by the Mustangs. The season was a month old before SMU yielded a score, to Washington University, but the Mustangs went on to win, 35-6. Indeed, of the four teams that scored on SMU during the 1935 season, only TCU would tally more than six points.

Southwest Conference scorer Bobby Wilson led the offense. SMU often scored or set up scores with punt returns, and Wilson made more yardage on returns than on runs from the line of scrimmage. Wilson also was an excellent pass receiver, and so was rangy end Maco Stewart. Top substitutes Bob Finley and J.R. "Jack Rabbit" Smith were fine offensive performers.

Leo Robert "Dutch" Meyer, who began his long association with TCU football as a boy growing up in Waco, coached the Horned Frogs. Texas Christian University was located in Waco during his boyhood, and in 1909, when he was eleven, little Dutch Meyer was the water boy for the football team. A few years later Meyer played football at Waco High, tutored by Paul Tyson, the first great Texas high school football coach. Tyson was so far ahead of other high school coaches that sports-crazy Dutch Meyer was inspired to follow him into the coaching profession.

In 1910 fire ravaged the TCU campus. Fort Worth officials offered TCU fifty acres of land for a campus and $200,000 to move the school to Fort Worth. Dutch Meyer later followed TCU to Fort Worth, and plunged into the sports program. Although short of stature, Meyer was quick and aggressive, and he earned eleven varsity letters in three sports: football, baseball, and basketball. Following graduation he played a little minor league baseball, before a brief coaching stint at a Fort Worth high school. In 1923 he returned to TCU as freshman football coach. He also served several seasons as varsity baseball coach, and during his first three years as head football coach, he simultaneously led TCU's basketball team. While working as a freshman coach from 1923-1934, his football duties included scouting, always a vivid learning experience for a young coach. "It was the greatest thing to happen to me," he reminisced. "As a scout I saw the different phases of coaching from different people, top men like Knute Rockne, Ray Morrison [of SMU] and D.X. Bible. That gave me ideas I wouldn't have gotten otherwise."[7]

Meyer's other principal element as a coach was a rugged approach as a disciplinarian. He was called "Old Iron Pants," as well as "Mr. Football" and "The Saturday Fox," who often pulled off upsets. On the sideline Meyer was tough and fiery, sometimes hurling his Stetson to the ground and stomping it. "Fight 'em until hell freezes over," Meyer often shouted, "and then fight 'em on the ice." The phrase became a Horned Frog tradition.[8]

The most gifted player on the TCU squad was "Slingin' Sammy" Baugh. The tall, rangy farm boy from Sweetwater High School had a howitzer of a passing arm. His throwing ability made him a standout third baseman, and after college he would sign a professional contract with the St. Louis Cardinals organization. When Baugh was a raw newcomer at TCU, Dutch Meyer was a freshman football coach, as well as head baseball coach. Meyer was impressed by Baugh on the opening day of fall practice. The freshmen were tossing the ball around. "I looked over and there he was throwing the ball like I'd never seen it before."[9] Meyer recommended the six-foot-two youngster to head coach Francis Schmidt as a prospect in both football and baseball. Schmidt was dubious, but at the end of Baugh's freshman year the coach left for Ohio State.

Slingin' Sammy Baugh and teammates from the 1935 Horned Frogs
COURTESY BILL O'NEAL

With Schmidt's departure, Dutch Meyer was elevated to head football coach of his alma mater. His first season, 1934, was Baugh's initial year on the varsity, and the talented sophomore helped the Horned Frogs to an 8-4 record. Coach Meyer designed an offense built around the hard-throwing Baugh. The "Meyer Spread" split an end and a wingback several yards out from both sides of the line. Four receivers could run downfield on any down, and Slingin' Sammy could throw the ball as far as any of his receivers could sprint.

But Coach Meyer took advantage of Baugh's deep passing threat and designed a short passing game. Baugh told of the team meeting when Coach Meyer introduced this strategy.

> He has three S's up on a blackboard; nobody knew what that meant. Then he gives us a little talk and he says, "This is our passing game." He goes up to the blackboard and he writes three words that complete the S's: "Short, Sure and Safe." That was his philosophy —the

short pass. Everybody loved to throw the long pass. But the point Dutch Meyer made was, "Look at what the short pass can do for you." You could throw it for seven yards on first down, then run a play or two for a first down, do it all over again and control the ball. That way you could beat a better team.[10]

Baugh's versatility and stamina were keys to his value as a football player. As safety on defense he was a sure tackler, a far-ranging pass defender, and a dangerous punt returner who averaged almost thirteen yards on eighty-six returns at TCU. Baugh was a superb punter, kicking with power and accuracy. During his TCU career he averaged over forty yards per kick on 210 punts. (Later he led the NFL in punting for four consecutive seasons, including a 51.4 yard average in 1940.) At TCU Baugh sometimes played all sixty minutes of a game. As Flem Hall of the *Fort Worth Star-Telegram* insisted, Baugh "was the difference that lifted TCU out of the ordinary."[11] Slingin' Sammy was an All-American in both his junior and senior seasons as a Horned Frog.

Captain of the 1935 season was senior center Darrell Lester. A star at Jacksboro High School, Lester won nine varsity letters at TCU, pitching for the baseball Frogs and playing center on the basketball court. At six-foot-three and 220 pounds, Lester was one of the best college linemen in the nation. Jimmy Lawrence from Harlingen was a talented back who ran with speed and power (and who was the fifth pick in the NFL draft in 1936).

The Horned Frogs charged to a 41-0 victory over Howard Payne University to open the 1935 season. North Texas State fell next, after losing to SMU a week earlier. The TCU victories continued week after week, including 28-0 shutouts over Baylor (6-0 at the time) and Texas. In their first ten games, the

Horned Frogs scored 238 points and gave up only forty-five points, while recording five shutouts.

For the big game against the Mustangs, the Horned Frogs wore canvas pants with wide purple stripes on the back of each leg, white jerseys with small purple numerals, and black leather helmets. SMU players donned red and blue uniforms with dark leather helmets. As the two squads warmed up, fans cheered from close range. TCU's stadium wrapped snugly around the football field. There was no running track surrounding the gridiron. Concrete walls and seating loomed just behind the sideline benches, and in the end zones, seats and fencing came right up to the black lines.

A knee injury sidelined Harry Shuford, SMU tri-captain and star fullback. Coach Bell inserted Bob Finley into the starting lineup and assigned him play-calling duties. Confident in Finley's versatility, as well as the overall quality of his 10-0 team, Matty Bell used his customary cool, low-key approach before sending the Mustangs onto the field against the Horned Frogs.

The fire-eating Dutch Meyer took the opposite approach, delivering one of his typical explosive pre-game orations. Later he realized, "It was the worst thing I ever did." He often reflected on this early misstep as head coach. "Football taught me a lesson in '35. I sent our lads out there like it was a crusade. They had tears in their eyes when they left the dressing room—and it gave 'em butterfingers."[12]

Against the shutout-prone SMU defense, TCU relied upon the arm of Sammy Baugh. "Throw anytime you see a man open," Meyer instructed his talented passer. "I won't second-guess you."[13] Baugh threw forty-three passes against SMU, a virtually unprecedented aerial circus for the time. But during the first half, his receivers dropped pass after pass.

An excited young spectator was Dan Jenkins. Born and raised in Fort Worth, Jenkins would become a student at TCU and a member of the golf team. Jenkins became a top sportswriter working for newspapers in Fort Worth and Dallas, as well as *Sports Illustrated*. He became well-acquainted with Dutch Meyer and Sammy Baugh and Matty Bell, and he has written with depth about the 1935 Horned Frogs and Mustangs. Jenkins also reflected upon his vivid boyhood impressions of the big game. "What I mostly remember about the game was the constant noise in the stadium, SMU running sweeps and reverses in a blur of red and blue uniforms and the Frogs continually dropping Sam Baugh's passes, although he kept hitting his receivers in the chest and hands."[14]

"I threw the ball too damned hard and we dropped nine passes," Baugh said later with regret. "I always felt bad about that."[15] But TCU was ranked Number One in the nation with a 10-0 record, and at that level the blame belonged to receivers who coughed up accurately thrown passes.

With the TCU offense stymied by dropped passes and by SMU's rugged defense, the Mustangs threatened to run away with the game. Bill Cunningham of the *Boston Post* raved about SMU's offense, "led by their lizard-legged little bundle of mobile murder Bobby Wilson," and by a line anchored by "big Truman Spain, a tackle with walking beam shoulders. . . ."[16]

In the opening quarter SMU drove seventy-three yards, utilizing reverses, fake buck laterals, and "every known form of attack," according to Grantland Rice.[17] Fullback Bob Finley scored from one yard out, and after Maurice Orr's kick, the Mustangs led, 7-0. A second quarter drive featured a thirty-three-yard pass from Finley to Maco Stewart and a nine-yard sprint around the right end by Bobby Wilson. Orr's extra point made the score 14-0.

But before half-time Sammy Baugh punted the ball out-of-bounds on SMU's four-yard line. The Mustangs could not make a first down, and their return kick took a bad hop, bouncing out on SMU's twenty-six-yard line. Baugh then launched a pass for the end zone, and an interference call placed the ball to the one. With blockers in front of him, 190-pound Jimmy Lawrence scored over left tackle. In the casual style of the day, the kicker and holder—right end Walter Roach and Sammy Baugh—tossed their helmets onto nearby grass. The bare-headed duo registered the extra point, and the two teams went in at half-time with a 14-7 score.[18]

As the game progressed, Grantland Rice grew increasingly excited about the quality of football he was viewing. "Terrific line play by fast young giants—hard driving and elusive running backs—forward passing that electrified the packed stands—especially by Sammy Baugh —hard-blocking and even harder tackling—magnificent kicking—turned this climax game of 1935 into a combination of all-round skill and drama no other football crowd has ever seen this year."[19]

There was no scoring in the third quarter, but in the last period a TCU interception by Roach led to a scoring drive. Baugh fired a strike to Jimmy Lawrence from eight yards out. Baugh and Roach again dropped their helmets, and the kick was true to tie the game, 14-14. On the kickoff Jack Rabbit Smith raced into TCU territory as SMU fans screamed in triumph. But the drive gained little, and on fourth down from the TCU thirty-nine, Bob Finley dropped back to punt.

Finley had averaged forty-seven yards per punt during the game, but Matty Bell was unaware that a fake punt was called in the huddle. Wilson told Finley, "Throw it as far as you can. I'll be there."[20] Finley received the snap and started as though to kick, slowing the line rush. Then he backpedaled as Wilson streaked down the right side. From the forty-seven yard line Finley launched the ball forty-four yards in the air.

A TCU back was trying to keep up with Wilson, while Baugh desperately ran over to close the gap from his safety position. Wilson looked over his inside—left—shoulder, but game film shows the ball dropping down behind him, toward his right shoulder. With amazing footwork Wilson spun around and hauled in the ball while somehow whirling to his right without breaking stride. Two more quick steps and he was in the end zone, as the stadium erupted.[21] It hardly seemed to matter that Orr missed the extra point try.

There was still time on the clock, and Baugh rapidly moved his team downfield. On the last play he ran to his right and fired the ball to a receiver on the goal line, but a lone SMU defender knocked the pass away. The scoreboard read 20-14, and the Mustang band began playing "California Here I Come."[22]

SMU had one more Southwest Conference game, with Texas A & M. On December 7 the Mustangs earned their eighth shutout victory of the season, downing the Aggies 24-0. In 1935 SMU compiled a brilliant 12-0 record, outscoring their opponents 288-32. TCU also closed their season on December 7, with a non-conference game in California. The Horned Frogs beat the Santa Clara Broncos, 10-6 to finish their schedule at 11-1.

All but one poll issued final rankings at the end of the regular season. Bowl games at that time had scant effect on the standing of teams. In 1902 the Rose Bowl staged a game, but did not resume play until 1916, and remained the only bowl game for years. In January 1933 the Orange Bowl began play, and on January 1, 1935, the Sugar Bowl staged its first game. For years there had been only one bowl game, affecting the record of just two teams, so polls continued the custom of issuing final rankings shortly after the end of the regular season. The most anticipated award came from the Dickinson System, originated in 1926 by John Dickinson, economics professor at Illinois University. Dickinson designed a math-based formula, which since 1931 awarded the Knute Rockne Intercollegiate Memorial Trophy. The Rockne National Championship of 1935 was presented to Southern Methodist University—the first time a Texas team had been named national champions.

SMU's stellar record in 1935 brought an invitation to the Rose Bowl game in Pasadena. While "the Rose Bowl was a plum," conceded Harry Shuford, "the real plum was a 12–0 season, winning the Southwest Conference and being chosen to go to the Rose Bowl."[23] In addition, the Rose Bowl offered a payoff of $85,000. SMU still owed $75,000 in bonds for Ownby Stadium, which opened on campus in 1926. Following the win over TCU, SMU borrowed $75,000 from a Dallas bank, a loan which was paid off a month later, after the Mustangs returned from California. The game-winning throw from Bob Finley to Bobby Wilson began to be called, "The $85,000 Forward Pass."

The Southern Methodist football squad traveled by train to California for the January 1 game in Pasadena's vast stadium, which seated nearly 85,000. Thousands of Texans journeyed to California to see the big game, and for the first time in its history the Rose Bowl was a sellout. The Mustang opponent was Stanford University. The 7-1 Cardinals had lost the previous two Rose Bowls, and the "Vow Boys" vowed to win the 1936 Rose Bowl.

There was a traffic jam on the way to the stadium, and the bus bringing the Mustangs from their hotel arrived at the parking lot only twenty minutes before kickoff. The team left the bus and hustled across the auto-filled lot to the stadium. Without their usual pregame routine, the Mustangs got off to a

The 1935 National Champion SMU Mustangs

COURTESY BILL O'NEAL

slow start. The Cardinals scored from one yard out in the first quarter, and the Mustangs never managed to unleash their vaunted offense. The Mustangs lost, 7–0.

"They didn't win it," insisted SMU tackle William "Tugboat" Sanders. "We had so much better of a team, and we knew it. But that day, we just didn't have our heart in it."[24] Perhaps Coach Matty Bell's cool approach was a little too cool at the Rose Bowl.

Although the Mustangs finished the long season with a 12–1 record, SMU still held the Rockne trophy. And Ownby Stadium was paid for. Furthermore, one of the Texans who attended the Rose Bowl was Dallas oil man and promoter J. Curtis Sanford. From the Rose Bowl excursion Sanford conceived of creating a Cotton Bowl, and the first game would be played one year later at Fair Park Stadium in Dallas.

On the same afternoon that SMU lost the Rose Bowl, TCU was in New Orleans playing LSU in the second Sugar Bowl. The game was all defense, and TCU won, 3–2. TCU elevated its record to 12–1, with a bowl victory. The Williamson System, the only rating service to post its final ranking after the bowl games, declared TCU National Champions. Both SMU and TCU, therefore, could claim national championship recognition for 1935.

During the Great Depression, college athletic departments did not lavish scholarship perks on football players. Even Slingin' Sammy Baugh had only a partial scholarship at TCU. "A lot of boys didn't get full scholarships," related Baugh. "They'd let you sign a note to pay it out later. After my freshman and sophomore year, I didn't know how much I owed. I'd been waiting on the training table and cleaned the music room every night."[24]

By the end of his sophomore year, Baugh owed TCU $500. But he learned that anyone on a partial scholarship who made a B average would be elevated to full scholarship. "So I went to the library every night and the last two years, I didn't owe anything." Following graduation Baugh began a record-setting career in the National Football League. "After my first year in pro football," said Baugh, "I went back to TCU and paid them off."[25]

Mustang players at SMU faced similar circumstances. A football scholarship paid for the $228 annual tuition, but players had to work for room and board. A number of players were assigned to erect and dismantle temporary bleachers for sporting events and other college activities. Harry Shuford had enough savings to pay his freshman expenses, but the next year he dug ditches for campus shrubbery plants. As a junior, the star fullback was "promoted" to janitor, with the assignment of cleaning the athletic offices early each morning. Occasionally he slept late, and when called by an irate staff member, Shuford apologized and said he would immediately get to the offices.

"You better," came the reply, "or I'm going to cut your end of the training table off."

The nationwide attention that SMU and TCU brought to Texas football during their magical 1935 season soon paid major dividends. In 1938 Dutch Meyer coached the Horned Frogs to the national championship, while TCU star Davey O'Brien won the Heisman Trophy. The next year Texas A & M won the national championship. Arguably, these triumphant performances might have been overlooked if SMU and TCU had not opened the door in 1935. After national championships in 1935, 1938, and 1939, as well as the Heisman Trophy and several other important player awards, teams and athletes from the Southwest Conference were judged on performance, rather than being automatically relegated to a second tier. Thus the 37,000 football fans (and one "fly on the wall") who crowded into TCU Stadium on November 30, 1935, witnessed a pivotal event in the history of Texas sports.

———◆◆×◆◆———

I was born and raised in Corsicana, a hotbed of high school football. My father was an accomplished schoolboy athlete and a lifelong sports fan. The year he graduated from Texas A & M the Aggies won the 1939 National Championship in football. From boyhood on, I accompanied him to Aggie football games and, in the summers, to Texas League baseball games in Dallas. While playing high school football, I daily saw photos of the All-State players who had led CHS to the State Championship in 1932. One of those star athletes was Maco Stewart, an All-State end who became an All-American on SMU's 1935 championship team. Maco maintained a prominent voice in CHS athletics, and his daughter and my sister were close friends. I heard many stories about the 1932 Tigers and the 1935 Mustangs, and

I became aware of other CHS stars who also were stalwarts of SMU's great team. One of our CHS assistant coaches had played at TCU, and I began to learn about Horned Frog football.

I entered the coaching profession, serving as head football coach at both Anna and Waskom high schools. By the time I began teaching college history, I already had launched my writing career with technical articles in coaching magazines. For more than three decades I maintained my sports connection by broadcasting football and baseball games over KGAS Radio in Carthage, where I taught at Panola College. I had come to the realization that students could not thoroughly understand Texas history without studying the statewide passion for sports. I developed a lecture, "Sports in Texas," which I regularly tweaked. Through the years I have written six books of sports history, beginning with a centennial history of *The Texas League* (Eakin Press, 1987). I am aware of many exciting and consequential sporting events in Texas, but when called upon to make a "fly on the wall" selection, I quickly decided to eavesdrop on the SMU vs. TCU football game. Two 10-0 rival Texas teams were pitted against each other, with not only the Southwest Conference title on the line, but also a national championship and a Rose Bowl bid—both unprecedented honors for a college from the Lone Star State. The pivotal nature of this dramatic contest furthermore resulted in the creation of the Cotton Bowl the following year. Texas football thus shouldered its way onto the national sporting scene, where it has maintained a prominent presence for the past eighty years.

SELECTED BIBLIOGRAPHY

Baker, Dr. L.H. *Football: Facts and Figures*. New York: Farrar & Rinehart, Inc., 1945.

Canning, Whit, and Dan Jenkins, eds. *Sam Baugh: Best There Ever Was*. Indianapolis, IN: Masters Press, 1997.

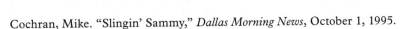

Cochran, Mike. "Slingin' Sammy," *Dallas Morning News*, October 1, 1995.

Coffey, Jerry. "At 77, Sammy Baugh Remembers His Fancy Passing." *Fort Worth Star-Telegram*, October 6, 1991.

Cunningham, Bill. "Wilson-Baugh Battle Thrills 35,000 Fans." *Boston Post*, December 1, 1935.

Davis, Steve. "Game to Remember: SMU's 1935 National Champions Recall Surprising Rose Bowl Loss." *Dallas Morning News*, October 3, 1995.

Hall, Colby. *History of Texas Christian University: A College of the Cattle Frontier.* Fort Worth: Texas Christian University Press, 1947.

Jenkins, Dan. "When Frogs Dipsy-doodled in the Wild and Woolly." *Dallas Morning News*, September 3, 1981.

Moore, Jerome A. *Texas Christian University: A Hundred Years of History*. Fort Worth: TexasbChristian University Press, 1973.

90 Great Moments in SMU Football History. SMUMUSTANGS.com— Official Athletic Site.

Perrin, Tom. *Football: A College History*. Jefferson, N.C.: McFarland & Company, Inc., 1987.

Rice, Grantland. "Wilson's Great Catch Beats Texas Christian." Syndicated Column, December 1, 1935.

Sherrington, Kevin. "SWC Played Fast and Loose, 1935 SZMU-TCZU Final Earned League Respect After Ragtag Start." *Dallas Morning News*, June 13, 2010.

"Texas Christian Bows to Southern Methodist Attack." *Universal Newsreel*. 1935 Football Game, SMU vs. TCU, SMU Heritage Hall Video.

Texas Sports Hall of Fame, Its Members and Their Deeds. n.p., n.d.

NOTES

1 Kevin Sherrington, "SWC Played Fast and Loose," *Dallas Morning News*, June 13, 2010.

2 Dan Jenkins, "When Frogs Dipsy-doodled in the Wild and Woolly," *Dallas Morning News*, September 3, 1981.

3 Grantland Rice, "Wilson's Great Catch Beats Texas Christian," Syndicated Column, December 1, 1930.

4 90 Great Moments in SMU Football History, "71. Bell Inducted into CFHZOF." SMUMUSTABGS.com – Official Athletic Site.

5 "Robert 'Bonny' Wilson," *Texas Sports Hall of Fame, Its Members and Their Deeds,* n.p., n.d. Pages are not numbered in this book, but entries are in alphabetical order.

6 "W.M. 'Matty' Bell," *Texas Sports Hall of Fame.*

7 "Leo 'Dutch' Meyer," *Texas Sports Hall of Fame.*

8 Ibid.

9 Ibid.

10 Jerry Coffey, "At 77, Sammy Baugh Remembers His Fancy Passing," *Fort Worth Star-Telegram*, October 6, 1991.

11 Jenkin, "When Frogs Dipsy-doodled...," *Dallas Morning News*, September 3, 1981.
12 Mike Cochran, "Slingin' Sammy," *Corsicana Daily Sun*, October 1, 1995.
13 Jenkins, "When Frogs Dipsy-doodled...," *Dallas Morning News*, September 3, 1981.
14 Mike Cochran, "Slingin' Sammy," *Corsicana Daily Sun*, October 1, 1995.
15 Bill Cunningham, "Wilson-Baugh Battle Thrills 35,000 Fans," *Boston Post*, December 1, 1935.
16 Rice, "Wilson's Great Catch . . . ," Syndicated column, December 1, 1935.
17 "Texas Christian Bows to Southern Methodist Attack," *University Newsreel*. 1935 Football Game, SMU vs TCU, SMU Heritage Hall Video.
18 Rice, "Wilson's Great Catch . . . ," Syndicated column, December 1, 1935.
19 90 Great Moments in SMU Football History, "71. Bell Inducted into CFHZOF." SMUMUSTABGS.com – Official Athletic Site.
20 "Texas Christian Bows to Southern Methodist Attack," *University Newsreel*. 1935 Football Game, SMU vs TCU, SMU Heritage Hall Video.
21 Jenkins, "When Frogs Dipsy-doodled...," *Dallas Morning News*, September 3, 1981.
22 Steve Davis, "Game to Remember," *Dallas Morning News*, October 3, 1995.
23 Ibid.
24 Frank Luska, "Slingin' Sammy at Short?" *Dallas Morning News*, February 19, 1996.
25 Steve Davis, "Game to Remember," *Dallas Morning News*, October 3, 1995.

CHAPTER TEN

The Firing of Homer Price Rainey, November 1, 1944

Light T. Cummins

THE BOARD OF REGENTS OF the University of Texas met at the Rice Hotel in Houston on Friday, October 27, 1944, for its regularly scheduled meeting. One of their members, however, was ill and did not attend. That regent passed away over the ensuing weekend. The regents temporarily adjourned their meeting to attend his services in Waco. Returning to the Rice Hotel, they resumed their sessions on Tuesday, October 31. In addition to the regents, those attending included University President Homer Price Rainey along with the usual assemblage of high-ranking administrators and senior staffers. The meeting also drew a committee of faculty members, a group from the Ex-Students Association, and a variety of other people interested in the school and its operation, including representatives of the press. In addition, three members of the Texas State Senate's Educational Investigation Committee and two observers from the American Association of University Professors also came to the meeting. All in all, a much larger group than usual assembled for this regents' meeting. Many of those present attended because the deliberations had potential to be unusually explosive. The Board of Regents and University President Rainey had been involved for some time in an increasingly public squabble between them. Both sides had been voicing a growing number of charges and counter-charges about how the University should be run, each disagreeing with the other. Their rhetoric at times had become impolite and shrill in tone.[1]

Each side was clearly exasperated with the other. On October 12, several weeks prior to the Houston meeting, President Rainey had given a speech to a large group of faculty and staff members on the Austin campus in which he enumerated a list of explicit criticisms about the regents and their policy decisions. Newspapers across the state had carried reports of his remarks. Now, as the regents assembled in Houston, tension filled the air because this would be the first time the board could react to Rainey's speech, something several members had already done individually and in strongly negative terms. Would there be further confrontation between Rainey and the regents? If so, what would be its nature? Events in Houston quickly brought an answer these questions once the meeting got underway. What transpired that week rocked higher education in the state with tremors that resonated for many years. It also marked in retrospect a pivotal moment in Texas politics.[2]

Routine business first occupied the board as the meeting resumed after the funeral in Waco, although the regents had no doubt discussed privately among themselves their feelings about Dr. Rainey. Some of them had previously gone on record individually as favoring the termination of the president while others had not declared themselves. Some non-regents, including faculty members and alumni loyal to Rainey, congregated in informal groups, mostly in their hotel rooms while the formal regents meeting proceeded elsewhere in the building. Many faculty members and alumni leaders who had come to Houston

hoped for a compromise that would calm differences and keep
the president in office. Representatives of the Ex-Students
Association in particular wished Rainey and the regents could
reach a workable solution. This alumni group included powerful and accomplished Texans who had much influence because of their commitment to the University. They included
W. R. Francis, Judge Joseph C. Hutcheson, and Robert Lee
Bobbitt, a leading attorney in the state. Additionally, alumnus
J. R. Parten, a wealthy oilman and former university regent,
also came to the meeting as an advocate for President Rainey,
although he did so as an individual not representing any official university entity. Parten had served as chair of the regents
in 1939 when Rainey had been selected as president, having
played a most significant role in choosing him for the position.
Parten and Rainey worked effectively together before the oilman left the Board of Regents and the two men had become
friends. Major Parten, as he was popularly known because of
his World War I military rank, took upon himself the task of
informally leading those at this meeting in Houston who advocated keeping the president in office.[3]

By Wednesday, November 1, the final day of the regents'
meeting, Parten's suite at the Rice Hotel had become an unofficial headquarters of sorts for the pro-Rainey faction. There,
in those quarters, faculty members, alumni, and friends of the
University planned strategy and discussed options on behalf
of Rainey while the regents met elsewhere in the hotel in their
official session. The regents consulted in their meeting with
representatives of the faculty, the Ex-Students Association,
and the A.A.U.P., all of whom sought a compromise between
President Rainey and the regents.[4] The regents, however, conducted their deliberations in executive session without the
participation of President Rainey. No outside observers were

permitted. Nonetheless, several faculty members and representatives of the alumni association who had testified before the regents at various times, brought reports back about what was happening to those waiting in Parten's suite. For the most part, the regents seemed very concerned with the contents of Dr. Rainey's October 12 speech to the University faculty. Some of them proved immoveable in their strident objections to many of the points he had raised. Those in Parten's hotel suite worked with President Rainey to fashion a compromise statement, softening some of what he had said several weeks earlier. In the end, however, neither side could agree to the terms desired by the other. Calling Dr. Rainey into their official meeting late that afternoon, the regents deliberated with him in executive session and, after additional discussion, they voted to terminate him. "It is therefore ordered by the Board of Regents of the University of Texas," as the scant and cryptic minutes of that executive session note, "that Dr. Homer Price Rainey be and he is hereby removed from office of the President of the University of Texas effective November 1, 1944." The regents gave no public explanations for their decision.[5]

The reasons for Homer P. Rainey's firing, however, were far from secret because almost all aware Texans at the time had a general appreciation of what had occurred. The firing was not an event that centered on the termination of a university president, *per se*. It was, instead, a very public battle between people of conflicting political beliefs regarding what philosophies would hold sway at the University of Texas. In that regard, the school was a reflection of political differences both across the state and at the national level. It was a controversy of core values about the role that higher education should play in American society. Rainey's progressive, pro-New Deal views held that a university should be a motivator for social change. His views came head to head with the corporate, business-oriented conservatism endemic on the Board of Regents. For Rainey, the conflict became one of academic freedom in the face of regent meddling. For the regents, the controversy centered on their maintaining what they believed was an even-handed, no-nonsense business supervision of the University that did not violate their conservative views of institutional management. The termination of Dr. Rainey had its fundamental motivations rooted in these political differences: one side liberal and the other conservative. And most everyone familiar with the on-going controversy between Rainey and the regents understood that these differences led to the president's dismissal.[6]

The two meetings at the Rice Hotel—the one in Parten's suite and the formal one that took place among the regents downstairs in a conference room on that fateful day—provide an historian with an eavesdropping moment to witness a microcosm highlighting two fundamental schools of political belief and orientation in Texas. Detailed knowledge about the discussions in both rooms, no doubt, would give much clarity in understanding the issues in play during the Rainey Controversy as a watershed moment in Texas political history. Both sides operated from clear-cut ideological assumptions about the role that university-level education played in American life generally, and about the place in particular of the University of Texas in the development of the state. Would it be a progressive force for change or a place for the reconfirmation of traditional values? As well, political viewpoints about the nature of proper administrative leadership, academic freedom of the faculty, and the defining of appropriate intellectual inquiry conducted with public funds all came into question, especially on the part of the Board of Regents. Importantly, discussions in both rooms that day likely turned on visions about how the best possible future for Texas could be achieved. Each side in the controversy was convinced theirs was the best answer. The outcome of Rainey's termination seemed, in retrospect, almost foreordained given the vitriol that had come to mark relations between the University president and the majority of regents by the time of the meetings on November 1, 1944. Sadly for historians, what was said, and by whom, in those two meetings remains mostly unknown.[7]

The end of the Rainey presidency that November proved all the more remarkable because of the high hopes and grand vision of the future widely held five years earlier at the time he had assumed office. Rainey was a native Texan who had graduated from Austin College in Sherman, been credentialed as a Baptist minister, earned a Ph.D. from the University of Chicago, and had taught on the faculty of the University of Oregon. Earlier he was president of Franklin College in Indiana followed by the presidency of Bucknell University in Pennsylvania. J. C. Parten, as a key regent who served on the selection committee, believed Rainey was the best person to head the University, as did many others including most of the faculty. The new president assumed office to popular acclaim and much public fanfare. His formal inauguration in 1939 attracted national attention, especially in academic circles, because it included a national conference held in Austin dealing with the role of university education in public life.[8] It had special personal meaning for Rainey because his own college mentor, President Thomas Stone Clyce of Austin College, participated in the inauguration ceremony and in the educational conference. By his second year in office, however, cracks began to appear in the façade of the Rainey administration, especially regarding the president's relations with the Board of

Regents. These came in large part because of growing political differences between progressive, New Deal-oriented Texans (a group that included Rainey and many faculty members) and conservative, traditionalist Texans who rejected many of the social, economic, and reformist programs advocated by the former group. These differences came to a head when a traditionalist group of new university regents joined the board during the several years after Rainey became president, all of them appointed by Governor W. Lee O'Daniel, a conservative businessman. He assumed office the same year Rainey had been inaugurated president.

A political outsider at the time of his 1938 election as governor, O'Daniel had astutely cultivated a popular image during the mid-1930s as a folksy and home-grown radio personality who pushed sales of his Hillbilly Flour by means of an entertaining musical program that swept the Texas airwaves with high ratings.[9] Nonetheless, O'Daniel held deeply conservative political viewpoints. The individuals the new governor selected as regents reflected his pro-business, anti-labor, and pro-*laissez faire* political opinions, tempered by a healthy measure of suspicion regarding intellectual commentary critical of social or economic matters. The O'Daniel regents also tended to view the University as a business establishment producing a product, thus making it subject to the sort of financial accountability and top-down management from the board-level accepted in corporate organization.

Rainey and his ally J. R. Parten, who had revolved off the Board of Regents at its February 1941 meeting, eventually came to the opinion that an organized conspiracy of political and business leaders, including Governor O'Daniel, were implementing a covert assault on the University in order to stifle progressive, liberal viewpoints on campus. This conspiracy

*Rainey Inauguration Ceremony, December 1939. (l. to r.) Governor W.
Lee O'Daniel; Rainey; Chester H. Rowell, guest speaker; J. R. Parten,
Regent, George W. Truett, Pastor First Baptist Church of Dallas; and
Thomas Stone Clyce, President of Austin College.*
J. R. PARTEN PAPERS, BRISCOE CENTER FOR
AMERICAN HISTORY, UNIVERSITY OF TEXAS AT AUSTIN

accelerated, they believed, shortly after O'Daniel was reelected
to a second term in November of 1940. The two university
men cited as their chief proof a secret meeting supposedly held
in Houston several months after that election, attended by
O'Daniel and a selected group of businessmen and corporate
executives who supported the governor. Attorney Robert Lee
Bobbitt, a staunch Rainey partisan and university alumnus who
had served as Attorney General of Texas, believed the purpose
of this meeting was to "secure control of the governing bodies of the major institutions of public higher education in the
state including the University of Texas as well as A&M, Texas

Tech, and A&I at Kingsville." The goal in so doing, according to Bobbitt, who did not attend as supporter of Rainey but who had received a report from someone who had been there, was to go about "limiting the academic freedom of some of our institutions of higher learning and of restricting the teaching of certain subjects and the getting rid of certain teachers."[10] Rainey would years later describe this Houston gathering of O'Daniel and conservative, anti-New Deal businessmen by telling an interviewer that the governor told those assembled: "Now gentlemen, the time has come for you representing these big organizations to take control of education in Texas and the University of Texas in particular because that's the place where all these radical ideas are coming from."[11] Later, historical research by modern scholars has questioned whether or not this secret meeting between O'Daniel and conservative business leaders actually took place. No records of it exist and those who supposedly attended later denied it had occurred. J. R. Parten's biographer, for example, could not prove that such a gathering with O'Daniel actually transpired.[12] Nonetheless, no matter if such a meeting took place or not, this anti-university viewpoint was a very real phenomenon in the state's conservative political community that proved palpable by 1940.

Such opinions became public earlier that year when United States Representative Martin Dies accused the University of harboring a communist cell. Dies went before the news media with much fanfare, promising a full-scale investigation on his part and eventually holding hearings in Austin that subpoenaed several students and a professor. Dies, trying as best he could, was unable to provide proof of his allegations, prompting President Rainey to take the hard line against him.[13] "Put up or shut up," Rainey told him, thus causing Dies to back down and move on to other concerns away from the University. The president's stern handling of Congressman Dies, however, did nothing to endear Rainey to Texas conservatives concerned about liberalism at the school. Influential Texas banker D. K. Martin of San Antonio, for example, observed there was a "far reaching evil" in Texas higher education where "unscrupulous, designing, subversive professors has been 'diggin in' in our schools more than we dare admit."[14] J. R. Parten characterized those who held such opinions by saying: "They have in mind that education is going to destroy the government and are dead serious about it." President Rainey even more explicitly described the agenda of his detractors when he noted "anything that was pro-labor was obnoxious to them." "Any friendliness shown to Negroes," he added, "or any proposals to secure better educational opportunities for them was radicalism, or any support for civil liberties, or any questioning of the economic system was heresy."[15]

Open and explicit conflict between Rainey and the new regents began as soon as O'Daniel's appointees took their seats. These regents particularly disliked two senior professors in the Department of Economics who had tenure: Clarence Ayers and Robert Montgomery, the latter one of the most popular teachers at the University. The O'Daniel regents paid particular attention to the Department of Economics because both Ayers and Montgomery had publicly advanced ideas the regents believed were too liberal. Ayers based his work on a complete freedom of economic inquiry wherever that led, while Montgomery was an ardent, vocal supporter of New Deal reforms. Early on at a board meeting, one O'Daniel regent handed President Rainey a card on which he had written the names of several professors in the Department of Economics, including Ayers and Montgomery. The regent told Rainey that he and other board members wanted those faculty members fired. When the president asked the reason, the regent stated: "We don't like what they are teaching." Rainey explained the rules of academic tenure as the reason why such could not take place. Another regent offered the opinion that it would be fine with him if the University dispensed with tenure altogether. He observed there were surely faculty members at lesser colleges and universities in Texas who would be glad to join the teaching staff in Austin as replacements for any professors who left should tenure be abolished. An additional attack against the department by the regents took place when a group of its younger professors attempted to attend a public rally held at the state fairgrounds in Dallas. This event had been organized by conservative Dallas businessman Karl Hoblitzelle for the purpose of publicly lambasting the Roosevelt Administration's Fair Labor Standards Act, a key piece of New Deal legislation anathema to the conservative establishment of corporate America. Newspaper advertisements placed around the state by the organizers contained—in the opinion of these four economic instructors—a number of misleading if not untrue statements about the content and scope of the act. They wrote a letter to the newspapers rebutting these assertions and travelled to Dallas where they hoped to speak at the event. Hoblitzelle, as its chair, refused to let them do so and, in his ensuring discussion with them, believed that the four economics professors had been rude and disrespectful to him. On their part, the four faculty members countered that the Dallas businessman had been rude to them. "He very curtly, and I thought uncivilly," one of them later remembered, "denied our request without any consideration of the issues involved or any consideration of the right of a public mass meeting to hear the facts of what they were concerned with."[16] Hoblitzelle wrote a stern letter of complaint to the regents decrying the behavior of the four professors. This mobilized the regents and, after several heated meetings during which some of the involved professors met with the board, a majority of regents voted not to rehire any of them since none of them held tenured appointments to the University. This occurred over Rainey's objections. W. N. Peach, one of these instructors, related years later: "President Rainey was absolutely behind us on this thing, although it caused him great difficulty and had something surely to do in contributing to him getting fired."[17]

By 1942, a second source of controversy between Rainey and some of the regents had further soured relations between them, namely, a struggle regarding administration of the University's medical school located in Galveston. Known formally as the Medical Branch, the school had been located there since 1881. When Rainey assumed the presidency, J. R. Parten observed that "he inherited one of the most difficult problems that any university President ever inherited with the Galveston Medical School in the shape it was in."[18] Such was the case because the school essentially operated as an independent fiefdom governed by a group of Galveston physicians and businessmen, some of whom were the same political conservatives who supported Governor O'Daniel. One of them, a Galveston physician who also served on the University board of regents, quickly became an avowed enemy of Rainey when the president attempted to reassert control over the medical school from the central, main university administration in Austin. Rainey supported the dean at the medical school in these efforts to change governance procedures and realign the relationships with the local teaching hospital in Galveston. The O'Daniel regents vehemently opposed these changes and, by the end of 1943, were in public conflict with Rainey regarding the president's efforts to effect changes at the medical branch. This conflict continued for several years thereafter as an ongoing point of profound difference between several conservative regents and President Rainey.[19]

The situation did not improve for Rainey when Lieutenant Governor Coke Stevenson became the governor of Texas after O'Daniel resigned to become a United States Senator. Stevenson proved to be even more politically conservative than his predecessor. This came to be reflected in Stevenson's appointment of new regents after his assuming the governor's office. "He appointed men of wealth and influence," as one student of the Rainey controversy had noted, "who were as strongly conservative in their views of education, race relations, and policies."[20] The majority of university regents were O'Daniel or Stevenson appointees by 1943. By that time, the regents had again become concerned that communists had infiltrated the University, although all investigative attempts to substantiate this had failed. Nonetheless, some of the regents tried to implement a loyalty oath for all university faculty and staff members. Rainey opposed this and nothing came of it in the end. However, the regents thereafter moved to weaken tenure rules, something opposed both by President Rainey and the American Association of University Professors. Rainey's strong opposition resulted in a compromise with the regents that resulted in a weakened tenure policy which, although not an abolition of it as desired by the majority of the board, did reduce contractual protections for the faculty. The Board of Regents at this time also turned toward involving itself in the outside reading requirements of a contemporary literature course being taught by the English Department. Faculty members in that department had placed John Dos Passos's *Big Money* on the reading list for one of their courses, thereby provoking much controversy with the board because this novel was seen by political conservatives as having inappropriate sexual content, along with making frank discussions of un-American ideas. Several regents railed against the book and the board passed a resolution banning it at the University. They also vowed to fire the faculty members who had put it on the reading list. Rainey worked hard to protect the involved professors during a flap about this book, which attracted much public attention.[21]

By 1944, Rainey and the board of regents had come to the point of generally operating at loggerheads with each other. The regents began to meet more and more in executive sessions that excluded the president from attending. Regents at these sessions often involved themselves in micro-managing various university policies in ways that guaranteed Rainey's disagreement when he learned about what had transpired. Rainey countered these developments by going on the offensive against the regents in many of his public speeches that carried his concerns about university governance to the people of Texas. This further infuriated the board.

Matters came to a contretemps when Rainey gave his candid and frankly worded speech to the faculty on October 12, 1944. He cataloged a list of indictments against the regents in condemnatory language that enraged the regents as soon as they learned about his remarks. It was this speech that remained very much on the minds of the regents as they met in Houston at the Rice Hotel in late October, resulting in Rainey's being fired on November 1. Rainey's termination rocked the state, was greeted with dismay by students in Austin who accordingly marched on the capitol, disgusted many faculty members, and resulted in an unsuccessful effort for several months afterwards to have him reinstated in the presidency. The Texas Senate held public hearings in the weeks thereafter at which supporters from both sides testified about what had

Front Page of Daily Texan, *November 2, 1944*

happened, with the result that many observers felt these proceedings had vindicated Rainey. In the end, however, efforts
to restore Rainey to the presidency of the University came to
nothing and the termination stood.[22]

Rainey quickly developed a public presence for himself as
a private citizen living in Austin and, across 1945, became increasingly active politically. He routinely spoke out on many of
the progressive viewpoints that had bothered the regents. In
1946 Rainey therefore decided to run for the governorship of
Texas. Liberal Democrats rallied to Rainey as a person who
clearly articulated their political viewpoints, while conservatives in the party tended to identify with the regents' opinions
about the former university president as a dangerous radical.
Some of his opponents attacked him as being pro-labor, in favor of increasing opportunities for African-Americans, and an
advocate for raising taxes to improve government programs,
all viewpoints that bore some measure of truth. Rainey conducted a spirited campaign that brought him into a runoff with
Beauford Jester, a businessman from Corsicana. Jester, who had
served on the board of regents prior to Rainey's tenure as university president, represented in his candidacy the conservative,
Anti-New Deal wing of the Democratic Party. The issues in the
campaign went far beyond discussion of Rainey's experiences
as university president to include a wide variety of matters on
which the two candidates generally manifested opposing viewpoints. Rainey lost the election and retired from public life. He
moved away from Texas the following year when he accepted
the presidency of Stephens College in Missouri. In 1956 he became a professor of education at the University of Colorado,
retiring from that position in 1964. Seven years later he wrote
a memoir about his controversy with the regents entitled *The*

Tower and the Dome in which he justified all he had done in Austin. Homer Price Rainey died on December 19, 1985.[23]

———◆▸)◖◂◆———

There is no comprehensive history of the Rainey Controversy. I believe the time is approaching for a historian to research and write one that examines all of its ramifications, something the foregoing essay fails to do given space limitations and the nature of this volume. An unbiased, academic history is now possible because the ardor and strong feelings surrounding Homer Price Rainey have faded considerably after almost eighty years. Those who participated in the controversy on both sides, including university students during the late 1930s and 1940s, have passed from the scene. The deep passions they once held have cooled considerably; but I know from personal experience how strong such feelings touching on the Rainey Controversy were for well over a generation afterwards.

I am a Texan born in the year Rainey ran for governor and I have heard over the course of my life many discussions about the firing of Homer Price Rainey. Indeed, my lifelong acquaintance with the Rainey Affair constitutes my motivation for writing this essay. My knowing about the controversy started in childhood with stories told by my father, who graduated from the University of Texas in the 1930s. Serving his senior year as president of the student body, my father maintained a keen interest in university matters as did my much older cousin Scott Miller, who also attended the University in those years and graduated from law school during the Rainey era. They and their lifelong college friends often talked in my presence throughout my childhood and adolescence about what had happened to Homer Price Rainey, a person they much admired. The late Robert Lee Bobbitt III, grandson of the former Texas Attorney General, was one of my closest friends in high school. I heard much from Bobby Bobbitt, who often talked about the role played by his grandfather as a key Rainey supporter.

William C. Pool, who taught me Texas history when I was a college student, had been an undergraduate during the Rainey era and later earned a Ph.D. in History from the University. Dr. Pool and I developed a friendship that lasted for the remainder of his life. He wrote a biography of university Professor Eugene C. Barker, who had been involved in the Rainey Controversy. This book provides much information about the entire affair. Dr. Pool was politically progressive and a staunch member of the liberal wing of the Texas Democratic Party, from whose ranks he drew many of his friends in the Austin area. I attended informal cookouts during the early 1970s at Bill Pool's country retreat on the banks of Onion Creek where some of the older attendees personally remembered the Rainey Controversy, including Bob Eckhardt, Jake Pickle, Creekmore Fath, and Joe B. Frantz, among others. Rainey was always one of the touchstones of their campfire talk. All of them had respect for Dr. Rainey and what he had stood for in the controversy. Eckhardt and Pickle had been active in campus politics as students in that era, while Fath had been a protégé of economics professor Robert Montgomery. Frantz was particularly critical of those individuals who had been Rainey detractors. This viewpoint permeates an informal history of the university he wrote in the early 1980s. "Rainey wanted to educate and humanize the students," Joe Frantz noted in it. "The regents, the governor, and their corporate handmaidens thought the purpose of education was to train and indoctrinate." Frantz also cast his net wide in placing ultimate blame for the entire affair: "Apparently, the people of Texas did not want a university president who believed in the freedom to read and write and think."[24]

Bill Pool also introduced me to two individuals who had much to say about the Rainey Controversy from personal experience: Robert Montgomery, who had been a target of the regents, and Richard T. Fleming, an outspoken attorney friend of J. R. Parten. "Dr. Bob," as Professor Montgomery like to be called, had retired to San Marcos in the 1960s and was sometimes in the company of Bill Pool. Fleming, a 1912 graduate of the University, became a colorful fixture around the University campus in Austin during his retirement years and was well-known for his strong opinions, some of which had to do with his never-dying support for Rainey.[25] I recall a spring day in 1971 when the four of us went for a long lunch at the Kreutz Market in Lockhart. For several hours, Montgomery and Fleming talked of nothing but Homer Price Rainey and their personal memories of the controversy. Dr. Montgomery said that, in his opinion, the firing of Rainey as university president was one of the most important events in twentieth century Texas political history because it was the precise moment when political conservatives realized they could definitively control the State of Texas. Fleming agreed.

My informal cognizance of the Rainey affair continued once I joined the Austin College faculty in the fall of 1978. John D. Moseley, the college president who hired me, had been a student at the university in the Rainey era and had great admiration for him. The fact that Homer Price Rainey had graduated from Austin College in 1919 further bolstered Dr. Moseley's high opinion of him. Rainey officially became a distinguished alumnus and today the most prestigious faculty award on campus bears his name. Each year the Homer Price Rainey Award goes to a faculty member who has rendered distinguished service to Austin College. I had the opportunity as a young faculty member to chat casually with Dr. Rainey at an Austin College alumni function before a series of strokes and Parkinson's disease clouded his final years. I did refrain on that occasion from discussing his time at the University of Texas. It must be noted, given the nature of what I have related in this and the immediately preceding paragraphs, my individual, personal sympathies lie with Homer Price Rainey instead of his detractors, as was also the case for most everyone I knew who talked to me about the controversy over my lifetime. And, having spent my entire adult career as a college professor, I remain absolutely committed to the canons of academic freedom and the sanctity of independent intellectual inquiry Rainey attempted to protect during his period of difficulties at the University of Texas. I was saddened when Professor Robert Montgomery passed away the year I joined the Austin College faculty. Were he still among us, I have confidence "Dr. Bob" would vigorously contend that, across the many years since our lunch together in Lockhart during the spring of 1971, the Homer Price Rainey Controversy still serves as an important moment and benchmark in the historical process that made Texas into the "Red State" we know today.

SUGGESTED READINGS

Carlton, Don E. *A Breed So Rare: The Life of J. R. Parten, Liberal Texas Oil Man, 1896-1992.* Austin: Texas State Historical Association, 1998.

Cox, Alice. "The Rainey Affair: A History of the Academic Freedom Controversy at the University of Texas, 1936-1946," Ph.D. Dissertation, University of Denver, 1970.

Dugger, Ronnie. *Our Invaded Universities: Form, Reform, and New Starts.* New York: Norton, 1974.

Green, George Norris. *The Establishment in Texas Politics: The Primitive Years, 1938-1957.* Norman: University of Oklahoma Press, 1979.

Pool, William C. *Eugene C. Barker: Historian.* Austin: Texas State Historical Association, 1971.

Porterfield, Nolan. *Last Cavalier: The Life and Times of John A. Lomax*. Urbana: University of Illinois Press, 1996.

Rainey, Homer Price. *The Tower and the Dome*. Boulder, CO: Pruett Publishing Company, 1971.

NOTES

1 Alice Carol Cox, "The Rainey Affair: A History of the Academic Freedom Controversy at the University of Texas, 1936-1946," Ph.D. Dissertation. University of Denver, 1970, pp. 1-5; Rainey later noted during his retirement that "the greatest way to injure a great state university is to have it fall victim to a political regime." Homer Price Rainey, *The Tower and the Dome* (Boulder, CO: Pruett Publishing Company, 1971), 3.

2 The complete transcript of Rainey's October 12, 1944, speech to the University of Texas faculty is found in Rainey, *The Tower and the Dome*, pp. 39-54. The length of this version is such that he clearly expanded his remarks from what he actually said since this printed version could not have been delivered in the time frame of the actual talk.

3 Don E. Carlton, *A Breed So Rare: The Life of J. R. Parten, Liberal Texas Oil Man, 1896-1992* (Austin: Texas State Historical Association, 1998), 197-252, 300-323, 350-374.

4 "Oral History Interview with J. R. Parten conducted by E. Dale Odum," October 17, 1967, Oral History Collection, Willis Library, University of North Texas, Denton, Texas.

5 "Multi-Millionaire Regents Fire Rainey," November 2, 1944. Newspaper Clipping, "Compilation of News Concerning the University Crisis Taken from the November, 1944 Files of the Austin American and American Statesman," Briscoe Center for American History, University of Texas at Austin, Austin, Texas.

6 George Norris Green, *The Establishment in Texas Politics: The Primitive Years, 1938-1957* (Norman: University of Oklahoma Press, 1979).

7 In the days and weeks after the event, most of the regents issued statements to the press about why they had voted to fire Rainey. Most of these were carefully crafted and lacked the frankness that was likely evidenced in the November 1 meeting. For an example, see: "Four Regents Explain Their Vote Against Rainey," undated newspaper clipping, Orville Lee Bullington Vertical File, Briscoe Center for American History, University of Texas, Austin, Texas.

8 *Inauguration of Homer Price Rainey as President of the University of Texas: December 9-19, 1939* (Austin: University of Texas, 1939); Carleton, *A Breed So Rare*, 228-30.

9 For discussions of O'Daniel's campaign styles and political beliefs see: Bill Crawford, *Please Pass the Biscuits, Pappy: Pictures of Governor W. Lee "Pappy" O'Daniel* (Austin: University of Texas Press, 2004); Dallas Lee Cothrum, "The Senatorial Campaigns of W. Lee O'Daniel," Senior

Honors Thesis, 1992, Abell Library, Austin College, Sherman, Texas: Seth Shepard McKay, *W. Lee O'Daniel and Texas Politics, 1938-1942* (Lubbock: Texas Tech University Press, 1944); and Green, *The Establishment in Texas Politics*.

10 Bobbitt made these remarks during his testimony at hearings on the firing of Rainey held by an investigating committee of the Texas State Senate in Austin. "Senate Investigation of the University of Texas, Hearings," 48th Texas Legislature, November 1944, Legislative Reference Library, Texas State Capitol, Austin, Texas, Vol. 4: 577. Quoted in Cox, "The Rainey Affair," 16.

11 "Oral History Interview with Homer Price Rainey conducted by Kendall Cochran," February 1967, Oral History Collection, Willis Library, University of North Texas, Denton, Texas Oral History Interview, Homer Price Rainey, 1967, 87.

12 This meeting eventually became known as the Houston "Gag" Conference and was much discussed by Rainey partisans in their unsuccessful efforts to have the university president reinstated. Don E. Carlton notes: "One problem with the 'Gag' Conference allegation was that every person accused of having attended the conference denied it strongly. Another problem was the Parten had no documentation." Carleton, *A Breed So Rare*, 316.

13 "Dies Quizzers Finish Role at University," August 4, 1940, *Dallas Morning News*; Nolan Porterfield, *Last Cavalier: The Life and Times of John A. Lomax* (Urbana: University of Illinois Press, 1996), 458.

14 Green, *The Establishment in Texas Politics*, 83.

15 Parten and Rainey quotes come from Cox, "The Rainey Affair," 17-18.

16 "Oral History Interview with J. Fagg Foster conducted by Kendall Cochran," April 1968, Oral History Collection, Willis Library, University of North Texas, Denton, Texas, 4.

17 "Oral History Interview with W. N. Peach conducted by Kendall Cochran," June 1966, Oral History Collection, Willis Library, University of North Texas, Denton, Texas, 9.

18 "Senate Investigation of the University of Texas, Hearings," 48th Texas Legislature, November 1944, Legislative Reference Library, Texas State Capitol, Austin, Texas, Vol. 3, 510.

19 A good contemporary summary is: "Rainey Duel With Regents Started Soon After He Took Position: Medical Branch Started Trouble," *Amarillo Daily News*, November 3, 1944. Cox, "The Rainey Affair," 19-29; Chester Burns, *Saving Lives, Training Caregivers, Making Discoveries: A Centennial History of the University of Texas Medical Branch at Galveston* (Austin: Texas State Historical Association, 2003), 53-56; Carleton, *A Breed So Rare*, 208-235

20 Cox, "The Rainey Affair," 31.

21 William C. Pool, *Eugene C. Barker: Historian* (Austin: Texas State Historical Association, 1971), 192.

22 For a summary of the Senate Hearings, see: Texas. Legislature. Senate. "Committee Investigating the University of Texas Controversy: An

Educational Crisis." Briscoe Center for American History, University of Texas, Austin, Texas.

23 "Academic Freedom Fighter Succumbs to Long Illness," *The Alcalde* 74, no. 4 (March/April 1986): 42; "In Memoriam: Homer Price Rainey," Documents of the General Faculty, Homer Price Rainey Vertical File, Briscoe Center for American History, University of Texas, Austin, Texas.

24 Joe B. Frantz, *The Forty-Acre Follies: An Opinionated History of the University of Texas* (Austin: Texas Monthly Press, 1983), 83-84. Bob Eckhardt worked on the Rainey campaign for governor. Gary Keith, *There Once was a Congressman from Texas* (Austin: University of Texas Press, 2007), 95. As a student, Creekmore Fath had been a protégé of economics professor Robert Montgomery while Pickle had been active in student politics on campus.

25 Robert Robertson, "Montgomery's Wars," *The Alcalde* 97, no. 5 (May/June 2009): 26-27; Joe B. Frantz, "On Richard Fleming: Tribute to Richard T. Fleming at Memorial Services, March 16, 1973," in *The Texas Book: Profiles, History, and Reminiscences of the University*, edited by Richard A. Holland (Austin: University of Texas, 2006), 45-51.

CHAPTER ELEVEN

"Harry, the President Is Dead": Speaker Sam Rayburn of Texas, Vice President Harry Truman, and Congressman Lyndon Johnson at the "Board of Education" on April 12, 1945

Patrick Cox

AMERICANS OF THE POSTWAR GENERATIONS recall their personal reactions to tragic events such as the assassination of President John F. Kennedy and the 9/11 attacks in 2001. Likewise, all Americans remember the fateful spring day as World War II drew to a close when President Franklin D. Roosevelt died in Warm Springs, Georgia, from a massive stroke. Speaker of the House Sam Rayburn of Texas and Vice President Harry Truman were crucial participants in the events surrounding the death of the president. Rayburn and

Truman were together when Truman unexpectedly took office April 12, 1945, as the 33rd president. But the events of the day and how Truman was notified of FDR's death were unusual and somewhat theatrical given the unforeseen events of that day. At the same time, it provides a unique moment for all Americans when four-term President Franklin Roosevelt, the leader of the free world, would no longer lead the nation or realize the successful end of World War II.

The focus of this essay will cover the similarities and the variations of the story from multiple viewpoints, including Truman's, Rayburn's, and Lyndon Johnson's recollections of the day's events. Further, it will explore accounts from other observers and historians who have written during this momentous period of American history. Statements from Truman, Rayburn, Johnson, and others will also reveal how they recalled and felt about this historic event.

Speaker of the House Sam Rayburn of Texas and Vice President Harry Truman were longtime friends and colleagues for years prior to the death of President Franklin D. Roosevelt. Rayburn first came to Congress in 1912 from Bonham, Texas. He was known affectionately by friends and members as "Mr. Sam" and still holds the record as the longest-serving Speaker of the House in the institution's history. Rising in the ranks of seniority and influence, in 1940 Rayburn became Speaker of the House after the death of Speaker William Bankhead. He remained Speaker, with only two exceptions in 1947-48 and 1953-54, when Republicans gained a House majority, until his death in 1961. At the time of his passing, John F. Kennedy was president and Rayburn's protégé Lyndon Johnson was vice president.[1]

Future President Harry S Truman, a decorated World War I veteran, was first elected in 1922 in Missouri as Jackson

President Harry Truman (left) with his longtime friend Speaker Sam Rayburn on the docks of the naval base at Key West, Fla., where the Chief Executive was vacationing on November 19, 1952. The Presidential yacht is in the background. Vice President Truman was in Speaker Rayburn's "Board of Education" when he received an urgent phone call to come to the White House on April 12, 1945.

SAM RAYBURN PAPERS, DI _ 07830, THE DOLPH BRISCOE CENTER FOR AMERICAN HISTORY, THE UNIVERSITY OF TEXAS AT AUSTIN.

County Court Judge with the support of Kansas City political boss Tom Pendergast. In 1934, Truman won election to the United States Senate. After being reelected in 1940, Truman gained national prominence as chairman of the Senate Special Committee to Investigate the National Defense Program, later known as the Truman Committee. In July 1944, the Democrats jettisoned Henry A. Wallace and nominated Truman to run for vice president with President Franklin D. Roosevelt. As vice president, he played only a minor role in foreign and domestic policy during Roosevelt's final year of office.[2]

In 1945 Lyndon B. Johnson, the future president, was a young, upcoming Congressman from Central Texas. President Roosevelt had appointed the twenty-six-year-old Johnson as Texas Director of the National Youth Administration in 1936. A year later, Johnson successfully ran for Congress from Central Texas when longtime Representative James P. Buchanan passed away. Once elected, Congressman Johnson quickly aligned himself with Rayburn and FDR. He was soon recognized as a Rayburn protégé and was often at Rayburn's side when the House was not in session.[3]

In early 1945, with World War II still raging on both the European and Pacific fronts, the Russians prepared to launch the massive assault on Berlin in what would be the final days of Hitler's Third Reich. American forces in the Pacific had captured the island of Iwo Jima from Japan after a bloody battle. They followed the victory with the invasion of Okinawa. President Roosevelt had recently returned from the climactic meeting of the Big Three in Yalta in February 1945, where FDR, Winston Churchill, and Joseph Stalin planned the final stages of the conflict and transition to the postwar world. While the end of World War II was in sight, much remained to be done to bring an end to the Axis Powers as the summer of 1945 approached.

The rainy Thursday afternoon of April 12, 1945, in Washington, D.C. appeared relatively uneventful. After an exhausting trip to Yalta and return to Washington, D.C., President Roosevelt had departed by train for one of his favorite retreats at Warm Springs, Georgia, arriving in time for Easter services on Sunday, April 1. FDR planned to relax and work on improving his health and stamina. First Lady Eleanor Roosevelt remained at the White House, working on the upcoming United Nations Conference in San Francisco. Vice President Truman presided over the Senate that day, steering a debate on a water treaty with Mexico. Truman was also preparing for his nationwide radio broadcast the following day. His Jefferson Day address to the nation would be followed by President Roosevelt's speech from his Warm Springs retreat.

Late in the afternoon of April 12, Truman left the Senate chamber and walked across the Capitol to see his longtime friend House Speaker Sam Rayburn. With the House of Representatives in recess, the Vice President entered the downstairs capitol office of Speaker Rayburn around 5 p.m. for their customary meeting in Rayburn's "Board of Education." Writing to his mother and sister a few days later, Truman said: "as soon as I came into the room Sam told me that Steve Early, the President's confidential press secretary, wanted to talk with me. I called the White House, and Steve told me to come to the White House 'as *quickly* and as quietly' as I could." Truman recalled: "I ran all the way to my office in the Senate by way of the unfrequented corridors in the Capitol, told my office force that I'd been summoned to the White House and to say nothing about it." Truman stopped by his office in the Senate, grabbed his hat, and had a brief conversation with his staff before heading to the limousine, without his Secret Service detail, that would whisk him to the White House.[4]

Truman arrived at the White House at 5:25 p.m. and was taken by elevator to First Lady Eleanor Roosevelt's second-floor study. As he emerged, Mrs. Roosevelt stepped forward and put her arm across his shoulders. "Harry," she said quietly, "the President is dead." For a minute Truman was too stunned to speak. Then, fighting off tears, he asked, "Is there anything I can do for you?" With her characteristic empathy, Mrs. Roosevelt replied, "Is there anything *we* can do for *you*? For you are the one in trouble now."[5]

In the next hour and a half Truman learned the details of Roosevelt's death at Warm Springs, gathered his composure, and prepared to take the oath of office in the presence of Congressional leaders, Cabinet members, his wife, Bess, and their daughter, Margaret. The president's poor health that spring was evident to many after his return from the Yalta Conference in February 1945. Following his message to Congress on March 1, 1945, where he noticeably struggled, the president was determined to travel to his retreat at Warm Springs, Georgia. Roosevelt's health briefly improved in the comfortable, mild weather at Warm Springs. As late as April 10, his physician Dr. Howard Bruenn noted that his "color was much better, and his appetite was good." But two days later, while sitting at a table and sorting mail, he complained of a "terrific pain in the back of my head." He slumped over the table, lost consciousness, and was taken to his bedroom. Dr. Bruenn arrived shortly thereafter and watched as the president's breathing became irregular and his eyes began to dilate. In a final effort to revive the dying president, Dr. Bruenn injected caffeine sodium benzoate into his heart. At 3:35 p.m. on April 12, Dr. Bruenn pronounced President Roosevelt dead.[6]

While historians have reached a general consensus on the events that day, there are a number of activities during that momentous time that have received little attention. Vice President Truman's meeting with Speaker Rayburn on this fateful day raises a few questions, especially for those unacquainted with Speaker Rayburn's habits. The importance of the "Board of Education," a small room on the ground floor of the Capitol, has also gone unnoticed. Moreover, oral histories and official accounts of April 12, 1945, reveal several conflicting stories as individuals recounted their version of the story.

Some fundamental questions arise from this event. What was the "Board of Education" and what role did it play in this event? Who was actually present at Sam Rayburn's office on the afternoon of April 12, 1945, and what did they recall about the events? What are the accounts and interpretations offered by historians? What conclusions can be drawn from the different stories of the event?

A quiet, small out-of-the-way room near the main floor of the U.S. Capitol, the "Board of Education" gained its reputation for being one of the most secretive, yet famous rooms in the historic building. According to the distinguished historian Robert Remini in his history of the House of Representatives, the location was "a regular hangout for Democratic leaders where important legislative business transpired." Speaker Rayburn enjoyed having his friends meet with colleagues and other special guests to discuss policy, as well as exchange stories about people and events. "In the Board of Education the boys would have a few pops, and Mr. Sam would hold forth on legislation, the various committee chairmen, history, world politics, and sports," according to future House Speaker Tip O'Neill.[7]

As Rayburn noted, the Board of Education had its origins in the 1920s under Republican Speaker Nicholas Longworth. His friend from across the aisle, Congressman John Nance Garner, attended those sessions with Longworth. When

Garner became Speaker, he carried on the tradition as the Great Depression descended on the nation. Garner maintained the former committee room as a retreat and a place for private conversations. He often took afternoon naps there and his wife Ettie often prepared lunch for him and his guests.

Rayburn continued this tradition when he became Speaker in 1940. Rayburn described the room as his "downstairs" location as opposed to the House floor that was "upstairs." During his tenure as Speaker, Rayburn utilized the already historic room for legislative discussions, socializing, and a place for his close friends to gather in the afternoon. They also carried on a tradition started by John Nance Garner: to "strike a blow for liberty" by having drinks, usually bourbon or another whiskey. A large refrigerator, camouflaged in a veneer box, stood at one end of the room, with a sink and small closet. Rayburn's desk was at the other end of the room along with several overstuffed chairs.[8]

As Speaker Rayburn explained in his understated manner: "There was a room back in the Longworth-Garner days that was called the 'Board of Education.' I have a hide-a-way where I can sometimes go and read a little or dictate my mail and late in the afternoon some of the boys come by, who are invited to come by, and we have a session." Rayburn stated that the discussions were usually in regard to the "legislative program." Those who attended included Senators and Representatives— both Democrats and Republicans.[9]

Only Speaker Rayburn determined who would attend the after-hour sessions. There were a number of regular members with standing invitations, but all others had to be invited. Invitees to the Board of Education were expected to adhere to Rayburn's rules. No conversations were to be repeated to outsiders. And there would be no excessive drinking or profane stories—unless Rayburn told them.

Celebrating John Nance Garner's 90th birthday at his Uvalde home were (left to right) Senator Lyndon Johnson, former President Harry Truman, former Vice President and Speaker Garner and Speaker Sam Rayburn. Another Uvalde resident shown behind Rayburn was future Texas Governor Dolph Briscoe. Rayburn maintained Garner's tradition of private meetings at the "Board of Education" after House of Representatives sessions adjourned. Truman, Johnson, and Rayburn all were at the U.S. Capitol when they learned of the death of President Franklin Roosevelt on April 12, 1945.

Sam Rayburn Papers, di _ 02065, The Dolph Briscoe Center
for American History, The University of Texas at Austin.

Regular attendees included: House Parliamentarian Lewis Deschler, Congressmen Lyndon Johnson (D-TX), Eugene Cox (D-GA), Wright Patman (D-TX), John McCormack (D-MA), and Homer Thornberry (D-TX). A later participant was Congressman Richard Bolling who was introduced by Congressman Patman. Bolling said in an oral history interview, "except for McCormack, there was hardly anybody there that didn't take a drink." Bolling emphasized the cordial yet strict rules that Rayburn enforced. "There was nobody there that couldn't keep his mouth shut, at least nobody lasted any length of time who couldn't keep quiet," Bolling recalled.[10]

Lady Bird Johnson never attended, but was fully aware of Rayburn's Board of Education. In an oral history, she stated that "if those walls could speak they would have some of the most interesting bits of history than any room in the country because along about dark, if they were still there, the Speaker would call them into that office." Those in attendance would "sit there and discuss the legislation and make plans and have a drink and get better acquainted."[11]

Gaylord Armstrong was a young aide to Texas Congressman Bob Poage who had a rare opportunity to visit the room. "I don't recall why I was taken there or permitted to enter because even after Speaker Rayburn's death in November, 1961, the 'Board of Education's' location was still considered a secret," Armstrong recalled. "I was a House floor assistant as well as working for a senior member, Congressman Bob Poage of Waco. I was impressed (or depressed) by a small barren room on the ground floor of the House side of the Capitol. As I recall, you entered through a small room to then enter a room not much larger with limited chairs and a table, and a desk," Armstrong said.[12]

As a freshman U.S. senator from Missouri, Truman befriended Vice President John Nance Garner and became a frequent guest at the "Board of Education." At one of those sessions in early 1935 Truman became acquainted with Congressman Sam Rayburn, the protégé of the powerful Vice President Garner. Just as he had done during his one term as Speaker, Garner utilized the private room for socializing, eating, and drinking good whiskey. While Truman primarily worked and socialized with other Senators, his growing friendship with Congressman Rayburn would come to benefit both of these leaders.

Truman's personal account of the day's events appeared in his memoirs published after the conclusion of his presidency in 1953. He remembered that his final meeting with President Roosevelt occurred a few weeks prior and immediately after a joint session of Congress. Truman said that following the president's speech, the two leaders had a brief conversation at the Capitol. "Clearly, he was a weary man," he noted. Truman stated that FDR hoped that his upcoming trip to Warm Springs, Georgia, would provide some resurgence to his health. "I can be in trim again if I can stay there for two or three weeks." That was the final conversation between the two leaders as FDR departed for Warm Springs on March 30, 1945.[13]

On April 12, 1945, after presiding over an afternoon debate concerning the treaty between the United States and Mexico over water in the Colorado River and the Rio Grande, Vice President Truman walked across the Capitol for the afternoon gathering at Speaker Rayburn's Board of Education. According to Truman, he went to see Rayburn "to discuss the domestic and world situation generally. As I entered, the Speaker told me that Steve Early, the President's press secretary, had just telephoned, requesting me to call the White House."

Truman recalled that Early insisted that he told him in "a strained voice" to come to the White House right away. "I turned to Rayburn, explaining that I had been summoned to the White House and would be back shortly. I did not know why I had been called, but I asked that no mention be made of the matter." Truman offered no other comments about others who were in the room that afternoon. He also provided no statement as to any other comments he made before leaving for the White House.

When he reached the White House at about 5:25 p.m., Truman said that he "knew at once that something unusual had taken place." He was escorted upstairs to Eleanor Roosevelt's study. In addition to Mrs. Roosevelt, Truman said that Colonel John and Mrs. Anna Roosevelt Boettiger and Steve Early were in the room. Mrs. Roosevelt told him, "Harry, the President is dead." Truman recalled that he was fighting off tears. "The overwhelming fact that faced me was hard to grasp. I had been afraid for many weeks that something might happen to this great leader, but now that the worst had happened I was unprepared for it."[14]

Historians have provided differing accounts of that day. Truman biographer Robert Donovan in *Conflict and Crisis* described the phone call from the White House and the reaction. After Truman arrived, Donovan related, he poured himself a bourbon and sat down in one of the Speaker's overstuffed black leather chairs that faced Rayburn's desk. House Parliamentarian Lewis Deschler reminded Speaker Rayburn that Truman was supposed to call the White House when he arrived. "Oh yeah, Harry, Steve Early wants you to call him right away." Truman then picked up the phone and called Early. The president's secretary directed him to come to the White House and enter by the north portico on Pennsylvania Avenue.

Truman, who was startled by Early's voice, hung up the phone and said, "Jesus Christ and General Jackson." Turning to Rayburn, Truman said that he had to go immediately and as he left, he turned around and said, "Boys, this is in the room. Something must have happened."[15]

Alonzo Hamby, another Truman biographer, provided his version of the account in *Man of the People: A Life of Harry S Truman*. Upon having the phone conversation with Steve Early, Truman sensed something was wrong. At first, he thought that

President Roosevelt had returned to Washington for the funeral of his long-time friend Bishop Julius Atwood. However, one of the men in the room described Truman as "ashen faced." Jumping up from his chair, he blurted an expletive, and said, "Boys, this is in the room. Something must have happened."[16]

Sam Rayburn's biographers D. B. Hardeman and Donald C Bacon in *Rayburn: A Biography* provided another twist to the account. As he departed from the Senate, Truman eluded his Secret Service guards and made his way to Rayburn's office below the House Chamber. After receiving the call from Steve Early, Truman "went pale" and uttered "Jesus Christ and General Jackson." In a later interview with author D.B. Hardeman, Truman said that he thought Episcopal Bishop Atwood's death had brought FDR back to Washington. "I thought he probably had come back up here for the funeral and wanted to see me before he went back to Warm Springs." Truman added that he "walked back through the basement of the Capitol to get my car. It was the only time that I needed the Secret Service men and they weren't there."[17]

After Truman's departure, Rayburn received another call from Early that confirmed the president's death. Rayburn stated: "The President is dead" and went limp in the chair. Just then, *New York Times* reporter William S. White stopped by the office where he encountered Congressman Lyndon Johnson, a protégé and close friend of Speaker Rayburn who frequented the Board of Education. White stated that Johnson "looked, in fact, very much like a man who had had far too much to drink, though this was not the case at all." Johnson sobbed and reached out to White and said, "He's dead, he's dead."

Rayburn went to his typewriter to try to type out a statement. Unable to type and overcome with emotion, he dictated to one of Congressman John McCormack's secretaries: "We know not how to interpret God—in the way he performs. The world has lost one of the great men of all time. President Roosevelt's passing will shock and sadden good people everywhere. The American nation has been well led in every crisis. In Harry Truman we have a leader in whom I have complete confidence."[18]

The close, personal relationship between Rayburn and Truman revealed itself four days later. On Monday, April 16, Truman appeared for his first address as president to a joint session of Congress in the House of Representatives. Speaker Rayburn presided over the joint session. The new president was apparently nervous, for as he took his place at the rostrum in front of Speaker Rayburn, he immediately began reading from his prepared speech. "Just a minute, Harry," Rayburn interrupted, "let me introduce you." Rayburn then looked at the combined session and stated: "The President of the United States."

Rayburn and Truman maintained their friendship through the remainder of their lives. Rayburn died while still Speaker in November 1961 and President Kennedy was in office with his protégé Lyndon Johnson as vice president.[19] In an interview years later with the *Capitol Cloakroom* (a Washington D.C. political report), Rayburn recalled the events of the day. "Vice President Truman was on his way to my office by invitation when President Roosevelt died," Rayburn said. "He [Truman] and I have been good friends the ten or eleven years he had been in the Senate and the Vice Presidency." Once Truman arrived, Rayburn said that he had a message from Steve Early at the White House. After a brief conversation, Rayburn stated that Truman left immediately. "All he said was that he had an emergency message and had to go to the White House immediately—he didn't say what the message was. A few minutes after that we had the flash that President Roosevelt was dead. Mr. Truman didn't know, when he left to go to the White House, what that message was."[20]

A few days later, Rayburn issued press statements on the deep personal loss that he felt following FDR's death. He also expressed confidence in his good friend Harry Truman who unexpectedly was now president. Commenting on FDR, Rayburn said, "He was our close friend even more than he was our great leader. We are each better and stronger because of him." In support of Truman as the new president, Rayburn reiterated again the shock and sadness experienced by the nation after Roosevelt's death, concluding that he had "complete confidence" in the new leader.[21]

Rayburn issued many statements of support in those first days of the Truman Administration. As the nation mourned FDR and began to accept that Truman was now president, Rayburn became one of his strongest and most vocal supporters. Rayburn continuously praised Truman for being "honest, able and courageous." Rayburn surmised that following the momentous day of April 12, Truman rose to the challenge. "For a fellow whose first reaction was that he felt as if a ton of bricks had fallen on him, President Truman learned mighty fast," the Speaker remarked.[22]

Lyndon Johnson recalled his learning of FDR's death in Rayburn's hideaway office and his story appeared the following day in William S. White's report in the *New York Times*. Johnson said that he showed up shortly after Truman left the scene, but he was present when Speaker Rayburn received his call from Steve Early. Johnson said, "He didn't say anything I could hear—just a kind of gulp. Then he hung up and looked at me. Finally, he said the President was dead."

President Roosevelt's passing had a profound impact and gave Johnson a real sense of loss. The death of FDR was like losing a member of his own family. Johnson remembered: "He was just like a daddy to me always; he always talked to me just that way . . . . I don't know that I'd ever have come to Congress if it hadn't been for him." His heartfelt description that day extended through Roosevelt's funeral. One of Johnson's staff members noted that his "grief was just unreal. He just literally wasn't taking phone calls and he just literally shut himself up. His grief was vast and deep and he was crying tears. Manly tears, but he actually felt . . . that it was like losing his father."[23]

In Merle Miller's *Lyndon: An Oral Biography*, the author recounted the same story from the *New York Times*. Johnson provided his immediate reaction to the reporter: "I was just looking up at a cartoon on the wall—a cartoon showing the president with that cigarette holder and his jaw stuck out like it always was. He had his head cocked back, you know. And then I thought of all the little folks, and what they had lost. 'He was just like a daddy to me always.'"[24]

Johnson's story, however, may have contained some embellishment. House Parliamentarian Lewis Deschler, who according to numerous accounts was present during that fateful afternoon, said Johnson was at the Board of Education that day, but arrived after Rayburn had departed. When Johnson arrived, Deschler recalled that Johnson asked him, "Where's everybody?" Thus, Deschler disputed both Johnson's arrival time and what he actually witnessed.[25]

So how do memory and a sense of place improve our understanding of history? Oral histories, interviews, memoirs, and written accounts often contain a blend of truth and fiction. In this instance of the assembling of the events of FDR's death and the notification of the new president, some of the information is verifiable, but often details and opinions are inconsistent. These events provide an example of how historians assemble their sources of information, analyze the accounts for consistency or inconsistency, and provide analysis.

Many "fly on the wall" moments in history can serve as a repository for various voices and opinions. The participants in this pivotal event had different memories, impressions, and recollections as time progressed. As no official records or proceedings were recorded directly during this episode, the only evidence comes from the statements later provided by participants. Some historians who discussed this event utilized selected statements and impressions to form their own interpretations. Consequently, their analysis may be subjective or unintentionally biased as a result of the selection of the individuals involved in the event.

With the variations in the statements of those involved in the proceedings on April 12, 1945, analysis of this event is not ultimately dependent on the veracity of each person's recollections. Instead, even with contradictions and differences, these stories provide key insights into both the historic occasion and the character of those involved. For example, based on the interviews and recollections of both Truman and Rayburn, there is little doubt that phone calls came from the White House to the Board of Education on that spring afternoon in 1945. Not surprisingly, the White House would have the location, phone number, and the knowledge that Vice President Truman would be with Speaker Rayburn following the official business that day. Truman arrived there a short time before the phone call came from White House aide Steve Early. Both Rayburn and Truman maintained a nearly identical account of the timing of events.

As for those in attendance in addition to Rayburn and Truman, the most likely person would be Lewis Deschler. Rayburn knew that Deschler would remain discreet. As House Parliamentarian, he was also a keen observer of the people whom Speaker Rayburn trusted. For corroboration of the accounts from Truman and Rayburn, Deschler would be counted as the best and most reliable source.

Truman and Rayburn each had different versions of the specifics about the phone call from the White House, which led to some uncertainty, causing future historians to wonder when Truman actually knew about FDR's death. Truman received word from Steve Early to come to the White House quickly, but Early most likely did not relay the news of FDR's demise over the telephone. Rayburn stated that they did not have the official information at that point. Truman apparently had a premonition or a strong feeling about what had transpired, although he did not officially hear the news until he reached the White House and was told officially by Eleanor Roosevelt.

However, several historical accounts note that Truman reacted with great alarm when he received Steve Early's call. Truman's exclamation, "Jesus Christ and General Jackson," is mentioned prominently in several accounts of the event. This type of colorful statement would seem to be in character with Truman's personality, but neither Rayburn nor Truman acknowledged it in their versions of the phone call. However, given the official nature of their statements, neither leader would likely quote Truman's curse words. Biographers of the three principal characters have not addressed the specificity of the comments made that day. The main references are to the William S. White's *New York Times* story, Lewis Deschler and the memoirs and statements by Truman, and Rayburn and Johnson. This provides an illustration of how time and perspective influence individual memory of specific events, especially the precise words that may or may not have been spoken that day. If one accepts that Truman may only have suspected FDR's death when he received Steve Early's call, then his comment of "Jesus Christ and General Jackson" is probably apocryphal. But this made for a better story for others to tell once the event passed into history. Rayburn received confirmation of FDR's death in the second phone call when he was still at his desk at the Board of Education. Rayburn's recollections would be highly accurate given his reputation for straight talk and succinct commentary. Deschler also substantiated his reaction. Rayburn was very emotional and stated that he tried immediately to type his own statement but was unsuccessful. His dictation and subsequent press statements and letters issued over the course of the next few days provide the best account of Speaker Rayburn's reaction to the event.

While the subject never apparently arose that day and is not often mentioned in histories of the event, once Truman took the oath of office as president, the vice presidency was vacant. At that point in time the next person in line was the Secretary of State Edward Stettinius. Two years later, the Presidential Act of 1947 changed the order of succession for the presidency. The House Speaker would follow after the vice president and before any appointed cabinet secretary. Truman actively campaigned for this change as the Speaker was the leader chosen by the "representatives of the people."[26]

As for Congressman Johnson's account of the day's events, he was at the Capitol and the Board of Education as documented by William S. White and Lewis Deschler. Johnson's timing is somewhat problematic, however, based on the conflicting stories as to when he arrived at the room. Johnson likely spoke with and talked to Rayburn after the event. In later

interviews and accounts, he also registered his own personal
and emotional reaction to Roosevelt's death. But his presence
at the time of the phone calls to Truman and Rayburn from
the White House remains murky. In the final analysis, Johnson
clearly was at the Board of Education after the phone calls, but
missed the critical event.

In 1972 historian Robert Donovan noted in his interview
with Lewis Deschler that he said, "Johnson did not arrive until
after Truman left." The author also stated that he had reviewed
the event with D. B Hardeman, Rayburn's biographer, and the
Speaker's former aide. Donovan emphasized that Hardeman
confirmed that on all occasions Johnson was not present in
the Board of Education when the crucial phone calls came in.
Donovan provided no additional comments on the exact statements from the participants that day.[27]

Along with conflicting memories, a sense of place provides
context to the historical narrative. Based on several accounts,
oral histories, and a visit by this author to the site in the U.S.
Capitol, the Board of Education was a defined location utilized
by the House Speaker and his colleagues for a substantial period. For this particular moment, the room also became the
site of one of the most famous yet little known transitions of
power in U.S. history.[28]

An identifiable location such as this small room at the U.S.
Capitol brings us closer to both the everyday and significant
events that took place under the Dome. Today, the room retains
its size and appearance with its single entryway. The built-in
cabinet where Rayburn kept his liquor and glassware is still in
its original location. The refrigerator is no longer present. A
large conference table with chairs is now in the center of the
room where Rayburn's desk and oversized chairs were once located. Rayburn's portrait of Robert E. Lee is also gone. On one

wall, a large painted mural with the Seal of the State of Texas is affixed to the wall for all to see when they enter the room.

A sense of place then is important for historians to connect with as part of the landscape and the narrative. Historic locations, whether it is a battlefield, a significant building, or a room in the Capitol, provide many clues for understanding the context, the story, and the people. Historians of all types—whether interested in social, cultural, political, public, or economic research—utilize structures, as well as landscapes and spaces, for just such understanding and interpretation.

Historical interpretation that relies on memory and place is like a river. At times the flow is clear, consistent, and predictable. On other occasions, the waters become turbulent, murky, and a hazard. At the Board of Education on April 12, 1945, this one metaphoric river was calm and stormy, predictable and uncertain—everything that contributes to significant history and an engaging "fly on the wall" moment.

<hr>

The idea of a story about the "Board of Education," a little known room in the U.S. Capitol, came to me after having the opportunity to visit the historic site during my research on Speaker of the House Sam Rayburn of Texas. Speaker Sam Rayburn and Vice President Harry Truman were longtime friends and colleagues for years prior to the death of President Franklin D. Roosevelt. Senator and then Vice President Truman was a frequent guest to the downstairs, small hideaway office. This secret enclave played a significant role in the management of important national legislation during Speaker Rayburn's many legislative terms. His role in politics and decisions of governance, many of which were discussed on the House floor and in the Board of Education, are revealed through his character and mannerisms, which provide an engaging study of national political leadership.

This room is now one of the private meeting rooms, but still retains its original configuration and character. But it is not on any of the Capitol tours and can only be accessed with special permission. As such, its existence provides a sense of place to a narrative on how legislation and history are made. These stories also give historical context to the times in which they occurred. Other than some references to the Board of Education and its attendees (as described in this essay), no extensive evaluation of the site and its role in history has been attempted. So that is why it was such an engaging moment in history when I wished I could have eavesdropped on Harry, "Mr. Sam," and Lyndon, on April 12, 1945.

SUGGESTED BIBLIOGRAPHY

Brands, H. W. *Traitor to His Class*: *The Privileged Life and Radical Presidency of Franklin Delano Roosevelt*. New York: Doubleday, 2008.

Caro, Robert A. *Means of Ascent (The Years of Lyndon Johnson)*. New York: Alfred A. Knopf, 1990.

Dallek, Robert. *Lone Star Rising: Lyndon Johnson and His Times 1908-1960*. New York: Oxford University Press, 1991.

Donovan, Robert J. *Conflict and Crisis: The Presidency of Harry S Truman, 1945-1948*. New York: W.W. Norton and Co., 1977.

Dulaney, H. G., and Edward Hake Phillips, eds. *Speak, Mr. Speaker*. Bonham, TX: Sam Rayburn Foundation, 1978.

Hamby, Alonzo L. *Man of the People*: *A Life of Harry S Truman*. New York: Oxford University Press, 1995.

Hardeman, D. B., and Donald C Bacon. *Rayburn: A Biography*. Austin: Texas Monthly Press, 1987.

Remini, Robert. *The House: The History of the House of Representatives*. New York: HarperCollins Inc., 2006

Truman, Harry S. *The Truman Memoirs, Vol. 1: The Year of Decisions, 1945*. London: Hodder and Stoughton, 1955.

NOTES

1 Robert Remini, *The House: The History of the House of Representatives* (New York: HarperCollins Inc., 2006): 314-315, 325.

2 Harry S. Truman biography, Harry S. Truman Library and Museum, http://www.trumanlibrary.org/hst-bio.htm, accessed August 1, 2015.

3 Lyndon B. Johnson biography, Lyndon B. Johnson Presidential Library, http://www.lbjlibrary.org/lyndon-baines-johnson/lbj-biography/, accessed August 1, 2015.

4 Robert J. Donovan, *Conflict and Crisis: The Presidency of Harry S Truman, 1945-1948* (New York: W.W. Norton and Co., 1977), 4-7.

5 Alden Whitman, "Harry S. Truman: Decisive President," http://www.pbs.org/wgbh/americanexperience/features/transcript/truman-transcript/. November 1, 2014.

6 H.W. Brands, *Traitor to His Class: The Privileged Life and Radical Presidency of Franklin Delano Roosevelt* (New York: Doubleday Publishing, 2008), 810-812.

7 Remini, *The House*, 342-343.

8 Ibid., 341-342.

9 Sam Rayburn, "Capitol Cloakroom interview, January 29, 1951," in H.G. Dulaney and Edward Hake Phillips, eds., *Speak, Mr. Speaker* (Bonham, TX: Sam Rayburn Foundation, 1978), 120.

10 Richard Bolling interview with Anthony Champagne, June 26, 1980. Transcript located in Oral History files at Sam Rayburn Library and Museum, Bonham, Tx.

11 Lady Bird Johnson interview with Anthony Champagne, November 13, 1979, Rayburn Library and Museum.

12 Gaylord Armstrong interview with author, March 3, 2015.

13 Harry S. Truman, *1945 Year of Decision, Memoirs*, Vol. 1.

14 Ibid.

15 Donovan, *Conflict and Crisis*, 4.

16 Alonzo L. Hamby, *Man of the People: A Life of Harry S Truman* (New York: Oxford University Press, 1995), 290.

17 D. B. Hardeman and Donald C Bacon, *Rayburn: A Biography* (Austin: Texas Monthly Press, 1987), 308-309.

18 Ibid.

19 Remini, *The House*, 343.

20 Sam Rayburn, Capitol Cloakroom interview, *Speak, Mr. Speaker*, 120.

21 Sam Rayburn Statement to Newspapers, April 16, 1945, *Speak, Mr. Speaker*, 120.

22 *Speak, Mr. Speaker*, 122-123.

23 Robert Dallek, *Lone Star Rising: Lyndon Johnson and His Times 1908-1960* (New York: Oxford University Press, 1991), 266.

24 Merle Miller, *Lyndon: An Oral Biography* (New York: Ballantine Books, 1980), 126-127.

25 Robert A. Caro, *Means of Ascent (The Years of Lyndon Johnson)* (New York: Alfred A. Knopf, 1990), 121.

26 Presidential Succession Act of 1947, http://www.senate.gov/artandhistory/ history/minute/Presidential_Succession_Act.htm, accessed August 12, 2015.

27 Donovan, *Conflict and Crisis,* 4-5, fn, 443.

28 Richard Candida Smith, Handbook of Interview Research - Context and Method, http://www.history.ucsb.edu/faculty/marcuse/projects/ oralhistory/2002Candida_SmithStrategiesOralHistoryInterviews.pdf., accessed August 2, 2015.

CHAPTER TWELVE

The Establishment of Texas Southern University, 1947

Merline Pitre

TEXAS SOUTHERN UNIVERSITY (TSU), LOCATED in Houston, Texas, is often described as an institution that "was conceived in sin." To put it another way, TSU was established in 1947 in a climate during which the state was desperately trying to prevent the integration of the University of Texas (UT). The establishment of TSU, then, can be regarded as a ploy by the State of Texas to influence the final decision in a case filed by Heman Marion Sweatt, a black student, to enter the University of Texas Law School, thereby forcing integration at the all-white institution.

Efforts to preserve segregation in higher education in Texas began much earlier in 1876 with the establishment of the University of Texas as an all-white institution and were followed by a call for a separate black university. The 1876 Texas Constitution, in making provision for separate schools, colleges, and universities, explicitly stated that "the Legislature shall also when deemed practicable, establish and provide for the maintenance of a College or Branch university for the instruction of colored youths of the State to be located by a vote of the people. . . ."[1] Almost from the time that this section was inserted into the constitution, both whites and blacks argued over its implementation. When Prairie View A & M College was established in 1878, the issue became even more complicated. Some individuals took the position that with the establishment of Prairie View, the constitutional mandate had been fulfilled. Others argued that Prairie View was only a normal school and could not be classified as a classical university. Still others believed that if blacks were to receive a liberal arts education, a separate university with a curriculum similar to that of the University of Texas was required.[2]

Although proponents for a classical university included African Americans from all walks of life—state representatives, black professionals, lay people, the Colored Teacher Association, and other black organizations, it was not until near the end of the first half of the twentieth century that the state took concrete action to address this issue. By that time there was a burgeoning civil rights movement in Texas, one focused on the white Democratic primary statute, which allowed only white men to vote in the Democratic primary. After a twenty-two-year court battle, victory came to African Americans when the Supreme Court in *Smith v Allwright* (1944) declared the white primary unconstitutional. This case not only allowed blacks to vote in the Democratic primary, but it opened the door for an impending attack on the white educational citadel that barred blacks from graduate and professional training both in Texas and throughout the South. The National Association for the Advancement of Colored People (NAACP), having used Texas as a proving ground in *Smith v Allwright*, decided that its next move would be to launch a frontal attack on segregation in higher education in Texas. By this time, black Texans had begun to express concern, not only about a branch university and equal opportunities in general, but also about the lack of graduate and professional training institutions for people of color. In the entire South, graduate and professional schools existed only at a few privately supported black institutions. The general feeling among African Americans was that each state should provide advanced training for its black, as well as its white citizens.[3]

In June 1945, the NAACP announced that it would challenge segregated public professional education in Texas. The state government's immediate response to this challenge was the passage of Senate Bill #228, a bill that changed the name of Prairie View State Normal and Industrial College to Prairie View State University. Additionally, the measure authorized the Texas A & M Board of Directors to provide at Prairie View, upon demand, training in law, medicine, engineering, pharmacy, and journalism, as well as any other courses taught at the University of Texas. Undeterred by the state's action, in October 1945, Lulu B. White, Executive Director of the Houston Chapter of the NAACP, wrote Thurgood Marshall, General Counsel for the national NAACP: "I think I have a plaintiff for the educational case." The individual was Heman Marion Sweatt, a thirty-three-year-old Houstonian with a Bachelor of Science degree from Wiley College, who was employed full-time by the post office and part-time by the *Houston Informer*.[4]

Urged on by the NAACP and accompanied by Lulu White and other supporters, Heman Sweatt attempted on February 26, 1949, to register at UT in Austin. After a discussion with President Theophilus Painter and other university officials, Sweatt left his application at the campus and returned to Houston, hoping for a quick answer. During his stay on campus, Sweatt made no mention of his intention to file a lawsuit; but given the wide publicity previously accorded the NAACP's plans, university officials realized that one was in the making. It is not surprising, then, that Painter wrote to Texas Attorney General Grover Sellers, asking for an opinion on Sweatt's application. "This is to be a test case on the question of admission of Negro students in higher education of the state. . . . This applicant is duly qualified for admission to the Law School, save and except for the fact that he is a Negro, [Please advise]." Sellers' ruling did not come until March 16, at which time he upheld Texas law, which read, "No African or persons of African descent should be admitted to the University of Texas." Adding insult to injury, Sellers noted that Sweatt could apply for legal training at Prairie View, since in 1945 Senate Bill #228 had made it (on paper) a university.[5]

Sellers' opinion set things in motion, signaling the beginning of a concerted campaign to end segregated education in Texas. Conversely, it stimulated the thinking of some blacks who wanted a separate but equal university. Shortly after Sellers issued his opinion, A. Maceo Smith, NAACP Director of State Branches, wrote to Carter Wesley, editor of the *Houston Informer*, that the Sweatt case should be pursued although "realism dictates that a special university is about all we are going to get." Wesley countered that "mule" caution should guide blacks in accepting such an alternative. "The seeming advantage," he reasoned, "that we might have in putting them on the spot, might trap us." Wesley was very perceptive. Sweatt's registration attempt mobilized the political establishment to press for a black university.[6]

Refused admittance, Sweatt commenced legal proceedings against the University of Texas, asking the court for a writ of mandamus that would compel the University of Texas to admit him. After Sweatt sued university officials on May 16, 1946, for denying him admission, Dudley K. Woodward, Jr., chair

Heman Marion Sweatt, speaking at a rally, c. 1947

of the UT Board of Regents, began to talk about making provisions for a black university. He took the lead in advancing the cause of a black university, not for humanitarian reasons, but to ensure that "a branch university for colored youths," required by the state constitution, would not threaten UT's Permanent University Fund. In Woodward's opinion, having a black university share the endowment would "entail consequences of [the] most destructive character." Creating another black university by statute would avoid this possibility since a state law mandated only UT and Texas A & M as benefactors of the Permanent University Fund. "It is of great importance," Woodward wrote, "that the [constitutional option] be effectually destroyed."[7]

On June 17, 1946, Judge Roy Archer made public his decision to postpone issuing a writ of mandamus to compel UT to admit Sweatt. This ruling not only delayed Sweatt's action, but also allowed the Texas legislature enough time to create a black statutory university that would be substantially "equal to whites." Subsequent to Archer's ruling, which set December 17, 1946, as the date for final execution of the judgment, officials from UT and Texas A & M College, charged in 1945 with studying Negro education, held a joint meeting to address the issue. In essence, this joint committee recommended that a black statutory institution of higher education be established, and that the governor appoint a biracial committee to study its report. But before the biracial committee convened and before a report was presented to the governor, A. Maceo Smith called a meeting of ninety-six black leaders from throughout the state, to take place on August 3, 1946. Eighty-three of the leaders agreed that they should base any actions on Article 7, Section 14, of the Texas Constitution. Blacks interpreted Section 14 to mean that such a university would share in UT's endowment fund and would not exclude blacks from attending classes at the main UT campus. Further, they made it clear that they were not interested in a legislative arrangement by which a makeshift university would be established.[8]

Responding to this group, UT's President Theophilus Painter asserted that a black statutory university would be established. In an effort to head off integration of other professional programs, Painter told his audience that this university should be located in Houston, not only because the state of Texas would purchase Houston College for Negroes for this purpose, but also because the city's two black hospitals would enable the black university to establish its own medical school. In a heated debate, Lulu White attacked Painter's statement as an insult to black people. She pointed out that the hospitals referred to were separate and unequal; one of them, Jefferson Davis, had refused to treat black patients. Painter's suggestion, she charged, was simply a ploy to prevent blacks from attending UT.[9]

Meanwhile, during the interim between Judge Archer's initial ruling in June 1946 and his decision in December 1946 to deny Sweatt admittance to UT, the state decided to apply Senate Bill #228 to the creation of a law school at 409 1/2 Milam Street in Houston under the auspices of Prairie View University. When no qualified black applicant sought admission, including Sweatt, the school was permanently closed in February 1947. The UT Board of Regents then took further steps to counter Sweatt's challenge. On February 28, 1947, a black law school was established in the basement of the Supreme Court Building at 104 East 13th Street in downtown Austin. While three black students did enroll at the new school, Sweatt did not on the grounds that this law school was unequal to that of any white school. Going back to the drawing board, the state came up with its final offer to keep Sweatt out of UT. On March 3, 1947, the Texas Legislature passed Senate Bill #140 and House Bill #780. The former provided for the "establishment of a three-million dollar Negro University, including a law school to be located in Houston," while the latter allowed for the purchase of a fifty-three acres site which housed Houston College for Negroes. The passage of these bills was made easier by the fact that Houston College for Negroes was under the supervision of the University of Houston, which was experiencing financial problems. So, when the State of Texas made an offer to purchase Houston College for Negroes, those in charge responded affirmatively. Thus, Texas State University for Negroes (TSUN), later called Texas Southern University, became a state chartered institution of higher learning.[10]

After the passage of Senate Bill #140, the 50th Texas Legislature moved rapidly in coming to grips with the awkward situation of establishing a university for the "special purpose of providing at once similar courses for Negro citizens as were offered to white students at the University of Texas"— courses that were found in arts and sciences, literature, law medicine, pharmacy, journalism, and other professions.[11] With this act, an actual emergency was not only declared and recognized, but was accepted by the state as its obligation to its black citizens. Because the state deemed it impractical to establish a branch of the University of Texas for the instruction of colored people, it established an entirely separate and (at least on paper) equivalent university of the first class for the same purpose. Yet the problems inherited in the establishment, operation, and maintenance of Texas State University for Negroes were considerable. "To begin the operation of a first-class institution in a hurry entail[ed] not only expenses, but problems not commonly found in the path of normalcy."[12]

Since the legislature had established Texas State University for Negroes to satisfy an emergency in education and since the university had to qualify for first-class status in a hurry, there were a number of items that the state had to address very rapidly in order to prepare for the opening of the university in September 1947. First was the arrangement for the transfer of properties from Houston College for Negroes (HCN) to Texas State University for Negroes (TSUN). In addition to the task of negotiating a satisfactory contract with the University of Houston, arrangements had to be made for a complete audit of the financial statements of Houston College for Negroes by a certified public accountant. Accounting procedures and methods of operating the institution had to be changed almost overnight from methods used by a private educational institution to those used in state institutions. As such, a completely new system of accounting was established, and under the direction of the state's auditor office, a manual of accounting and purchasing procedures was prepared.[13]

In order to effect, facilitate, or implement any contractual agreement, in April 1947 the governor appointed a Board of Directors, but it was not sworn in until May 7, 1947. Meanwhile, during the interim between the establishment of TSUN and the swearing in of board members, Attorney General Price Daniel served as temporary chairman of the university. As the board members were selected, Daniel told them that it was their duty to sell the school to blacks and to convince them that the state, via the establishment of TSUN, had fulfilled its obligation to provide graduate and professional training. Not all blacks took kindly to his advice. Those who were active in the NAACP scoffed at the idea. Others were concerned with the composition of the board and requested an all-black board

Heman Marion Sweatt in line to register at the University of Texas for the fall semester of 1950

or at least a majority of black members. The latter request was denied as the governor appointed five whites and four blacks.[14]

In keeping with the state and board's directives, the faculty, staff, administration, and other employees of Houston College for Negroes had to transfer to TSUN effective September 1, 1947. Ordinarily, a faculty is selected in keeping with the normal appetite of an institution's growth, but this was not the case. The great majority of the faculty did not have the necessary credentials to meet the needs of the new university. Those who did not have a master's degree had three years to get one. Those who wanted better salaries had to acquire more college hours. Although there were concerns as to whether the new university would pay its faculty with equal rank as UT, this was not the case. Yet, it was logical for the faculty at TSUN to expect the same salaries as their white counterparts, not only because the enabling act implied equality, but also because Texas black public school teachers had just won a salary equalization case.[15]

On September 8, 1947, TSUN opened its doors for registration and began classes September 14 with an enrollment of 2,303 students in the College of Arts and Sciences, the College of Industrial and Vocational Education, the School of Law, and the Graduate School. An enrollment of 2,303 students taxed the institution's facilities. When the university opened its doors it had available for use the following buildings: one classroom building; one automobile shop building; five other shop buildings that had been built by the vocational department of Houston College for Negroes; and twelve buildings that had been moved from Camp Wallace by arrangement with the University of Houston.[16]

In terms of its programs, the legislature designed Senate Bill #140 to transform TSUN from an emergency university to one of first class, but several elements in the state, as well as the university, mitigated against such. For one thing, building a segregated university of the first class was not only expensive, but one for which the state would not and did not commit sufficient dollars. Equally important was the part of the bill that called for providing courses "on demand for any and all Negro students of the State of Texas." This charge placed the university in a precarious position. It worked both for and against the university. For example, various departments added courses without long-range planning and instead of a school or colleges being scientifically developed, it might have been better to say they simply came into existence. In the beginning, departments not only created courses on the basis of the slightest demands, but many times new programs were placed into the catalogue, which caused unnecessary duplication. In a few cases, departments operated as independent units, rather than as part of the college in which they were housed. For example, the School of Pharmacy had its origin in the College of Arts and Sciences as a department in the division of Natural Science and Mathematics, but became a school in 1948 because of the demand from six students.[17]

The selection of a president for TSUN was almost as chaotic as establishing the university itself. The Board of Directors believed that it was necessary to find someone who had a national stature in the black community, who had experience in higher education, and who had popularity among the rank-and-file in Houston and in Texas in order to effect a smooth transition for its "colored statutory university." But more importantly, the state wanted the Board to hurriedly find someone to foil Sweatt's attempt to enter the University of Texas. Raphael O'Hara Lanier fell into all of these categories. Lanier was no stranger to blacks either in Houston or in the Southwest for that matter. Not only had he been a former dean at Houston College for Negroes from 1933 to 1938, and a former acting president at Hampton Institute, but he also had served as United States Minister to Liberia before resigning to accept his current post. His academic credentials included a bachelor's degree in English from Lincoln University and a master's degree in English from Leland Stanford University in California.[18]

The announcement of Lanier as president was met with mixed reactions from the faculty, general public, and the various factions who were for or against the establishment of Texas State University for Negroes. While there was some satisfaction among rank-and-file Houstonians, many faculty members did not appear impressed with Lanier's credentials since he did not hold a terminal degree—something they argued was needed for a first-class university. Members of the NAACP and other black liberal groups in the community, who knew of Lanier's temperament and his advocacy for equality of blacks, argued that he had become the Boards' choice in an attempt to put down the opposition to a segregated institution.

Lanier was not unmindful that he had a daunting task before him. In his first presentation to the Board, he thanked the members for the confidence that they had shown in him and informed them that he had met with the following audiences: the administration committee, academic committee, graduate council, students, and the faculty. Most importantly, he wanted to let the Board know about the questions that he received from people in the community. Upon his arrival, the following questions were posted: What is the present status of the law school? How soon will vocational education on campus be removed? Should the president take orders from John H. Robertson, the white executive assistant to the University Board? Why does the institution have to carry the label "for Negroes"? What provision will be made for medicine, pharmacy, and dentistry? What is to be the status of students who completed their work under the auspices of Houston College? Of the above questions, the ones that were most troubling for Lanier dealt with vocational and industrial education and the medical school.[19]

At the beginning of his administration, Lanier had to decide whether to move forward with the four academic units that were part of the Houston College for Negroes—the College of Arts and Sciences, the Graduate School, the Law School, and the Vocational and Industrial Education School, or whether to exclude the latter. Many individuals thought that if TSUN were to become a university of the first class, the vocational unit should be removed. During the transitional period, black intellectuals staged a protest to have it removed from the new university. As the verbal war intensified, Lanier not only asked the Commissioner of Education for a decision on this issue, but suggested that the vocational unit be transferred to Prairie View. Board member Willette R. Banks objected, arguing that the transfer would in effect place Prairie View under TSUN. In a haste to get the university off the ground, the Commissioner sided with Banks. Lanier was now in a quandary. He knew firsthand the long arduous fight that he and other blacks had waged for vocational schools in Texas when he served as dean of HCN. Academically, vocational and industrial education does not belong in a first class institution; therefore; it should have been placed at Prairie View just as the War Training Program had been placed at Texas A & M University. But on this issue, Lanier succumbed to his superior. He simply accepted the Commissioner's position and allowed the unit to remain as part of the university program.[20]

Meanwhile, Lanier focused on his first priority—to build a first-class university by hiring individuals with terminal degrees (Ph.Ds) and meeting accreditation standards for the various units. To that end, he immediately went out and hired eight individuals with terminal degrees and then moved toward accreditation. But accreditation was expensive, and the university needed monies if the above goals were to be achieved. So, Lanier wrote the State Board of Education and asked it to reconsider TSUN's biennial appropriation over and beyond the state formula that determines higher education funding. "Our institution is an emergency case, just one year old—not being in a position to properly request the funds necessary for adequate development of a first class institution, the university is required by law to offer courses on demand which places it in a position of always trying to anticipate future demands," said Lanier.[21] Cognizant of the fact that accreditation also required the university to have adequate buildings to accommodate programs and students' needs, Lanier requested that the legislature give consideration to the following: a science building, a men's dormitory, a women's dormitory, a law school building, a gymnasium, an athletic field, a library building, a fine arts and music building, a medical administration building for a medical school, and a medical laboratory (although money had not yet been appropriated for a medical school). Lanier's request did not fall on deaf ears. On June 29, 1949, Governor Beauford Jester advised Craig F. Cullinan, Chair of the TSUN Board, that he had signed Senate Bill #253 providing $300,000 in emergency appropriation for TSUN.[22]

Accreditation of professional and non-professional programs was essential to the survival of the new university. Before Lanier arrived on campus and before Senate Bill #253 was finalized, the Board designated Dean Wesley J. Lyda to prepare a self-study for the College of Arts and Sciences for approval by the Southern Association of Colleges and Schools

(SACS). After a site visit, SACS reported that the institution had met the minimum requirements in most areas, but had failed in others. The university was sharply criticized for the condition of the registrar's office, for inadequacy of the university library, and for insufficient equipment in scientific laboratories. The Board moved quickly to allay the fear that the college would not be approved by its accrediting agency by telling the visiting team that the Board would provide the necessary monies to purchase books and equipment. While the committee was pleased to hear of the Board's commitment, it was nevertheless concerned about the registrar's records. Dean Lyda, who had worked diligently to secure approval, told the Board that he would take corrective action and would report to the Board weekly on the progress made on correcting the registrar's records.[23]

Following accreditation of Arts and Sciences, the university then focused its attention on the Law School, which had been moved in June 1948 to TSUN in Houston by statutory rule. Since accreditation was expected to satisfy Sweatt, as well as to foil his attempt for admission to the University of Texas, the Law School quickly became a favorite of the Board of Directors. Not only did the board select the Dean of the Law School, Ozie L. Johnson, before the arrival of Lanier, but it also later passed a resolution giving authority to the dean over faculty, budget, facilities, and equipment. So, Johnson started to make application for approval by the State Board of Examiners and the American Bar Association (ABA) in the fall of 1948. Pleased with Johnson's interest, efforts, and attempts to get approval from the Texas Board of Examiners, Governor Beauford Jester summoned Johnson to his office and asked him if anything needed to be done that required action by the legislature before it convened in January 1949.

According to Johnson, this was the first time that the governor had intimated that the school would be maintained as a state institution regardless of the outcome of the *Sweatt* case. Johnson therefore continued to work on accreditation. In October 1949, Texas State Board of Law Examiners approved the law school. Similarly, in September 1949, the ABA granted provisional approval with the stipulation that the ABA make periodic inspections each year. The school was supposed to go up for accreditation in 1950, but the Executive Committee of the ABA postponed the hearing on the application until after a decision was rendered in the *Sweatt* case.[24]

Meanwhile, as Lanier dealt with the law school, black citizens pressured him to do something about the promise the state had made for a medical school. When the legislature decided to create TSUN as a bulwark against integration, it paid little more than lip service to creating a medical school for African Americans. Eventually, the legislature provided UT's President Theophilus Painter with an estimated budget of $192,000 for the first two years of operation of the "colored" medical school. Prospective black students made inquiries immediately when they heard of the legislature's action, and two of them actually applied for medical school when TSUN opened in September 1947. Others sought the advice of black board member Willette R. Banks, president emeritus of Prairie View. Rather than working behind the scenes to help establish this medical school, Banks told Painter that these students did not want to embarrass the state, so he had suggested that they attend Meharry Medical College in Nashville, Tennessee.[25]

Not only did some blacks, including those members of the NAACP who were in Lulu White's camp, vigorously protest Banks' stance, but they also continued to remind the state of the need to train blacks in the medical profession. Under

continued pressure to provide blacks with equal medical training, in 1948 Painter announced that he would support establishing a regional black medical school. The NAACP refused
to accept this alternative. While intimating that the reason
TSUN did not have a medical school was that its board had
not pushed for it, Painter early in 1948 predicted that "[if the
State of Texas] does not make adequate provisions for a medical school before September, we are going to have a hard time
keeping Negroes out of Medical and Dental schools."[26]

In July of 1949, Painter's prophecy came true when Herman
Barnett applied for medical school. The state legislature then
belatedly appropriated $175,000 for a medical school at TSUN.
Many, however, regarded the state's action as suspect. If the
basement law school had proven unsuccessful, why should anyone expect a medical school, which was more expensive and
required more expertise, to be different? Responding as it had
when Sweatt applied to the UT Law School, the state asked UT
to contract with TSUN to provide the necessary professional
training in medicine for blacks. Under this plan, Barnett would
register at TSUN, but would take classes along with white students at the University of Texas Medical Branch at Galveston
(UTMB) until the state had time to provide medical training
at TSUN. As it turned out, the medical school, contingent to
a certain extent on the *Sweatt* case, never materialized, and
Barnett received his medical degree from UTMB in 1953.[27]

On June 5, 1950, the Supreme Court announced its findings in *Sweatt v. Painter*. In a unanimous decision, the court
ordered Sweatt admitted to UT. Speaking for the majority
of the Court, Chief Justice Fred Vinson asserted that there
was no comparison between the two law schools—Texas State
University for Negroes and the University of Texas. TSUN
had twenty-three students, compared to 880 at UT. At the

time TSUN had less than one-third the number of full-time instructors, and its library was one-fourth the size of UT's. Unlike TSUN, UT published a law journal and had moot court facilities, scholarships, and many alumni.[28]

The impact of this case was stunning. This decision not only required admission of blacks to graduate and professional schools in the state, but it also established precedent for *Brown v. Board of Education.* In the *Sweatt* case, the court implied that the doctrine of separate but equal was unconstitutional. In *Brown,* the doctrine was declared null and void. Striking a major blow at the separate but equal doctrine, the *Sweatt* case had a far reaching implication for the State of Texas. It meant that *de jure* Jim Crow was on the descent and that segregation was not only costly, but would become increasingly so over the years. Its overall impact was generally interpreted not only as ordering Sweatt's matriculation at the University of Texas, but also as nullifying the racial restrictions written into the legislation establishing Texas State University for Negroes. In effect, this decision said that UT could no longer be for whites only nor could TSUN be for Negroes only. This decision then had the prodigious effect of eliminating the legal support for racial segregation in all of American higher education.

Obviously, the months that followed the *Sweatt* decision were critical for TSUN. The State of Texas had made an investment, albeit not a preemptive one, in TSUN. Whatever the motive the state had for establishing TSUN, the court declared such a motive illegal. If the state's official interest in the promulgation of the new institution was indeed confined to the preservation of racial segregation in public colleges and universities, the immediate concern was the future of the institution, which was the state's main tool for the implementation of a position which was now legally discredited.

Although an official reaction to the *Sweatt* case in legislative terms was expected soon, it did not come until the Texas Legislature convened in January 1951. At that time, the state demonstrated its commitment to TSUN in a rather strange way. It slashed TSUN appropriations from $1,570,000 to $958,672. But the budget was not the only issue involving the new university. TSUN students held a demonstration at the Capitol for a name change for their university. Noting that the racial phrase "for Negroes," in the official designation of their institution was no longer valid, they suggested that the name be officially changed to Texas State University. This demonstration soon caught the attention of officials from the University of Texas who objected to the designation "Texas State University" because of what they perceived as confusion that may arise from both institutions having "Texas" and "University" in their names. The 52nd Legislature then struck a balance between the two positions. Noting the fact that the present name, Texas State University for Negroes, did not properly designate the new institution, the legislature changed the name of the institution (via an amendment to the original name bill) to Texas Southern University, effective on June 1, 1951.[29]

The original name of the institution at the time of its establishment strongly implied a second-class status. The action of the legislature in changing the name of the university, however, did not necessarily remove whatever onus may have been attached to the original name. The legislation that changed the name specifically reiterated the continuing commitment of the state to the applicable purpose and objectives of the original institution. While the university could not operate exclusively for Negroes, the legislation preserved intact "applicable laws and appropriations heretofore and hereafter. . . . relating to Texas State University for Negroes as applicable and relating to Texas Southern University." Here, then, was a legislative confirmation of the state's expectation of developing a first-class institution in Houston. Although the court ruling was not followed by a change in the law creating the university, it was followed by a change in attitude toward the infant university, in that its financial support became influenced more by the court's decision than by the legislation which created it.

Even after the legislature verified the continued existence of the University in 1951, there were those Texans who interpreted the action of the legislature as a hopeful effort to divert what might well have been a large influx of black students into previously all-white colleges into what was now permissively a university of their own. Though there was nothing in the 1951 legislation to suggest such a strategy, it is true that some state officials, including Governor Allan Shivers who assumed office upon the death of Beauford Jester, publicly declared a renewed intention to make the university so attractive that it would be the institution of first preference for its perspective students—presumably blacks students.[30] What attraction these officials envisioned in such statements is unknown. For Texas Southern University administration, such attraction rested on the relevance and excellence of its academic and service programs, its institutional ability to address the real needs and problems of its several clienteles, and the quality of the institutional staff which was steadily growing in size and in experiential expertise.

In sum, despite the negative factors associated with the State of Texas's interest in preserving segregation in graduate and professional training, the circumstances surrounding the establishment of TSU dictated that it was and is a special institution. In spite of it being "conceived in sin," these circumstances also indicated that there was a credible public

ADMINISTRATION & CLASSROOM BUILDING
AND
AUDITORIUM

THE TEXAS STATE UNIVERSITY FOR NEGROES
REDESIGNATED
TEXAS SOUTHERN UNIVERSITY
BY ACT OF THE LEGISLATURE
1951

Cornerstone of Texas Southern University

intent, however conceived, to provide a university for African Americans, which could achieve more than a nominal or quasi-legal status as a first-class institution.

In 1947, the State of Texas officials were acutely, some say painfully, aware of the changing climate of judicial opinion with regard to denying graduate and professional training to African Americans in southern states. There were also indications that the racial customs of segregation were softening after World War II. Yet, the follies of Jim Crow died hard and I have always been intrigued by that fact. As such, I would like to have been a "fly on the wall" and eavesdrop when Heman Marion Sweatt presented his application to the University of Texas. Was there panic on the part of the UT officials? If so, what happened when the legislature became involved in this controversy? Further, I would love to have been a fly on the legislative wall when Senate Bill #228 was passed in November 1946 to change Prairie View College to Prairie View University. This seemed a bit baffling. Why would the legislature make

Prairie View a university without according the same status to its counterpart, Texas A & M?

Likewise, my interest to eavesdrop would have peaked when the 49th legislature passed Senate Bill #140 and House Bill #780. What were the debates, if any, about the creation of a segregated, makeshift law school? And what were the reactions of these elected officials with the creation of an "emergency," first-class university in "a hurry"?

I would also have loved to have been a "fly on the wall" in the Supreme Court building when Attorney General Price Daniel argued that TSU law school was equal to UT. Did he really believe this? Was he saying that UT law school had not grown at all in its seventy-five years of existence? Or did he not know that segregation was costly and would continue to be? In the process of defending a racist policy and practice, Daniel displayed a limited vision of the present and the future, and his only argument was the southern Jim Crow tradition, which by 1947 could no longer stand up to the shifting legal, social, and political realities of a new era.

SELECTED BIBLIOGRAPHY

Bryant, Ira B. *Texas Southern University: Its Antecedents, Political Origin and Future.* Houston: Armstrong, 1975.

Gillette, Michael L. "Blacks Challenge the White University." *Southwestern Historical Quarterly* 86 (October1982): 321-344.

Hine, Darlene Clark. *The Rise and Fall of the White Democratic Primary.* Columbia: University of Missouri Press, 2003.

Hornsby, Alton, Jr. "The Colored Branch University Issue—Prelude to *Sweatt v. Painter.*" *Journal of Negro History* 61 (January 1976): 51-76.

Johnson, Ozie L. *The Price of Freedom.* Houston, privately published, 1954.

Lavergne, Gary M. *Before Brown: Heman Marion Sweatt, Thurgood Marshall and the Long Road to Justice.* Austin: University of Texas Press, 2012.

Pitre, Merline. *In Struggle against Jim Crow: Lulu B. White and the NAACP 1900-1957.* College Station: Texas A & M University Press, 1999.

Sapper, Neil. "The Rise and Fall of the NAACP in Texas." *Houston Review,* 7 (1985): 53-68.

Shabazz, Amilcar. *Advancing Democracy: African Americans and the Struggle for Access and Equity in Higher Education in Texas.* Chapel Hill: University of North Carolina Press, 2004.

Texas Southern University. "The Stepchild of the Texas Higher Education System." *Journal of Black Higher Education* 25 (October 31, 1999): 64-66.

NOTES

1 Texas *Constitution* (1876) Article 7, Section 14. See also *A Symposium Program,* "Lawyers in America Today," *Harvard Law School Bulletin* 22 (1971): 6, 28.

2 Alton Hornsby Jr., "The Colored Branch University Issue in Texas—Prelude to *Sweatt v. Painter,*" *Journal of Negro History* 61 (January, 1976): 51-55. See also George P. Woolfolk, *Prairie View A&M University: A Study in Public Conscience, 1878-1946* (New York: Pageant Press, 1962); Merline Pitre, *Through Many Dangers, Toils, and Snares: The Black Leadership of Texas, 1868-1898* (Austin: Eakin Press, 1997).

3 W.H. Holland to O.M. Roberts, September 28, 1882 in O.M. Roberts Papers, Texas State Archives, (Austin 1882); *Galveston Daily News,* January 23, 1888; *Texas Legislature, House Journal of the Twenty-third Legislature, Regular Session* (Austin, 1893):75, 422; *Galveston Daily News,* March 17, 1891; *Texas Legislature House Journal of Twenty-fifth Legislature, First Session:* 62, 11, 153, 428; *Texas School Journal* 14 (May 1896): 191; Ibid., 15 (February 1897): 75; *Texas Legislature, House Journal of Twenty-fifth Legislature, First Session:* 62, 22, 153; Darlene C. Hine, *Black Victory: The Rise and Fall of the White Primary in Texas* (Columbia: University of Missouri Press 2003), 16-19; *Smith v Allwright* 321, US 657, 64 Sup. Ct. 757 (1944).

4 *Texas Legislature, Texas General Laws of the State of Texas passed by the Regular Session for the 49th Legislature, Senate Bill #228* (Austin, 1945), 506; Lulu B. White to Thurgood Marshall, Oct. 10, 1945; A Maceo Smith to Lulu B. White, November 19, 1945; William J. Durham to Thurgood Marshall, January 28, 1946 in NAACP Files, Manuscript Division, Library of Congress (all letters to and from Lulu B. White will be referred to as LBW). See also Merline Pitre, *In Struggle against Jim Crow: Lulu B. White and the NAACP, 1900-1957* (College Station: Texas: A & M University Press, 1999).

5 Theophilus S. Painter to Grover Sellers, February 26, 1946. This letter was leaked by the *Houston Informer,* March 2, 1946; See Texas Attorney General Opinion, Texas, no. 0-7126; See also Senate Bill #228, *Texas Legislature, General and Special Laws of the State of Texas, Passed by the Regular Session of the 49th Legislature* (Austin, 1945).

6 A. Maceo Smith to Carter Wesley, March 21, 1946; Wesley to Smith, March 30, 1046; Wesley to William J. Durham, March 22, 1946, NAACP Files.

7 Dudley K. Woodward to Gibb Glilchist, June 20, 1946 in General Files, "Negroes in Colleges 1939-1954," University of Texas President's Office Records (UTPOR), History Center University of Texas at Austin.

8 A. Maceo Smith to Robert L. Carter, August 9, 1946; Mack Magee to Coke Stevenson, December 6, 1946; *Bi-Racial Commission Report*, December 17, 1946 in General Files, "Negroes in Colleges 1939-54," UTPOR; *Houston Chronicle*, May 17, 1946; LBW to Thurgood Marshall, July 30, 1946; A. Maceo Smith to Robert L. Carter, August 9, 1946; *Houston Post*, August 9, 1946; "Resolution of the Texas Council of Negro Organization to the Governor's Biracial Commission," August 8, 1940, in NAACP File.

9 *Houston Post*, August 9, 1946. See also LBW to Marshal, July 30, 1946.

10 *Texan Legislature, General and Special Laws Passed in Regular Session of 50th Legislature* (Austin, 1947), Senate Bill #140 and House Bill #780, 36-40; Pitre, *In Struggle*, 97-98; Mark Magee to Coke Stevenson, December 17, 1946; *Bi-Racial Commission Report*, December 9, 1946 in General File, "Negroes in Colleges, 1939-1954," UTPOR; *Houston Post*, February 25, 1947.

11 *Texas Legislature Senate and House, General and Specific Laws Passed in the Regular Session of the 50th Legislature*, Senate Bill #140 and House Bill #780 (Austin,1947).

12 *Second Draft: Report to the Governor by Board of Regents 1949* in Raphael O'Hara Lanier's Files in Heartman Collection TSU.

13 Ibid.

14 See LBW to Gloster Current, May 9, 1947, NAACP Files; Ira B. Bryant, *Texas Southern University: Its Antecedents, Political Origin and Future* (Houston, Armstrong, 1975), 51-53; Price Daniel to Allan Shivers, May 9, 1950, in HCN Files; see Beauford Jester's Address at Texas Southern University Commencement Exercise, May 30, 1949 and Lanier Presidential in Papers, Heartman Collection, TSU.

15 Minutes of Administrative Committee Meeting of Houston College for Negroes, March 1, 1946 in HNC Files, Heartman Collection, TSU; W. W. Kemmer to Allen Norton, December 1, 1947; Norton to William Bell, November 4, 1947, in Houston College for Negroes Files (HCN) at TSU; *Paige v The Board of Education, City of Dallas*.

16 See *Texas State University Catalogue 1947*; See also Minutes of the TSU Board of Directors, August 5, 8, 1947 in HCN Files.

17 See Texas 50th Legislature, Regular Session, Senate Bill #140.

18 Ralphael O'Hara Lanier's Biography in the Lanier File, Heartman Collection; Bryant, *Texas Southern University*, 9. See also "Houston College for Negroes," *University of Houston Herald* 8 (1934); Minutes of the Houston College for Negroes Board Meeting, September 8, 1931, HCN Files; *Houston Informer*, August *18, 1951; Dallas Post*, February *16, 1952; Houston Defender*, August *11, 1953*.

19 Presidential Report to the Board July 13, 1948, Minutes of the Board Regular Meeting of TSUN July 13, 1948, TSUN Files at TSU

20 Bryant, *Texas Southern University*, 1-3.

21 Ralphael O. Lanier to State Board of Education, November 8, 1948 in Lanier Papers; *Texas Legislature, House and Senate Journals of the 49th Legislature. Senate Bill #253, House Bill #379, General in Specific Laws Passed in the Regular Session of the Legislature (Austin, 1949);* See also William A. Miller Jr. to John H. Robertson, July 9 1949; John H. Robertson to Major Bell, July 6, 1949; Craig F. Cullinan to Governor Beauford H. Jester, June 29, 1949; John H. Robertson to William A. Miller Jr., July 9, 1949, in TSUN Files.

22 *Ibid.*

23 Ozie L. Johnson, *The Price of Freedom* (Houston: Armstrong, 1975), 55-65.

24 *Ibid.*; John E. Henry to Lanier, December 9, 1947; Johnson to Craig F. Cullinan, February 11, 1949, in TSUN Files.

25 Pitre, *In Struggle*, 101; J.H. Robertson to Major T. Bell July 6, 1949; TSUN Minutes of the Regular Board Meeting, August 9, 1949; William A. Miller Jr. to J.H. Robertson June 29, 1949, TSUN Files.

26 Pitre, *In Struggle*, 101-102; Painter to I.M. Maddox, September 1, 1949, in Negro College, 1939-45; Craig F. Cullinan to Theophilus Painter, July 13, 1949, both in the General Subject Files, "Texas State University for Negroes 1949-1952," UTPOR in History Center at the University of Texas at Austin.

27 Pitre, *In Struggle*, 101-102; Minutes of Regular HNC Board Meeting, August 2, 1946; *Houston Informer*, August 27, 1946. See also Michael Gillette "Blacks Challenge the White University," *Southwestern Historical Quarterly* 96 (Oct 1982): 321-344; Neil Sapper, "The Rise and Fall of the NAACP in Texas," *The Houston Review* 7 (1985), 53-68.

28 *Sweatt v. Painter* 339 US 629, 70 848-51 (1950); Pitre, *In Struggle*, 103.

29 *Texas Legislature. House and Senate, General and Specific Laws Passed in Regular Session of 52nd Legislature, House Bill #82.*

30 Allan Shivers' Speech at TSU's Commencement, March 16, 1956, in Samuel M. Nabrit Presidential Papers, Heartman Collection, Texas Southern University.

CHAPTER THIRTEEN

"The Loneliest Job in the World": The Day Lyndon Johnson Became President, November 22, 1963

Michael Collins

FOR THE FIFTY-FIVE-YEAR-OLD VICE PRESIDENT of the United States the sight of cheering crowds along sun-spangled streets must have been a mixed blessing. Tens of thousands had turned out to greet the president and first lady. Thankfully, the rain clouds had lifted and the sun had broken through. It was a glorious autumn day made all the warmer by the welcome of so many who had lined the curbs and sidewalks along Harwood Street in Dallas, Texas. Almost all were waving, smiling, applauding, with some holding placards expressing their adoration for the handsome and charismatic young president and his stylish, elegant wife. The outpouring of affection surprised the vice president who had privately held reservations about whether an ultra-conservative city like Dallas could be on its best behavior. Now the turnout along the motorcade route from Love Field through downtown exceeded his expectations and encouraged the president and vice president to look forward to launching a difficult and even bruising reelection campaign. In their last conversation earlier that day at the Hotel Texas in Fort Worth, a smiling president had joked that their ticket would carry two states next year if they did not carry any others. Understanding the reference to Massachusetts and Texas, the vice president had acknowledged, "Oh, we are going to do better than that, Mr. President."[1]

As the motorcade turned right onto Houston Street the vice president gazed ahead through his sunglasses and as far as he could see the crowds spilled over the curbs, fifteen to twenty deep in places, confetti drifting down on them. He could not have asked for a more enthusiastic reception from his fellow Texans. Riding in a rented silver-blue Lincoln convertible—just two cars behind the president's gunmetal blue limousine—he grinned and waved at well-wishers. But the crowds were not cheering for him, and he knew it.[2]

Favorite son or not, Lyndon Baines Johnson could never compete with the glamour of the Kennedys. He knew that too. His loving wife Lady Bird sat beside him, and to her left rode United States Senator Ralph Yarborough, the combative leader of the liberal wing of the Texas Democratic Party. State highway patrolman Hurchel Jacks drove the Lincoln convertible, and Secret Service agent Rufus Youngblood, a balding, soft-spoken southerner, sat in the front passenger seat. Hardly anyone paid attention to them, however. All eyes were on the president's open limousine, which also carried longtime Johnson protégé, Texas Governor John B. Connally, and his wife Nellie.[3]

From the teeming ravine of Main Street the police mo-
torcycle escort and presidential motorcade turned right onto
Houston Street. On the left the crowds thinned out along
the grounds of Dealey Plaza. Facing a sharp left turn on Elm
Street, the lead vehicles slowed. Directly across the street from
Johnson's limousine appeared an ordinary seven-story orange
brick building. Above the white stone cornice crowning the
first floor entrance read "Texas School Book Depository," an
odd name for a building. It wouldn't be long now—maybe five
minutes—before the motorcade arrived at the Dallas Trade
Mart, where President John F. Kennedy was scheduled to deliver a luncheon address. The clock on the Hertz Rent-a-Car
sign above the textbook warehouse read 12:30 p.m.[4]

"Suddenly, there was an explosive noise—distinct, sharp,
resounding," Youngblood recalled. "The movements in the
President's car were not normal . . . . I turned instinctively
and with my left hand I grasped Lyndon Johnson's right shoulder with all the leverage I could exert . . . and I forced him
downward." As the car paused then lurched forward and accelerated, Youngblood vaulted into the back seat. "Get down,"
Youngblood shouted. "Get down," he repeated the command
as he sat on Johnson, forcing him to the seat and floorboard,
face down. Seconds later, Johnson heard two other loud reports, which he later described as "explosions." But he could
only see Lady Bird and Senator Yarborough slumped in the
seat beside him. Then Johnson heard a voice on Youngblood's
radio screaming, "let's get out of here."[5]

Trooper Jacks steered right and stomped on the accelerator,
causing the vice president's Lincoln to swerve toward the curb
on the north side of Elm. Regaining control, Jacks sped away
behind the president's limousine and follow-up car. The next
five minutes seemed like a blur of confusion. "Stay with them,

and keep close," Youngblood yelled to Jacks. The limousine raced down Stemmons Freeway in a desperate attempt to catch up as the lead cars reached speeds in excess of 80 miles per hour. Still sprawled beneath the six-foot, boney frame of agent Youngblood, Johnson could barely make out the garbled, crackling radio transmissions. For the most part the frantic voices were drowned out by static, the blare of sirens, and the rushing noise of wind whipping over the car. LBJ asked Youngblood what was happening. "He said that he was not sure," Johnson recalled, "but he heard that the motorcade was headed for the hospital." Youngblood peered above the windshield and saw ahead the outstretched figure of Secret Service agent Clint Hill sprawled across the back seat of President Kennedy's limousine. In frustration, Hill was pounding his fist on the trunk of the car. Hearing over the radio that the president had been shot, Youngblood leaned back and shouted to Johnson, "We are going into the hospital and we aren't gonna stop for anything or anybody." Youngblood remembered that Johnson— still pinned beneath him—answered "Okay pardner."[6]

Lyndon Johnson was not a man who liked to take orders from anyone. But he trusted Youngblood with his life and agreed to do as he was told. At 12:35 p.m. patrolman Jacks wheeled the Lincoln to the right, then to the left, and right again. "Then suddenly, the brakes were put on so hard that I wondered if we were going to make it," Mrs. Johnson remembered. "Secret service men began to pull, lead, guide, and hustle us out," she recalled. With the help of Youngblood, Johnson crawled from the back seat and straightened up. Once upright, he began rubbing his chest and twisting his shoulders. Having a two-hundred pound man on top of him, with his knees in his back for five minutes, felt like the weight of the world had fallen on him.[7]

Soon Johnson would realize that it had. At least five Secret Service agents, several with guns drawn, immediately encircled Johnson and his wife and rushed them through the ambulance bay and into the emergency entrance. So hurriedly did they push past President Kennedy's open limousine that Johnson was shielded, unable to glance a few feet over his left shoulder. He was thus spared a macabre scene that almost defied description: a blood-splattered Jacqueline Kennedy leaning over her lifeless husband, holding his broken head, and a critically wounded Governor Connally lying semiconscious, cradled in the lap of his wife. Amid the whining sound of police sirens and the desperate shouts of Secret Service men, the agents spirited Johnson down a corridor to the left and into an examination room. "Minor Medicine," the sign above the doors read, the words failing to convey the grave nature of the situation. [8]

A nurse and patient stood nearby. Stunned by the commotion, both could only gawk at the unexpected invasion of armed men in dark suits. They probably did not even recognize the vice president of the United States, much less his wife. But Youngblood still ordered the other agents to clear the room. "Get them out of here," he screamed to agent Jerry Kivett while directing Johnson and Lady Bird into a small cubicle secluded in the back corner of the room. Then Youngblood drew what he described as a "sheet-like curtain" and commanded agent Woody Taylor to flip off the light switches and close all the window blinds.[9]

"I'm sticking to you like glue," Youngblood told a dazed Lyndon Johnson. For the next forty-five minutes Johnson remained in the dimmed, dreary cubicle that could not have been more isolated from the rest of the world. Incredibly, for all practical purposes Johnson was already the 36th president of the United States. He just did not yet know it. Minutes passed before anyone explained that Kennedy had been critically, perhaps mortally wounded. More astonishingly, for the next forty minutes Johnson would not know as much as virtually everyone else in the hospital about the frantic scene unfolding down the hallway in Trauma Room One, or for that matter, the more than forty million Americans who were already tuning into the breaking news on their televisions and radios. In more ways than one, Johnson would be kept in the dark for nearly three quarters of an hour.[10]

For what seemed like an eternity, Johnson stood with Lady Bird. Two folding chairs had been carried in, but he refused to sit. A deathly hush settled over the soundproof room. Johnson's first thoughts were of his daughters, Lynda and Luci. He asked that Youngblood contact his superiors and ensure that they receive Secret Service protection immediately. After a few minutes Kennedy aides began moving in and out of the secure area where Johnson waited. White House Special Assistant Kenny O'Donnell and Assistant White House Press Secretary Malcolm Kilduff entered then left the darkened cubicle, but apparently neither informed Johnson that the president's condition was hopeless and that Governor Connally had also been seriously wounded. But their faces conveyed the desperation of the situation. "Kenny, I'm in your hands," Johnson offered. Not until agent Emory Roberts entered the cubicle did anyone tell Johnson the gruesome truth. "It looks bad," Roberts began, drawing a deep breath. "I don't know about the governor's condition, but I have seen the president and don't believe he can make it."[11]

"I was stunned," Johnson recalled. "The day which had begun so cheerfully had turned into a nightmare." Moments later a distraught O'Donnell reentered the room and urged Johnson to leave the hospital immediately. "You'd better get the hell out of here and back to Washington." After O'Donnell left the room, Roberts and Youngblood concurred. Understandably shaken but composed, Johnson asked if Air Force One should be moved from Love Field to a more secure location, perhaps Carswell Air Force Base in Fort Worth. No, Roberts and Youngblood answered, the aircraft should be left at its present location, which already enjoyed a protective perimeter.[12]

Despite the consensus of advice that he should leave the hospital immediately, Johnson made his first executive decision: to remain on the scene. Shaking his head, he declared that it would be "unthinkable" for him to leave while President Kennedy's life was "hanging in the balance." Nor would he leave Mrs. Kennedy behind. "He understood our point of view, and we understood his," Youngblood put it succinctly. "His prevailed."[13]

In the meantime Congressman Homer Thornberry of Texas, a longtime LBJ loyalist, was allowed to see his old mentor. "This is a time for prayer, Homer, if there ever was one," Johnson told his protégé. Thornberry later expressed his frustration at the lack of information channeled to the vice president. "We didn't know what was happening," he later claimed. "I walked out once to try to see if I could find out what was going on, but either nobody knew or they wouldn't tell me." During this time Congressman Jack Brooks of Beaumont walked in to reassure Johnson by his presence. Johnson aide and troubleshooter Cliff Carter likewise joined his boss and expressed the opinion that the vice president must return to Washington without further delay.[14]

But Johnson remained adamant. Turning to the man who had been at his side all day, he pleaded, "Rufus, would it be alright [sic] if Mrs. Johnson and I went to see Mrs. Kennedy and Mrs. Connally?" "No Sir," the stoic Secret Service veteran answered. "Can Mrs. Johnson go?" the vice president pleaded. Youngblood nodded his approval and agreed, "all right." Accompanied by Congressman Brooks, Mrs. Johnson was hurriedly guided down a corridor and around the corner to the hallway outside Trauma Room One, where she caught sight of Jackie Kennedy. "I don't believe I ever saw anyone so alone," Lady Bird wrote in her diary. The two ladies held hands but, for the most part, their eyes spoke for them. Before returning to the Minor Medicine exam room, Lady Bird made her way a short distance down the hall to visit briefly with her old friend Nellie Connally. The women exchanged embraces, but little was said.[15]

In the meantime, Lyndon Johnson paced back and forth, at times stopping to stare at the curtains in the small cubicle that confined him. But mostly he stood vigil, fittingly with his back to the wall. There was nothing to do now but wait. After a few minutes, a grim-faced Lady Bird returned to her husband's side, but had little to report.

Johnson broke the silence. "Bird, why don't you take some notes?" The minutes passed ever so slowly. Not until almost 1:20 p.m. did Johnson receive confirmation of what almost everyone else around him had known for more than twenty minutes. O'Donnell returned, this time with Secret Service agent Roy Kellerman, the head of the presidential detail who had ridden in the front seat of Kennedy's limousine. As he walked into the room O'Donnell's pained expression and clinched jaw said it all even before he spoke. "He's gone," O'Donnell forced the words from his throat. After repeating his insistence that Johnson depart the hospital immediately and fly back to the nation's capital, he walked out. Then Mac Kilduff entered the room. Addressing Johnson as "Mr. President," Kilduff thus became the first person that afternoon to state the appropriate formality. He asked Johnson for permission to issue a statement to the press, officially announcing President Kennedy's death. Without hesitation, Johnson told him to wait until after he and Lady Bird had left for the airport. Youngblood agreed. At that moment, according to Congressman Thornberry, LBJ "took charge."[16]

All things considered, that interminable hour at Parkland Hospital had been numbing, even surreal. Yet as Lady Bird remembered, "through it all Lyndon was remarkably calm and quiet." Like the eye at the center of the storm, he seemed serene, though surrounded by a whirlwind of fear and uncertainty. Observing the strength and self-confidence that her husband exuded, Lady Bird could only think of how she had often said that Lyndon had always been "a good man to have in a tight spot."[17]

Roberts returned to the cubicle and officially confirmed Kennedy's death. At 1:30 p.m. Johnson considered preparations to depart for Love Field and Air Force One. He understood that Jacqueline Kennedy would not leave without her slain husband's body, and he remained just as determined not to leave without her. Youngblood then spoke up and suggested that, at the least, they should return to Air Force One and wait there. So it was Youngblood, Roberts, and other agents on the detail who decided that security protocols and superior aircraft communications dictated that the new president must fly Air Force One back to Washington rather than the vice presidential plane, Air Force Two.[18]

Johnson's hurried and unannounced exit from Parkland offered its own share of drama. "Our departure from the hospital . . . was one of the swiftest walks I have ever made," Mrs. Johnson recollected. While hurrying to an awaiting unmarked police car with Congressman Brooks and agents Taylor and Kivett, she looked up and noticed that, even though Kennedy's death had not been officially announced, a nearby American flag had already been lowered to half-mast. "That was when the enormity of what had just happened first struck me," she wrote. Surrounded by armed agents directing their every move, Lyndon Johnson left through the emergency entrance and stepped into another unmarked car driven by Dallas Police Chief Jesse Curry. On Youngblood's command, LBJ slid down in the back seat and lowered his head from view. He had never ducked from trouble in his life, but today would be an exception. Congressman Thornberry jumped in the front seat and Youngblood commanded, "Let's go." But as the vehicles rolled away, with the new president's car in the lead, a man in a dark suit darted out, waving his arms in an attempt to stop them. Apparently unaware that Johnson sat in the rear seat, Congressman Albert Thomas of Houston recognized his colleague Homer Thornberry seated in the front. "Stop and let him in," LBJ ordered, "It's all right." As Thomas climbed in the front seat, Johnson directed, "hurry up and close the door, Albert." Then, moving to the middle of the seat, Johnson told Thornberry to crawl into the back seat next to the door. With no further delay Curry drove away.[19]

"The journey to Love Field took less than ten minutes," Johnson remembered, "but those few minutes were as crucial as any I have ever spent. I knew from the moment President Kennedy died I must assume the awesome responsibility of uniting the country." Already a cascade of emotions were beginning to rush over him, and all he could think of was how "unbearable" it all was for the country, and even more devastating to him, in part because it had happened in his own beloved home state. "I was a man in trouble in a world that is never more than minutes away from a catastrophe," Johnson continued in reference to the ever present specter of nuclear war. "Most of all I realized that, ready or not, new and immeasurable duties had been thrust upon me . . . . I was catapulted into the most difficult job any mortal can hold. My duties would not wait a week, or a day, or even an hour." As Johnson confessed, "The first thought I had was that this might be an international conspiracy [and] . . . I was on my own."[20]

Winding through the back streets of northwest Dallas, Chief Curry drove the president past the entrance of Love Field, through security, and onto the tarmac where just over two hours earlier the Kennedys had been greeted by a huge crowd. But the scene was strikingly different now as only a wall of policemen and sheriff's deputies formed a defensive perimeter. Curry pulled up to Gate 27 of the East Terminal, alongside the gleaming blue and white Boeing jet with the presidential seal and the words United States of America stretching down the length of the aircraft. Following Youngblood, the Johnsons and their security detail scrambled up the ramp. Once inside, Youngblood commanded the other agents to close the window shades. Resting quietly, like a military outpost guarded by armed sentries, Air Force One became the setting for the next act of this historical drama.[21]

Johnson once described the American presidency as the "loneliest job in the world." The moment he entered Air Force One that painful fact set in immediately. "When I walked in everybody stood up," he remembered. "I still recall the deep emotion I felt. Here were close friends and aides who were like members of my family; here were secret service agents . . . . All of them were on their feet. It was at that moment that I realized that nothing would ever be the same again."[22]

The majesty of the office had already settled upon him, along with the burdens. Indeed, Lyndon Johnson was the only person in America who had no time to grieve. There was work to be done, decisions to be made, and he knew that every one of his moves would be scrutinized to the extreme. Entering the so-called stateroom, Johnson refused to sit in Kennedy's chair, the one with the presidential seal emblazoned upon the back. For a few moments he conferred with aide Cliff Carter before retreating into the presidential cabin, where he telephoned the slain president's brother, Attorney General Robert F. Kennedy. Briefly, Johnson expressed his sympathy before turning to the practical matter at hand. "There are some folks down here who feel that I ought to take the office here in Dallas," he explained. "I need your opinion on this." Youngblood remembered that Johnson paused, looked up and repeated Bobby Kennedy's response. "You feel it should be administered as soon as possible then. Who in Dallas should administer it?" Johnson questioned, and could someone provide the wording of the oath. While LBJ and RFK would later remember that short conversation differently, neither disputed one thing: Kennedy said that he would contact Assistant Attorney General Nicholas Katzenbach for the answers.[23]

Robert Kennedy later claimed that he never advised the vice president to take the oath of office in Dallas, while Johnson stubbornly insisted that he did. The controversy did not end there. None of President Kennedy's staff was closer to the attorney general than Kenny O'Donnell, who later disparaged LBJ, first for insisting that he had advised the vice president to take Air Force One (instead of Air Force Two) back to Washington— when in fact he had not—then for refusing to leave Dallas until he could be sworn into the presidency. "I asked a formerly close associate of Johnson's why Lyndon goes to the trouble of slanting such incidents." According to O'Donnell, the man claimed that "Lyndon himself doesn't know why he does it, but he soon convinces himself that his version of the story is the gospel truth." As for RFK, he was less tactful: Johnson was "incapable of telling the truth. . . . He just lies continuously about everything. . . . he lies even when he doesn't have to."[24]

At 2:15 p.m. the moment Johnson dreaded to the depths of his being arrived. The white ambulance carrying President Kennedy's body pulled up on the runway. Johnson most likely could not see the commotion or hear the sounds of men weeping and moaning, even cursing, as they lifted the casket and tilted, shoved, and pushed it through the narrow door at the rear of the plane. In that small cabin they gently lowered the coffin where Secret Service men had hurriedly removed two rows of seats to accommodate the remains of the 35th president of the United States.[25]

The Johnsons soon encountered Jackie Kennedy, her pink suit and white gloves caked with her husband's blood. It was an awkward moment, soon made worse. Among those accompanying Kennedy's body was Air Force General Godfrey McHugh. Intensely loyal to the Kennedys, McHugh took it upon himself to march into the cockpit and order the pilot, Colonel James Swindal, to take off immediately. Confused, Colonel Swindal responded that he had orders from the president to wait for further instructions. The president wanted his and Mrs. Johnson's luggage transferred from Air Force Two, he explained. "President?" McHugh interrupted, pointing to the coffin in the rear compartment. "I have only one president on this plane, and he is lying back in that cabin." After stalking through the sweltering aircraft, according to Johnson aide and confidant Jack Valenti "threatening anyone who came near him," McHugh cornered Kilduff and demanded that Air Force One take off immediately. Kilduff explained that they were still waiting for Lady Bird's luggage to be loaded and for members of the press to arrive.[26]

General McHugh exploded. "She's on the other plane with LBJ." Now realizing that McHugh was the only person on Air Force One who was unaware of Johnson's presence, Kilduff responded angrily. "Then you go back and tell that six-foot four Texan he's not Lyndon Johnson."[27]

By all accounts no member of Kennedy's staff held greater contempt for Lyndon Johnson than General McHugh, the president's Air Force aide and liaison. If true, what the French-born general later alleged about his brief encounter with Johnson that afternoon on Air Force One would be a sensational revelation. McHugh claimed that, after searching the cabin, he finally located Vice President Johnson "hiding" behind a curtain in the toilet of the bedroom compartment. According to McHugh, LBJ was "hysterical," crying, muttering his fear of a wider conspiracy. "They're going to get us all," McHugh quoted a frightened and sniffling Johnson as saying repeatedly. "It's a plot, it's a plot."[28]

But there remains good reason to doubt the story. Most importantly, this account contradicts all other eyewitness testimony that depicts Johnson as calm and poised during the crisis. In other words, the account remains more consistent with McHugh's disdain for Johnson than with other firsthand versions of events. Besides, the highly emotional McHugh apparently never mentioned the incident to other Kennedy confidants or anyone else until fifteen years after the fact. Even then, the transcript of the interview would be sealed, at McHugh's request, for another thirty years, buried in files and awaiting discovery by tabloid writers and pseudo historians, one of whom claimed that McHugh had slapped his new commander-in-chief to bring him out of his breakdown.[29]

Ken O'Donnell was more diplomatic than McHugh. "I went up forward to talk with Johnson and asked him if we could take off without further delay." O'Donnell informed Johnson that back at the hospital the Dallas County medical examiner had tried to prevent the president's staff and Secret Service detail from removing the body until an autopsy could be performed as required by state law. It was an ugly custody battle that turned physical, O'Donnell told Johnson. Only by forcing the casket out of the emergency area and shoving local officials aside had they managed to leave, he later recounted about the confrontation. It would be inexcusable for Mrs. Kennedy to be subjected to any further harassment by Dallas authorities, O'Donnell insisted. According to O'Donnell, Johnson then interjected: "We can't leave here until I take the oath of office." He had spoken with "Bobby," LBJ continued, and he agreed. Besides, Johnson's old friend, Federal Judge Sarah T. Hughes, was already on her way to the airport to conduct the ceremony.[30]

By the time Judge Hughes arrived shortly before 2:30 p.m., Air Force One had been idle on the runway for almost three hours. Powered down, with the air conditioning off, the cabin had become stifling hot, almost suffocating. Johnson had passed the word that anyone on the plane who wished to step into the forward cabin to witness the historic moment could do so. Motioning to staff, he insisted that "Mrs. Kennedy wants to be here. We'll wait for her."[31]

Speechless, O'Donnell reluctantly walked back to the first lady's dressing room, only to find the door closed. He knocked on the door and Jackie Kennedy appeared, still wearing the blood-stained pink suit. Resentful at the suggestion that she should be imposed upon, O'Donnell still asked if she wished to witness the swearing in, though "it would not be necessary" if she "did not feel up to it." Surprisingly, she answered bravely, "I think I ought to. In the light of history, it would be better if I was there."[32]

Lyndon Johnson taking the oath of office aboard Air Force One with Jackie Kennedy and Lady Bird Johnson

COURTESY THE LYNDON B. JOHNSON
PRESIDENTIAL LIBRARY

Meanwhile, White House photographer Cecil Stoughton had climbed upon a sofa and staged what would become one of the most iconic moments and photographs in modern American history. Sitting less than three feet from Johnson, Kilduff held the microphone of a dictation machine—the only device on hand. As Johnson raised his right hand, placing his left on a Roman Catholic missal that had been retrieved from Kennedy's quarters, Stoughton and Kilduff recorded the moment for posterity. Other than the shuttering of the camera, the only sounds heard were Judge Hughes' quivering voice and the subdued monotone of Lyndon Johnson repeating the oath. "I solemnly swear that I will faithfully execute the office of President of the United States, and will to the best of my ability preserve, protect and defend the Constitution of the United States. So help me God." Johnson then kissed his wife and hugged Mrs. Kennedy. It all took less than two minutes.[33]

As the cabin emptied, President Johnson turned to the pilot and declared: "Let's get this plane airborne." At 2:40 p.m. Air Force One lifted off, carrying two presidents back to Washington. A few minutes into the flight the steaming cabin began to cool, but the mood onboard seemed much colder, especially between the Johnson people and the Kennedy loyalists. For the most part, a tomblike stillness settled through the narrow confines of the aircraft. "The flight . . . was silent, each sitting with his own thoughts," Lady Bird recalled. Although the flight lasted only two hours and eighteen minutes, it must have seemed much longer.[34]

Understandably, those closest to President Kennedy were overwhelmed with grief and disbelief. Even so, Johnson reached out. He sent his press secretary Bill Moyers to ask Kennedy confidants Kenny O'Donnell and Larry O'Brien to sit down with him. The Constitution had placed him in the White House, he explained, almost apologetically. He urged both to "stay on." Then he pleaded, "I need you more than President Kennedy ever did."[35]

The aircraft had not been in the air thirty minutes when Johnson asked to be connected by telephone to Mrs. Rose Kennedy, the late president's mother. Once reached, she began graciously by addressing Johnson as "Mr. President." How difficult that call must have been for both. "Mrs. Kennedy, I wish to God there was something that I could do, and I wanted to tell you that we are all grieving with you." "Yes, well thank you very much," the aging matriarch uttered in a trembling voice. "I know that you loved Jack and he loved you." At that point Johnson choked up and handed the phone to Lady Bird, who shared her condolences.[36]

The next hour and a half passed, as Kilduff put it, with Kennedy's people surrounding the coffin in the rear of the plane, "looking backward," as Johnson's staff huddled quietly around the new president "looking forward." Johnson understood that his countrymen must receive some reassurance from their new president. After reflection, he scribbled a short message and handed it to his young secretary Marie Fehmer, who typed the text and returned it to him shortly before landing. JFK's closest advisers sat quietly drinking scotch, thinking of what might have been as the plane hurtled toward Washington. At 5:59 p.m. the landing gear of Air Force One touched down at Andrews Air Force Base. While the entire nation and world watched on television, military personnel and presidential aides lowered President Kennedy's coffin on a hydraulic conveyor. Robert Kennedy, who had pushed his way through the crowded cabin as soon as it landed, walked with the president's widow behind the casket.[37]

As the ambulance pulled away, President Johnson—who had intended to accompany Kennedy's coffin—learned that the press awaited his announcement. Glancing around the stateroom, he growled, "Rufus, where's my hat?" Puzzled and surprised by the question, and by Johnson's harsh tone, Youngblood responded: "Your hat, sir?" The last time he saw the Stetson it was on the floorboard of the limousine in Dallas, Youngblood responded. "Well, get the damned thing," the president snapped. "Call back to Dallas and have one of your men get it." "I'll see to the hat, sir," a compliant Youngblood assured his boss. "This man had kept his composure. He had been forceful but cooperative, but now the safety valve eased open for a moment," Youngblood recalled, "and I had the dubious honor of being the first to be chewed out by the new President." In that moment it was as if Lyndon Johnson—the mercurial, smothering presence that Youngblood had come to know so well during the past three years—suddenly reappeared.[38]

Johnson looked around the cabin one last time. "Bird?" he called out. Seconds later the president and first lady descended the steps of the ramp, into the blinding glare of television lights and to a podium bristling with microphones. His message was brief and somber, but reassuring. "This is a sad time for all people. We have suffered a loss that cannot be weighed. For me it is a deep personal tragedy. I know the world shares the sorrow that Mrs. Kennedy and her family bear. I will do my best," he pledged. "That is all I can do. I ask for your help—and God's."[39]

With that, Johnson reached for Lady Bird's arm and walked toward an awaiting army helicopter for the seven-minute ride to the White House. Secretary of Defense Robert McNamara, Assistant Secretary of State George Ball, and National Security Adviser McGeorge Bundy stepped into the helicopter with the Johnsons. Into the night sky they floated over the Potomac River, past the Lincoln Memorial, the Washington Monument, and the Ellipse where so many flags flew at half-mast. Finally, the White House illumined against the backdrop of a silent city.[40]

Bill Moyers recalled that when the presidential party landed on the south grounds of the White House, they "walked in the dark . . . [to] the Rose Garden, toward the Oval office. We got to the porch outside. I was walking immediately behind Mr. Johnson and he didn't stop. He just veered to the right." The doors of the Oval office were open, the lights on, and Kennedy's desk, personal effects and favorite rocking chair sat in plain view. But instead of entering the slain president's inner sanctum, Johnson turned and barked out, "I'll use my office in the EOB." Escorted by a ring of Secret Service, he walked briskly into the Executive Office Building across the street, then up the stairs to his suite on the second floor.[41]

His first task was a heartbreaking one. He requested two pages of White House stationery and asked to be alone. He needed less than ten minutes to compose the first two letters of his presidency: one to each of President Kennedy's children, two-year-old John and five-year-old Caroline.[42]

That done, he went to work. The next two hours became a whirlwind of activity as President Johnson telephoned former presidents Dwight Eisenhower and Harry Truman, Democratic Party Treasurer Richard McGuire, and Supreme Court Justice Arthur Goldberg. Afterward, for more than forty minutes, he met with a bipartisan delegation of congressional leaders. In simple terms he asked all of them for their help and their support. Despite the horrific tragedy, the people's business must go on, he implored. Moreover, Soviet leaders in Moscow must not sense any weakness or indecision in the councils of the United States government. His message could be summarized in three words—unity, strength, and continuity.[43]

Next he met with members of his staff and charted a course for the coming days and weeks. Johnson troubleshooters Cliff Carter and Walter Jenkins joined Valenti and Moyers at the president's side. Shortly after 9:30 p.m. Johnson called Kennedy speechwriter Ted Sorensen to express his sympathies and offer some comfort to the grieving White House special assistant. "Kindly, strongly, generously, he told me how sorry he was, how deeply he felt for me, and that he . . . needed me," Sorensen remembered. A few minutes later agent Youngblood and a cadre of Secret Service men escorted Johnson to a limousine and departed.[44]

The fifteen-minute ride to the vice presidential residence seemed eerie. Down an empty Pennsylvania Avenue to M Street, then westward through the enclaves of Georgetown to 52nd Street, the limousine and follow-up cars rolled past darkened government buildings and rows of dimly lit brownstone homes and shops. The capital city appeared strangely deserted as streets were virtually clear of traffic. Restaurants and stores had all closed early. Like everyone else, residents of Washington had retreated indoors and huddled around their televisions. The Johnsons' home, known as "The Elms," a two-story French chateau-style house at 4040 52nd Street, peeked through the trees ahead.[45]

Johnson might have relaxed, except for the fact that a legion of Secret Service and police cordoned the iron gate. A makeshift guardhouse stood outside the entrance. While a few clusters of the curious gathered and gawked from the shadows, a throng of press stood vigil on both sides of the entrance. Inside the gate the silhouettes of heavily armed government agents could be seen darting about in the darkness of the grounds. "When we arrived at the circular driveway at the entrance to the home it had all the appearance of a convention," Valenti remembered. Youngblood informed Johnson that his home was now "a communications center" patched into the White House situation room switchboard.[46]

Johnson climbed the steps to the front door of the house. Inside, the scene provided a welcomed contrast to the pandemonium of the past nine hours. Several staff members and confidants greeted the president as he walked in with Rufus Youngblood still at his side; but the familiar faces were accompanied by an unfamiliar restraint and deference. From the terrace room down the hallway Johnson's speechwriter Horace Busby and his wife, Mary, peered out, both of them expressionless. Behind them a concerned Dr. Willis Hurst, the brilliant young Emory University cardiologist whom Johnson credited with saving his life eight years earlier, nodded a formal hello. Having heard of the specious reports that Johnson had suffered a heart attack in Dallas, he wanted to be on hand.

Only when Lady Bird rushed down the stairway with arms outreached did Johnson feel at home. Dressed in a house robe and slippers, she embraced her husband, held him tightly, and said in her soothing voice that she and her secretary Liz Carpenter had prepared a fried chicken dinner. "I should have called from the office. I had something to eat there," Johnson apologized.[47]

LBJ walked across the hall to his library and sank into his favorite easy chair, a green leather recliner. Moments later Lady Bird brought him a glass of orange juice on ice, just the way he liked it. An awkward hush fell over the room. It was as if everyone present held their breath in anticipation of some executive proclamation while Johnson sipped on his drink. Above the fireplace hearth a large portrait of Johnson's late mentor, Speaker of the House Sam Rayburn, peered down upon the new president. "Oh, Mr. Speaker," LBJ said under his breath, holding the glass upward, "how I wish you were here now when I need you."[48]

Johnson's youngest daughter, Luci, entered the room and approached her father. At first unable to speak, she leaned over, placed a hand on his cheek and managed just three words. "I love you," the others overheard her say as they looked away, allowing the president and his youngest child this private moment. LBJ and Luci held each other tightly and whispered to each other. Luci could only wipe away her tears and excuse herself. Her daddy no longer belonged just to her and her mother and sister.[49]

After commenting that he probably "knew less than anybody about what's happening," Johnson asked for the television to be turned on. Scanning the channels, he expected to see some news updates. Instead, the networks were airing a biographical documentary about President Kennedy, black and white footage of events during his administration, and images of JFK with his wife and children. "Turn it off," a shaken Johnson buried his face in his hands. "It's all too fresh. I can't watch it."[50]

It was getting late. "I want to talk some more," Johnson spoke softly. "We've got a lot of work ahead." Around midnight the president climbed the stairs and directed four of his most trusted aides to follow him. Then he pointed to the adjacent and upstairs bedrooms available for each of them. Moyers, Carter, Valenti, and Busby: they knew him better than any other men, and yet they hardly knew him at all. Retreating into the president's bedroom at the end of the hall, they sat beside his bed, as if gathering around a mysterious Oracle of Delphi. Moyers sat on the right, Valenti and Busby on the left, with Carter pulling up a chair at the foot of the bed. Johnson changed into his pajamas, stretched out, and propped himself up with pillows. Then he requested that the television to be turned on again. The pale glow of the screen illumined the room as the news reports confirmed what Johnson had already learned from aides. A former United States Marine and Soviet defector, Lee Harvey Oswald, had been formally charged with killing Kennedy, then murdering Dallas police officer J. D. Tippet.[51]

Busby remembered that his boss seemed "more controlled than calm," and his voice was strong but "barely audible" above the television. Valenti busily scribbled on a notepad, recording Johnson's every thought. At one point, when the network commentator called Oswald a "confessed communist" and raised the fear of a Russian or Cuban conspiracy, Johnson stiffened up and blurted out "no," as if ordering the newsman to stop. "We must not have that. It could tear the country apart."[52]

Sometime before 1:00 a.m. Busby drove home, leaving the others with the boss. Around 2:15 a.m. Secret Service agent Gerald Blaine stood at his assigned post at the rear corner of the house. Suffering from fatigue and lack of sleep, he could be forgiven for yawning and rubbing his eyes. He expected to rotate stations with one of his fellow agents, but not for another fifteen minutes. As was their procedure, every half hour members of the presidential security detail would be relieved by another agent approaching from a *counter-clockwise* direction.[53]

Aside from the .38 caliber pistol in his shoulder holster, Blaine carried a Thompson submachine gun. Like other agents he knew the wild rumors, the gnawing uncertainty, the dreadful fear that, for all they knew, other assassins might be lurking in the dark and that President Kennedy's murder might have been the result of an international conspiracy: the Soviets, the Cubans, or maybe the Mafia? Surely, the shooting was not the work of a lone nut, most assumed. Or was it? No one knew the answers yet, but rumors ran rampant.

So tired he could hardly stand, Blaine heard the sound of footsteps approaching from his left, from a *clockwise* direction. Swinging the weapon up to his shoulder, he saw a figure emerging from the shadows. Blaine pulled the bolt of his weapon, the racking sound piercing the silence. His finger on the trigger, he aimed for the chest. Blaine paused as the footsteps came closer, then emerged from the darkness. Only then did he recognize that the tall figure was that of Lyndon Johnson. "In the blackness of night," Blaine later recalled, "Johnson's face went completely white." Saying nothing, Johnson turned and walked back into the house. Nobody had thought to brief him on Secret Service procedures regarding a security lockdown after dark. It was a close call.[54]

Returning upstairs, the president continued his bedside staff meeting for another hour. Exhausted, he finally nodded off. Around 3:30 a.m. Johnson opened his eyes again. "Good night, boys," he whispered. "Get some sleep . . . . It's going to be a long day tomorrow." Indeed, it would be another long day and a long time before they could all go home to Texas again. Johnson's ranch house on the banks of the Pedernales seemed a world away now. Quietly Moyers, Valenti, and Carter slipped out, leaving the president alone. Stillness settled over Lyndon Baines Johnson, though not a sense of personal peace. As he drifted into a restless slumber, his mind must have churned over the many decisions that awaited him in the coming days, critically important decisions, hundreds of decisions that would be his and his alone.[55]

———◆◆▶◆◀◆———

Like everyone else who is old enough to remember the trauma of November 22, 1963, I will never forget where I was and what I was doing when I first heard that President Kennedy had been shot. As an impressionable eighth grader living in Denton, Texas—only thirty-eight miles from Dallas—I first heard the news when our junior high school principal broke in over the PA system to announce the initial, confusing reports of the shooting. My classmates and I sat stunned and in disbelief. After more than fifty years what stands out most in mind is the memory of my algebra teacher, Mr. Browning, asking his students to pray for the president and governor—and to my astonishment—"the man who did this terrible thing."

Almost as an afterthought, he also asked us to remember Vice President Johnson, who was rumored to have suffered a heart attack in the aftermath of the shooting. Still I recall school being dismissed early and how frightened I was walking home alone, down Congress Street to our residence on Crescent. The streets were empty, and to the best of my recollection, the neighborhood seemed like a ghost town.

The events of that somber weekend are forever seared into my memory as they are etched into our national consciousness. The indelible image of CBS news anchor Walter Cronkite announcing the president's death; the chaotic scenes at the Dallas police department headquarters; the shock of Jack Ruby's murder of Lee Harvey Oswald on live national television; the horse-drawn caisson, the riderless horse, the muffled drums, two-year-old John saluting the flag-draped coffin of his fallen father, the haunting sound of taps breaking over the shadowed slopes of Arlington National Cemetery—television brought it all into our home, as it happened.

I cannot claim that I came of age that weekend, but at thirteen I first became aware that life—and history—can change in the flash of a moment. In that sense, my childhood, my innocence—our collective innocence—seemed somehow lost on that fateful day and moment, November 22, 1963.

SELECTED BIBLIOGRAPHY

Bishop, Jim. *The Day Kennedy Was Shot.* New York: Harper Collins, 1968.

Busby, Horace. *The Thirty-First of March: An Intimate Portrait of Lyndon Johnson's Final Days in Office.* New York: Farrar, Straus and Giroux, 2005.

Caro, Robert. *The Years of Lyndon Johnson: The Passage of Power.* New York: Alfred A. Knopf, 2012.

Gillon, Steven M. *The Kennedy Assassination: 24 Hours After.* New York: Basic Books, 2009.

Johnson, Lady Bird. *A White House Diary.* Austin: University of Texas Press, 1970.

Johnson, Lyndon Baines. *The Vantage Point: Perspectives on the Presidency, 1963-1969*. New York: Holt, Rinehart and Winston, 1971.

Knebel, Fletcher. "After the Shots: The Ordeal of Lyndon Johnson." *Look*. March 10, 1964, 26-33.

Miller, Merle. *Lyndon: An Oral Biography*. New York: G. P. Putnam's Sons, 1980.

O'Donnell, Kenneth P., and David Powers. *Johnny We Hardly Knew Ye: Memories of John Fitzgerald Kennedy*. Boston: Little, Brown and Company, 1970.

Valenti, Jack. *A Very Human President*. New York: W. W. Norton and Company, 1975.

Youngblood, Rufus. *Twenty Years in the Secret Service: My Life with Five Presidents*. New York: Simon and Schuster, 1973.

Notes

1 Lyndon Baines Johnson, *The Vantage Point: Perspectives on the Presidency, 1963-1969* (New York: Holt, Rinehart and Winston, 1971), 2; Lady Bird Johnson, *A White House Diary* (Austin: University of Texas Press, 1970), 3.

2 Johnson, *A White House Diary*, 3; Johnson, *The Vantage Point*, 2-7; Robert Caro, *The Years of Lyndon Johnson: The Passage of Power* (New York: Alfred A. Knopf, 2012), 311-313.

3 Caro, *The Years of Lyndon Johnson*, 311-313.

4 Jim Bishop, *The Day Kennedy Was Shot* (New York: Harper Collins, 1968), 169-170.

5 Rufus Youngblood, *20 Years in the Secret Service: My Life with Five Presidents* (New York: Simon and Schuster, 1973), 112-113; Johnson, *The Vantage Point*, 7-8.

6 Johnson, *The Vantage Point*, 7-8; Youngblood, *20 Years*, 114-115.

7 Youngblood, *20 Years*, 114-115; Lady Bird Johnson, *A White House Diary*, 2, 4.

8 Steven M. Gillon, *The Kennedy Assassination: 24 Hours After* (New York: Basic Books, 2009), 54-55.

9 Youngblood, *20 Years*, 116.

10 Youngblood, *20 Years*, 116; Gillon, *The Kennedy Assassination*, 58-60.

11 Gillon, *The Kennedy Assassination*, 58-60; Kenneth P. O'Donnell and David Powers, *Johnny We Hardly Knew Ye: Memories of John Fitzgerald Kennedy* (Boston: Little, Brown and Company, 1970), 31-32; Johnson, *The Vantage Point*, 9-10.

12 Johnson, *The Vantage Point*, 9-10; O'Donnell and Powers, *Johnny We Hardly Knew Ye*, 34.

13 Youngblood, *20 Years*, 116-117; Johnson, *The Vantage Point*, 9.

14 Johnson, *The Vantage Point*, 9; Youngblood *20 Years*, 116-117.

15 Youngblood, *20 Years*, 117; Johnson, *The Vantage Point*, 10; Lady Bird Johnson, *A White House Diary*, 4-5.

16 Lyndon Johnson, *The Vantage Point*, 10-11; Lady Bird Johnson, *A White House Diary*, 4-5; Youngblood, *20 Years*, 118-119.

17 Lady Bird Johnson, *A White House Diary*, 4, 6.

18 Youngblood, *20 Years*, 119-120.

19 Johnson, *The Vantage Point*, 11-12; Lady Bird Johnson, *A White House Diary*, 6; Youngblood, *20 Years*, 120.

20 Johnson, *The Vantage Point*, 12.

21 Fletcher Knebel, "After the Shots: The Ordeal of Lyndon Johnson," *Look*, March 10, 1964, 28-30; Gillon, *The Kennedy Assassination*, 103.

22 Johnson, *The Vantage Point*, 12-13, 17.

23 Johnson, *The Vantage Point*, 14; Youngblood, *20 Years*, 124-125; O'Donnell and Powers, *Johnny We Hardly Knew Ye*, 38-39.

24 O'Donnell and Powers, *Johnny We Hardly Knew Ye*, 44; Edwin O. Guthman and Jeffrey Shulman, eds., *Robert Kennedy in His Own Words: The Unpublished Recollections of the Kennedy Years* (London: Bantam Press, 1988), 26.

25 Guthman and Shulman, *Robert Kennedy in His Own Words*, 26; Johnson, *The Vantage Point*, 14.

26 Gillon, *The Kennedy Assassination*, 123-132.

27 Gillon, *The Kennedy Assassination*, 123-132.

28 Gillon, *The Kennedy Assassination*, 124-130.

29 Ibid.

30 O'Donnell and Powers, *Johnny We Hardly Knew Ye*, 38-39; Johnson *The Vantage Point*, 15; Youngblood, *20 Years*, 125.

31 Gillon *The Kennedy Assassination*, 136-138.

32 O'Donnell and Powers, *Johnny We Hardly Knew Ye*, 38-40.

33 Gollon, *The Kennedy Assassination*, 137-140; Johnson, *The Vantage Point*, 15.

34 Lady Bird Johnson, *A White House Diary*, 5-6.

35 O'Donnell and Powers, *Johnny We Hardly Knew Ye*, 40-42; Johnson, *The Vantage Point*, 14-15.

36 Michael Beschloss, ed., *Taking Charge: The Johnson White House Tapes, 1963-1964* (New York: Simon and Schuster, 1997), 17-18.

37 Gillon, *The Kennedy Assassination*, 158.

38 Youngblood, *20 Years*, 134-135.

39 Johnson, *The Vantage Point*, 15.

40 Jack Valenti, *A Very Human President* (New York: W. W. Norton and Company, 1975), 3-4.

41 Merle Miller, *Lyndon: An Oral Biography* (New York: G. P. Putnam's Sons, 1980), 322-333.

42 Gillon, *The Kennedy Assassination*, 179.

43 Ibid., 172-179; Beschloss, *Taking Charge*, 19-21.

44 Ted Sorensen, *Counselor: A Life at the Edge of History* (New York: Harper Collins, 2008), 630.

45 Valenti, *A Very Human President*, 6-7.

46 Ibid.; Horace Busby, *The Thirty-First of March: An Intimate Portrait of Lyndon Johnson's Final Days in Office* (New York: Farrar, Straus and Giroux, 2005), 149-152; Youngblood, *20 Years*, 136-138.

47 Youngblood, *20 Years*, 136-138; Valenti, *A Very Human President*, 7; Busby, *The Thirty-First*, 152.

48 Valenti, *A Very Human President*, 7.

49 Miller, *Lyndon*, 324.

50 Ibid. Valenti, *A Very Human President*, 7-9; Busby, *The Thirty-First*, 153.

51 Knebel, "After the Shots," 33; Busby, *The Thirty-First*, 153-155; Valenti, *A Very Human President*, 8-9.

52 Valenti, *A Very Human President*, 8-9; Busby, *The Thirty-First*, 154-156.

53 Busby, *The Thirty-First*, 154-156; Gerald Blaine, *The Kennedy Detail: JFK's Secret Service Agents Break Their Silence* (New York: Gallery Books, 2010), 264-265.

54 Blaine, *The Kennedy Detail*, 264-265.

55 Valenti, *A Very Human President*, 9; Knebel, "After the Shots," 33.

CHAPTER FOURTEEN

"I Remember It Well. I Lived It": Louise Ballerstedt Raggio and the Passage of the Marital Property Act of 1967

Nancy E. Baker

ON MAY 29, 1967, GOVERNOR John Connally signed the Marital Property Act, a law that changed Texas women's lives dramatically.[1] Although now forgotten by most, the Marital Property Act granted married women legal equal rights with their husbands, allowing them to sell their own property, sign their own contracts, and control their own earnings, among other rights.[2] Before this law existed, married women in the state suffered under "the most restrictive laws in the country" and were considered equivalent "with infants, idiots, and the incarcerated."[3] Legal reformer Louise Ballerstedt Raggio had labored for years to accomplish this change for married women, enduring steep personal costs and sharp divisions among the small community of women's rights reformers in mid-century Texas. The story of Raggio's triumph has its roots in the woman suffrage movement, the immigrant experience,

Cold War anti-communist hysteria, and Raggio's reliance upon traditional femininity to accomplish revolutionary goals.[4] As such, the passage of the Marital Property Act in 1967 provides a unique moment when one individual was able to advance the cause of women's rights in Texas.

Born in 1919 in Austin and raised in a small, immigrant farming community in Central Texas, Louise held fast to Swedish and German culture. Although her grandparents had immigrated into the United States and her parents had been born here, Raggio thought of herself as having immigrant status in the eyes of others, sometimes describing herself as "the offspring of immigrants."[5] Growing up, she routinely experienced outsider status, considered too poor and too ethnic to be invited to classmates' social gatherings, promoted to third grade while only six years old, and perceived as bookish and unpopular.[6] The Ballerstedts belonged to the Swedish Lutheran church, and religion dominated her daily life. She accepted her minister's authority on issues such as the sinfulness of alcohol and her grandmother's belief that "card-playing was the work of the devil." She also did not question the racial segregation that was the norm in Texas.[7] Her ethnic ancestry and religious upbringing were instrumental in shaping her identity and worldview.[8]

Louise's parents valued education and political participation, to a degree that some relatives and neighbors considered them eccentric. Economic necessity had denied her parents more than a sixth grade education, and Louise's mother was particularly determined that Louise would reach her full potential, whether she wanted to or not. At the time people criticized her mother for wasting resources on, and having ambitions for, a mere girl. Nevertheless, her mother instilled in Louise a relentless work ethic and need to excel, merely to be

Louise B. Raggio, State Bar of Texas meeting, 1967

COURTESY THE TEXAS BAR JOURNAL,
ARCHIVES OF THE STATE BAR OF TEXAS

considered acceptable; Louise found such exacting standards difficult, but recognized throughout her life that she owed a great deal of her success to her mother.[9] Her parents' political participation made an impression, too. During the woman

suffrage movement, Louise's mother spent three years cam-
paigning, driving a Model T Ford with her sister and niece to
all the area farms to persuade people to support the Nineteenth
Amendment. Although this occurred before Louise was born,
her mother spoke of it and was fiercely proud of Texas for having quickly ratified the Nineteenth Amendment, the ninth
state in the Union to do so.[10] Louise's father was politically active as well, serving as Democratic precinct chairman. Known
for his love of democracy, he focused his efforts on ensuring
that all registered voters cast their ballots. More than once, his
precinct was noted for having the highest voter turn-out rate
in the state of Texas, with a precinct record of 97 percent one
year.[11] On her own, Louise's love of reading and lack of suitable
material led her to read the entire newspaper daily by age six.
This lifelong habit of being knowledgeable contributed to her
active interest in current events and politics.[12]

Louise was a driven, successful student. She graduated
high school in 1936, the valedictorian of her class and only sixteen years old. Within three years, she had completed a bachelor's degree in government and history from the University of
Texas in Austin with highest honors (second in her class) and
received her teaching certificate. In 1939 the National Institute
of Public Affairs awarded her a year-long Washington, D.C.
internship, a special program in government leadership funded
by a Rockefeller grant.[13]

Attending college and then living in Washington, D.C.
changed Louise's life. At the University of Texas, Louise for
the first time encountered ideas and people who caused her to
question her faith and what she had been taught to believe.[14]
In Washington, D.C., Louise met and dined with First Lady
Eleanor Roosevelt, who was to become her role model.[15] For
the first time, Louise saw possibilities beyond the plan of

becoming a rural schoolteacher that her father had for her. When she returned to Texas, Louise worked for the National Youth Administration in Austin, a New Deal agency, and she traveled throughout sixteen counties to recruit young men for job training programs.[16]

There, Louise met Grier Raggio, an intellectually restless and idealistic man whom she would marry in 1941. Grier served in World War II in some of the bloodiest battles of the South Pacific, and, though he returned to the U.S. in 1945, he suffered post-traumatic stress for the rest of his life.[17] Grier's work for the federal government as a sort of "secret agent for the U.S. Agriculture Department" would cause the two of them grief, leading as it did to a bizarre chain of events that resulted in accusations of communist sympathies and un-American activities. These accusations and the subsequent investigations would hound them for decades, resurfacing periodically over the slightest possible imagined missteps on their part.[18]

The investigations caused Louise and Grier economic insecurity and fear for the well-being of their family, especially their three children. Never free of the fear that the FBI would at some point return, Louise worried that Grier would be considered untouchable by employers. She therefore felt compelled to prepare herself to be the breadwinner for her family.

Raggio earned her law degree from Southern Methodist University in Dallas as briskly as she could, bringing her children to the library, when necessary, and relying on her husband for childcare while she attended night classes.[19] During her law school years, she had an unplanned pregnancy that her doctor warned could kill her. Though she and Grier chose to continue the pregnancy and were fortunate to have a healthy third child, Louise would always remember this dilemma and remain committed to supporting a woman's right to choose.[20]

She completed her degree in 1952, the only woman in a class of 100 students.[21] Impressive as Raggio was, employers considered her unemployable due to her sex. "[A]n attorney whose firm wanted her to head its typing pool" extended the only job offer she received after earning her law degree.[22]

With the aid of pioneering feminist and district court judge Sarah Hughes, Louise Raggio won her first job in the office of the Dallas District Attorney Henry Wade in 1954.[23] The D.A.'s office paid Raggio only $350 a month, while male attorneys made twice that amount.[24] Taking the work scorned by other attorneys in the office, Raggio quickly discovered that family law was an area with an enormous backlog of cases and a great many problems in need of reform.[25] As she attempted to make a difference for troubled families, Raggio encountered her own familial challenges—"a surge of community opposition" to her professional role, with a steady stream of people pronouncing her "an unnatural woman who would destroy [her] . . . life and [her] . . . marriage, and rear three juvenile delinquents."[26] One of her three sons found the transition to a mother working full-time outside the home difficult as well, and let her know it.[27] Though she would go on to work in private practice with her husband, Raggio's heart never truly left behind the misery she had witnessed in the cluttered and dingy quarters she inhabited while working for Wade.

Determined to make a difference, Raggio set about improving conditions for married women and for families. She continued to work on family law, and "perhaps because of, not in spite of . . . being a woman, [she] . . . built a family law practice that [became] nationally recognized[.]"[28] Soon enough, however, she ran headlong into conflict with another determined reformer who was leading a crusade for equal rights in Texas: Hermine Tobolowsky.

Tobolowky had tried to change the law governing married women's property. Meeting with hostility from the State Legislature, she vowed to amend the state constitution rather than seek piecemeal reform. Never one to suffer fools gladly or to avoid confrontation, Tobolowsky believed that she had softened her hard edges with a carefully cultivated ladylike persona.

Raggio saw her rival differently. Realizing that some legislators loathed Tobolowsky, she perceived that they objected to her overbearing manner. Resolving not to be dismissed in the same fashion, Raggio consciously employed traditional femininity in winning over male allies and champions for her ideas.[29] Taking advantage of an inebriated and flirtatious president of the Texas State Bar Association, Raggio coaxed him into assigning a Marital Property Bill to the Family Law Section of which she was chairman. Expecting inertia at best from her male-dominated section, she wrote a letter announcing that this bill had been assigned to them to write and gave them a deadline for replying. Only one responded by the deadline, after which she wrote again to thank everyone for their support.[30]

Then began the truly difficult work. Raggio's task force for creating the bill included Hank Hudspeath, Charles Saunders, Angus McSwain, Eugene Smith, Joe McKnight, Dewey Lawrence, William Huie, and Bob Johnson.[31] The process of then shepherding the bill through the State Legislature was lengthy and painstaking, and all the task force members used every bit of political influence they had, with Raggio relying upon "charm and shenanigans" when necessary.[32] Her most vocal opponents were four women from the Texas Federation of Business and Professional Women's Clubs (TX-BPW), to which she and Tobolowsky belonged.[33] Tobolowsky and three other members of the TX-BPW testified against the Marital Property Act, believing it to be a distraction from the real reform

needed – their proposed Equal Legal Rights Amendment
(ELRA), a state equal rights amendment. Tobolowsky's campaign for the ELRA had alienated many of the legislators, and
her testimony against the Marital Property Act had the effect
of an endorsement of it for those who disliked Tobolowsky.[34]
Finally, after two years and seven drafts of the bill and drawing
upon "some of the best legal minds in the state," the bill passed
with unanimous support in the House and nearly unanimous
support in the Senate. It was then signed into law on May 29,
1967, by Governor John Connally. When Raggio shared her
triumph with Judge Sarah Hughes, she exclaimed, "Oh, no,
Louise! That bill couldn't possibly have passed. It will take 20
years to make all of those changes in Texas law."[35]

For Raggio, accomplishing such a landmark change did not
come without a price. In her autobiography, Raggio unflinch-
ingly described bleak periods of depression and extreme exhaustion.[36] Her husband's trauma from war and the repeated
anti-communist investigations marred her marriage, leaving
her painfully aware at all times of how precarious family fi-
nances, careers, and friendships could be.[37]

In response to these extreme circumstances, Raggio found
ways to pursue her daring reform goals in the most subtle, traditional ways possible. Cultivating male allies and mentors,
Raggio used gender expectations to her advantage; if suggest-
ing ideas to men privately and then praising them publicly for
her work would get her goals accomplished, Raggio did it. If
enduring flirtations from men (well into her 70s!) seemed essential to maintaining her network of allies, she smiled graciously and appeared flattered. Whether baking cookies at all
hours for male colleagues or spending her weekends entertaining them with home-cooked, family meals, Raggio appeared
to be the epitome of the domestically inclined, Cold War-era

female. Little did her male colleagues know that she did her best to fulfill standard gender roles and succeed at her career at the cost of time for herself and her mental health.

With the death on April 10, 1988, of her husband, whom she loved dearly, Raggio gave herself permission to champion openly women's rights and gender equality. Now in her 70s and 80s, Raggio embraced women's professional networks and also spent a great deal of time with women as allies and friends.[38]

In 1992, Raggio went public with the high personal costs of her professional accomplishments. She wrote, "Throughout history, the women have been the maids [and the helpers] . . . But the moment a woman becomes serious about her career . . . a tidal wave hits her. I remember it well. I lived it."[39] She spoke in more overtly feminist terms than she would ever have dared at that time, stating, "We will not tolerate having to live roles assigned to us by old, white men. We demand that women be free to choose and we will support and honor their choice—full-time homemaker, or homemaker plus career."[40] Even with this daring call to action for women, her use of the traditional role of the homemaker tempered Raggio's feminism. For example, Raggio's effort to balance family duties with work typically had meant planning ahead a month's meals and spending her weekends ironing clothes and cooking meals for the entire week. Necessity dictated that Raggio require her sons to help with all manner of household chores, regardless of their gender. Nowhere in her 1992 opinion piece did she discuss women who choose something other than heterosexual marriage and children. Throughout her career, Raggio had done her best to fulfill her traditional role as a mother and a wife, while pursuing her career—no matter how difficult this became for her.[41]

Raggio thought the Marital Property Act affected much of the substantive change she and other women's rights activists had been working towards for decades. Previously, married women in Texas were governed by the most restrictive laws of any state in the nation, with their rights reduced in the same manner as those of children, prisoners, and the mentally incompetent. The Marital Property Act revolutionized married women's rights, recognizing them as legal equals to their husbands. For the first time, married women in Texas could sell their own property, sign their own contracts, and control their own earnings. However, because enforcement of the Marital Property Act was uneven and gradual, activists such as Tobolowsky believed that the law had changed little and continued to fight for a state Equal Legal Rights Amendment, which voters approved in November 1972.[42] Looking back on this divisive and decisive moment among women's rights activists, Raggio concluded that the well-researched Marital Property Act, changing all of the most essential laws, had been needed to pave the way for the constitutional amendment to succeed in the legislature.[43] The divisions among Texas feminists Raggio regarded as unfortunate but unavoidable. In Raggio's experience, practical, smaller steps with no fanfare were achievable and could lead to bigger things. How big, she did not completely know at the time.

Eavesdropping on this important moment that mild and rainy Monday in May would have confirmed the making of a landmark decision in Texas women's and legal history. As an elated Raggio quietly looked on, Governor John Connally picked up a pen and signed her bill into law—with a flourish. Though the press at the time paid scant attention, this event deserves to be remembered as a turning point for all Texas women. The Marital Property Act not only changed the past, but also heralded the future, bringing with it significant improvements for women and families. Louise Ballerstedt Raggio's leadership on the Marital Property Act led to the Texas State Bar president entrusting to Raggio a complete overhaul of the Family Code. As a result of Raggio's efforts, Texas, once the worst state in the nation for married women's rights, would go on to become the first state in the nation with a unified, reformed family code and would serve as a model to other states.[44]

———————◆◆⟩◍⟨◆◆———————

The story of Louise Ballerstedt Raggio's efforts to reform Texas law and improve women's lives has intrigued me since I first researched and wrote about Hermine Tobolowsky and the Texas Equal Legal Rights Amendment. I puzzled over why another feminist lawyer would oppose Tobolowsky's ELRA. Raggio's published autobiography and my archival research in Raggio's papers allowed me a deeper understanding of the challenges confronting Raggio (nothing brings this home like seeing an enormous FBI file on the Raggios, based on so very little actual evidence). I developed a great admiration for her commitment to making a difference for women and families, especially at such devastating personal cost and with so little personal glory at the time. I would have liked to have been present to eavesdrop as Governor Connally signed the Marital Property Act. I could have seen the look on Raggio's face as she became the most important agent of change for Texas women in the twentieth century. Characteristically, Raggio was self-effacing to a fault about this historic triumph. Nevertheless, I would have loved to have been able to congratulate her, thank her, and shake her hand, as all women in Texas owe her so much for the rights they enjoy today.

SELECTED BIBLIOGRAPHY

McArthur, Judith N., and Harold L. Smith. *Texas Through Women's Eyes: The Twentieth Century Experience.* Austin: University of Texas Press, 2010.

Pierce, P.J. *"Let Me Tell You What I've Learned": Wisewomen of Texas Speak.* Austin: University of Texas Press, 2010.

Raggio, Louise. Texas Political History Oral History Project and the Women's Studies Oral History Project. Interview by Gerald D. Saxon. Dallas Public Library. 31 October 1980. University of North Texas Library.

Raggio, Louise Ballerstedt. Texas Bar Foundation. Interview by Sheree Scarborough. 2003. (Austin, TX: Texas Bar Foundation, 2003).

Raggio, Louise Ballerstedt, and Reba Graham Rasor. 1974. "From Dream to Reality—How to Get a New Code on the Books." *Family Law Quarterly* 8 (2). American Bar Association: 105–34. Accessed 17 November 2015. http://www.jstor.org/stable/25739086

Raggio, Louise Ballerstedt with Vivian Anderson Castleberry. *Texas Tornado: The Autobiography of a Crusader for Women's Rights and Family Justice.* New York: Citadel Press, 2003.

"Texas Trailblazer: Louise Raggio." 2008. Dallas, TX: KERA-TV video, 2008. DVD.

NOTES

1 60th Texas State Legislature, "A Bill to be Entitled An Act relating to the rights, duties, privileges, powers, and liabilities of spouses . . ." (Senate Bill 33) 1966-67 Regular Session, Texas State Senate. Last accessed 10 November 2015.
http://www.lrl.state.tx.us/LASDOCS/60R/SB33/SB33_60R.pdf#page=54
The Marital Property Act was later codified in Title I of the Texas Family Code. See Tex. Fam. Code Ann. 1.01-5.87, (Vernon 1975 and Vernon Supp. 1988); originally cited in Thomas M. Featherston, Jr. and Julie A. Springer, "Marital Property Law in Texas: The Past, Present and Future," *Baylor Law Review* (Fall 1987): 7n55.

2 "Dallas Domestic Courts Bill Signed by Connally," *Dallas Morning News,* 30 May 1967, 1. The article states that Connally signed several bills on Monday, which would have been the day before this newspaper was printed. Scholars have paid little attention to the Marital Property Act of 1967, preferring instead to study the Texas Equal Legal Rights Amendment (ELRA).

3 Louise Ballerstedt Raggio with Vivian Anderson Castleberry, *Texas Tornado: The Autobiography of a Crusader for Women's Rights and Family Justice* (New York: Citadel Press, 2003), 3. Raggio Book Summary, p. 18; Series 2, Box 9, unlabeled folder, Louise Raggio Collection, SMU, Dallas, TX.

4 Elizabeth Enstam has observed that the ELRA was of far less immediate, practical importance to women than the Marital Property Act,

"which amounted to a virtual revolution for women in Texas." Elizabeth York Enstam, "WOMEN AND THE LAW," *Handbook of Texas Online* (http://www.tshaonline.org/handbook/online/articles/jsw02), accessed September 8, 2015. Uploaded on June 15, 2010. Published by the Texas State Historical Association.

5 Raggio, *Texas Tornado*, 6.

6 Ibid., 6, 20, 27-32.

7 Ibid., 16-17.

8 Ibid., 3-26; Raggio described her upbringing and emphasized the importance of her ethnic and religious identity. For more on the ways in which German ethnicity and Lutheranism shaped Texan women's identities, see Lauren Ann Kattner, "Growing Up Female in New Braunfels: Social and Cultural Adaptation in a German-Texan Town," *Journal of American Ethnic History* 9 (Spring 1990): 49-72; and Mary Fehler Knarr, "Faith, Frauen, and the Formation of an Ethnic Identity: German Lutheran Women in South and Central Texas, 1831-1890" (Ph.D. dissertation, Texas Christian University, 2009). For insight into the experiences of Raggio's grandmother, see the related book: Charles H. Russell, *Undaunted: A Norwegian Woman in Frontier Texas* (College Station: Texas A&M University Press, 2006).

9 Raggio, *Texas Tornado*, 20-21, 22, 26-27, 29, 34.

10 Ibid., 21-22. Her mother campaigned in 1916-1918, and women got the right to vote nationwide in 1920.

11 Ibid., 21. The precinct was the Littig Precinct of Travis County, and her father's voter turn-out rate tended to be at least 90 percent.

12 Ibid., 27-28.

13 Raggio Book Summary, pp. 1-2; Series 2, Box 9, unlabeled folder, Louise Raggio Collection, SMU, Dallas, TX. Hereafter referred to as Raggio Book Summary. Raggio, *Texas Tornado*, 32-33, 45, 47.

14 Raggio, *Texas Tornado*, 34-35. When Louise asked her minister how to reconcile information from her geology class that implied the Earth was millions of years old with the Biblically-based claim that the Earth was created in 4004 B.C., her minister exploded at her, yelling, "I told your parents to send you to a church school! The University of Texas is a training ground for hell!"

15 Raggio Book Summary, 1-2.

16 Ibid., 2-3.

17 Ibid., 3.

18 Ibid., 3, 4, 6. For reasons he never discovered, Grier had first been suspected of Communist sympathies in 1942 while in the Army, dashing his hopes of a career as an officer. Later, Grier was a fraud investigator for the U.S. Department of Agriculture and was accused in 1948 of being a Communist. Raggio, *Texas Tornado*, 251-255.

19 Louise Raggio, "Far Right Still Fighting Women's Rights," *Dallas Morning News*, 13 September 1992, 6J; Box 1 of 5, unlabeled folder, Raggio collec-

tion, SMU, Dallas, TX. See her autobiography for how she brought her kids to the library.

20 Raggio Book Summary, 8.

21 Ibid., 1.

22 Ibid., 10.

23 Ibid., 11-12. Raggio held this job for two years. During her second year, she was responsible for "the first time in Texas history a case was heard by an all-woman jury" (p. 14). Wade was best known for his anti-abortion role in the Supreme Court case *Roe v. Wade* (1973), despite his personal belief that abortion should be legal. See Raggio, *Texas Tornado*, 137, 145, 156-157. President Kennedy appointed Hughes a federal court judge in 1962. She was an important mentor and friend to Raggio. Raggio once said that she was "Tonto and Hughes . . . the Lone Ranger." Darwin Payne, *Indomitable Sarah: The Life of Judge Sarah T. Hughes* (Dallas, TX: Southern Methodist University Press, 2004) 173, 230-231.

24 Louise Raggio, "Far Right Still Fighting Women's Rights." For the pay gap, see "Texas Trailblazer: Louise Raggio" (2008, 28 minutes). Raggio Book Summary, 11-12.

25 Raggio, *Texas Tornado*, 150-151, 153.

26 Louise Raggio, "Far Right Still Fighting Women's Rights."

27 Raggio Book Summary, 12.

28 Louise Raggio, "Far Right Still Fighting Women's Rights."

29 Raggio, *Texas Tornado*, 202. For example, Raggio made a backroom deal with the Speaker of the House Ben Barnes that she would oppose publicly the ELRA if he would ensure her Marital Property Act passed.

30 Ibid., 178-179.

31 Raggio Book Summary, 19. Hank Hudspeath and Charles Saunders chaired the State Bar's Real Estate/Probate Section. Angus McSwain was the dean of the Baylor Law School. Eugene Smith and Joe McKnight were faculty at the SMU School of Law. Dewey Lawrence was a well-known and respected lawyer from Tyler. William Huie was a faculty member at UT Austin's law school. Former state legislator Bob Johnson was the head of legislative services for the State Bar. For a detailed explanation of the intricacies and political realities of the process of reforming the marital property laws, see Raggio's own account: Louise Ballerstedt Raggio and Reba Graham Rasor, "From Dream to Reality—How to Get a New Code on the Books," *Family Law Quarterly* 8:2 (1974) 105-134. Last accessed 17 November 2015 at http://www.jstor.org/stable/25739086. Note that Raggio describes the reform of the marital property laws as part of the Texas State Bar's larger plan to develop a comprehensive Family Code, a description of the State Bar's intention that contrasts sharply with her more personal accounts of the process.

32 Raggio Book Summary, 19.

33 That both Raggio and Tobolowsky were members of the TX-BPW should not be surprising, given that they were both lawyers seeking social connections for the sake of their law practices and that they were both interested

in reforms to end gender inequality. The National Federation of Business and Professional Women's Clubs was an organization that attracted women interested in such reform, as the organization endorsed the federal Equal Rights Amendment in 1937, promoted the amendment nationally as of 1946, and sought other measures to increase gender equality. For more on this, see Kathleen A. Laughlin, "Civic Feminists: The Politics of the Minnesota Federation of Business and Professional Women's Clubs, 1942-1965," in Kathleen A. Laughlin and Jacqueline L. Castledine, eds. *Breaking the Wave: Women, Their Organizations, and Feminism, 1945-1985* (New York: Routledge, 2011) 11-27.

34 Raggio Book Summary, 19.

35 Ibid., 20.

36 Raggio, *Texas Tornado*, chapter 16, passim.

37 See Ibid., 118, for an example of how she lost friends and had no one to turn to for help or emotional support during the first of several anti-communist investigations of her husband.

38 Ibid., 216-217, 236, 244-246, 250, 262. Grier died nine days before their forty-seventh wedding anniversary.

39 Louise Raggio, "Far Right Still Fighting Women's Rights." Raggio, *Texas Tornado*, 218-219 describes some of the sexual harassment she routinely dealt with throughout her entire career.

40 Louise Raggio, "Far Right Still Fighting Women's Rights."

41 Raggio, *Texas Tornado*, 148-149. Chapter 16 of the book describes her struggles with depression and exhaustion (and how she continued to try and be all things to all people at work and at home). On page 258, Raggio's focus on the traditional family unit comes through when she says, "I have spent both my personal and my professional life committed to families and believe there is no substitute for family as the basic and most enduring human structure."

42 Nancy E. Baker, "Hermine Tobolowsky: A Feminist's Fight for Equal Rights," in Elizabeth Hayes Turner, Stephanie Cole and Rebecca Sharpless, eds., *Texas Women: Their Histories, Their Lives* (Athens, GA: University of Georgia Press, 2015), 446-447. Tobolowsky claimed that, in 1970, businesses and the state government persisted in requiring husbands' signatures for married women seeking credit or attempting to manage their own property. Tobolowsky saw this as proof that little had changed. In 1971, the Texas State Legislature passed the state ELRA. In 1972, Texas voters approved the state ELRA and the amendment became part of the Texas State Constitution.

43 Raggio, *Texas Tornado*, 178, 202.

44 Ibid., 183-184, 196-197. In 1976, Raggio would become the first woman elected to chair the American Bar Association's Family Law Section. In 1979, Raggio was the first woman elected to director of the State Bar of Texas. Numerous states called upon her expertise in family law and women's rights as they sought to reform their own Family Law Codes and model themselves after Texas. Raggio died in 2011.

CONTRIBUTORS

Watson Arnold is an Adjunct Professor of history at Texas Christian University where he currently teaches the history of medicine. Arnold attended Tulane University, receiving a B.A. degree, followed by Southwestern Medical School at Dallas where he earned a MD. He later returned to school and received his Ph.D.in history from Texas Christian University. He recently served as president of the Texas State Historical Association and as an officer in numerous other historical organizations. He has published over 100 articles and chapters on medicine and now, in his second career, has published several chapters in books, four articles, and numerous book reviews. He is currently working on a chapter on smallpox in Texas.

Nancy E. Baker is an Associate Professor of history at Sam Houston State University. In 2003 Baker earned her doctorate in history from Harvard University. She is the author of *Unequaled: Rescission and the Equal Rights Amendment, Texas Feminism Between and Beyond the Waves,* "'Focus on the Family': Twentieth-Century Conservative Texas Women and the Lone Star Right," in *Texas Right: The Radical Roots of Lone Star Conservatism,* and "Hermine Tobolowsky: A Feminist's Fight for Equal Rights," in *Texas Women: Their Histories, Their Lives.*

Paul H. Carlson is an Emeritus Professor of history at Texas Tech University where he earned his Ph.D. in history. Carlson has published twenty-two books and numerous articles, is a member of the Texas Institute of Letters and the Philosophical Society of Texas, and is a Fellow of the Texas State Historical Association. A recipient of six university teaching awards, he is currently working on a study of the Llano Estacado.

Michael Collins served Midwestern State University for twenty-seven years before retiring in 2012. He earned his B.A., M.A., and Ph. D degrees in history from Texas Christian University. In 2006 the MSU Board of Regents selected Dr. Collins as a Regents Professor and named him the Hardin Distinguished Professor of American History in 2008. A fellow of the Texas State Historical Association, he is a specialist in the American West and Texas as well as twentieth-century U.S. political and diplomatic history. His publications include five books, among them: *Texas Devils: Rangers and Regulars on the Lower Rio Grande, 1846-1861*; *That Damned Cowboy: Theodore Roosevelt and the American West, 1883-1898*; and *Profiles in Power: Twentieth Century Texans in Washington*. In 2008 the Minnie Stevens Piper Foundation of San Antonio honored him for his lifetime commitment to teaching excellence. He is now an independent scholar living in New Braunfels, Texas.

Patrick Cox is an historical consultant after having retired as Associate Director of the Dolph Briscoe Center for American History at the University of Texas at Austin. He received a B.A. from the University of Texas, an M.A. in History from Southwest Texas State University (now Texas State University), and a Ph.D. from the University of Texas. His books include *The First Texas News Barons*, *The House Will Come to Order*, *Writing the Story of Texas*, and *Ralph Yarborough: The People's*

Senator. He is currently working on a history of the W. W. Jones Ranch in South Texas.

Carolina Castillo Crimm is an Emeritus Professor of history and has spent her career entertaining and educating audiences with stories about inspirational historical characters. She received her Ph.D. in history from the University of Texas. Among her many publications is the award-winning *De Leon: A Tejano Family History*, a ground-breaking study of Latino empowerment. Carolina is a noted speaker and has appeared on numerous documentaries on PBS and The History Channel. She taught high school for twenty years then spent twenty years teaching on the university level, starting at Victoria College in 1990 then moving to Sam Houston State University in 1992. She is acclaimed for her teaching, winning local and state-wide teaching awards, including the prestigious Piper Award as one of the best teachers in Texas. Carolina serves on the Board of Directors for Humanities Texas and the Texas State Historical Association. She has also played an active role in the preservation of Huntsville's many log cabins. Carolina has begun work on several novels dealing with 1770s Spanish Texas.

Tom Crum is a retired State District Judge. He graduated from the University of Texas Law School. Crum has published several articles and book chapters and co-authored *Myth, Memory, and Massacre* with Paul Carlson. He is a past president of both the West Texas Historical Association and the East Texas Historical Association. Crum is also past counselor for the Texas Folklore Society and is currently chairman of the Advisory Council for the Center of Big Bend Studies at Sul Ross University.

Light T. Cummins is the Guy M. Bryan, Jr. Professor of History at Austin College. He received a B.S. in Ed. and an

M.A. from Southwest Texas State University (now Texas State University), and a Ph.D. from Tulane University. Cummins is the author or editor of twelve academic books and several dozen scholarly articles dealing with Texas and Gulf Coast history, along with two best-selling college textbooks, popular-oriented essays, and numerous book reviews. His most recent book is *Allie Victoria Tennant and the Visual Arts in Dallas* and he is currently working on a book dealing with women in early Texas art.

Victoria H. Cummins holds the A. M. Pate Jr. Endowed Chair of History at Austin College in Sherman, Texas. She received her Ph.D. in history from Tulane University. Her current research deals with 1920s and 1930s Texas art and artists. Recent publications include "Black Clubwomen and the Promotion of the Visual Arts in Early Twentieth-Century Texas" *Southwestern Historical Quarterly* (July 2015) and "Francis B. Fisk and the Promotion of the Visual Arts in Texas," in Stephanie Cole, Elizabeth Hayes Turner, and Rebecca Sharpless, eds. *Texas Women: Their Histories, Their Lives*, co-authored with Light Cummins. Her research on Texas-Louisiana regionalist artist Don Brown sparked her interest in Caddo Lake.

Bill O'Neal is currently serving his second term as State Historian of Texas. He received the B.A. and M.A. degrees from East Texas State University in Commerce, and in 2013 was awarded an honorary Doctor of Letters degree from Texas A&M University at Commerce. O'Neal has authored numerous books, including six on sports history and he has appeared on television documentaries for the A&E Channel, the History Channel, the American Heroes Channel, the Discovery Channel, TBS, and CMT. For thirty-five years he announced football and baseball games over KGAS radio in Carthage,

Texas. He is a Piper Professor and former president of the East Texas Historical Association and of the West Texas Historical Association. Recently, at the 2015 West Texas Book Festival in Abilene, O'Neal was presented the A. C. Greene Award for Lifetime Achievement.

Chuck Parsons is retired from the field of public school administration and supervision, having been a high school principal for eighteen years in schools in Minnesota and Wisconsin. He scribbled "G.T.T." on his front door and became a Texan by choice some twenty years ago. His recent books include *The Notorious Luke Short* (co-authored with Jack DeMattos); *Texas Ranger N.O. Reynolds: The Intrepid;* and *A Lawless Breed: John Wesley Hardin, Texas Reconstruction and Violence in the Wild West*. His biography *John R. Hughes, Lone Star Ranger* won the "Best Book of the Year" award in 2014 from the Wild West History Association. He now researches and writes on a variety of Texas figures, mainly outlaws and lawmen of the Wild West period. Parsons currently is working on a biography of State Police Captain Jack Helm, as well as a co-author of a biography of Ben Thompson.

Merline Pitre is a Professor of History at Texas Southern University and earned the Ph.D. degree in history from Temple University. Pitre has published four books: *Through Many Dangers, Toils and Snares: The Black Leadership of Texas 1868-1898; In Struggle against Jim Crow: Lulu B. White and the NAACP, 1900-1957; Black Women in Texas History;* and *Black Southern Women in the Civil Right Movement, 1954-1965*. Both of the latter books were co-edited with Bruce Glasrud, and won the Liz Carpenter Award in 2008 and 2013 for the best book published on women in Texas for that respective year. She currently serves as the managing editor of the *Handbook of Texas—African American*, an online encyclopedia. A former

President of the Texas State Historical Association (TSHA), Pitre is the first African American to head that august body. She is also a Fellow of the Texas State Historical and the East Texas Historical Associations. In 2013, she was the recipient of the Lorraine Williams Leadership Award given by the Association of Black Women Historians. In 2014, she won the TSU Presidential Achievement Medal for her work in teaching, research, and community service. Currently, she is writing a history of Texas Southern University.

Mary L. Scheer is Professor and Chair of the history department at Lamar University, Director of the Center for History and Culture of Southeast Texas and the Upper Gulf Coast, and editor of this volume. She received a B.S. and M.A. from Southwest Texas State University (now Texas State University), later earning a Ph.D. from Texas Christian University. She has authored *The Foundations of Texan Philanthropy, Twentieth-Century Texas: A Social and Cultural History*, co-edited with John Storey, *Women and the Texas Revolution*, an edited anthology which won the Liz Carpenter Award, and *Texan Identities: Moving Beyond Myth, Memory, and Fallacy in Texas History*, co-edited with Light Cummins. In 2004 Scheer was a Fulbright scholar at the University of Potsdam in Germany. She served on the board of the Texas State Historical Association and is a past president of the East Texas Historical Association. Scheer is currently researching the role of first lady Eleanor Roosevelt and the postwar American presidency.

Dan K. Utley is Chief Historian with the Center for Texas Public History at Texas State University. He holds degrees in history from the University of Texas at Austin and Sam Houston State University. He is the co-author of nine books on Texas history, including *History Ahead: Stories beyond the Texas Roadside Markers*, with Cynthia J. Beeman, recipient of the Philosophical Society of Texas Award of Merit, and *Just Between Us: Stories and Memories from the Texas Pines,* with Milton S. Jordan, honored with the Ottis Lock Award from the East Texas Historical Association. He is a Fellow of the Texas State Historical Association and the East Texas Historical Association. His recent works include *Echoes of Glory: Historic Military Sites Across Texas,* with Thomas E. Alexander, and a forthcoming oral history memoir of historian Archie P. McDonald. He is currently working on books about oral history and forgotten historic sites.

Heather Green Wooten is an independent historian and part-time instructor of History of Medicine at the University of Texas Medical Branch at Galveston (UTMB). She earned a Ph.D. in the Medical Humanities from UTMB in 2006. Wooten is the author of numerous publications. Her book, *The Polio Years in Texas: Battling a Terrifying Unknown,* was a recipient of the T. R. Fehrenbach Book Award by the Texas Historical Commission and the East Texas Historical Association's Ottis Lock Endowment Award in the best book category. In 2012 Wooten published *Old Red: Pioneering Medical Education in Texas* for the TSHA Fred Rider Cotten Popular History Series. She is active in many state and local historical organizations, having held positions in the East Texas Historical Association, the Texas State Historical Association and Galveston County Historical Commission. Wooten's latest projects include *Skilled Hands: Surgery at the University of Texas Medical School at Houston* co-authored with Dr. William H. Kellar, and an edited anthology of Texas medicine throughout the twentieth century.

Index

Page numbers in italics indicate illustrations

C

I

J